Extractivism across Production and Social Reproduction

Studies in Critical Social Sciences Book Series

Haymarket Books is proud to be working with Brill Academic Publishers (www.brill.nl) to republish the *Studies in Critical Social Sciences* book series in paperback editions. This peer-reviewed book series offers insights into our current reality by exploring the content and consequences of power relationships under capitalism, and by considering the spaces of opposition and resistance to these changes that have been defining our new age. Our full catalog of *SCSS* volumes can be viewed at https://www.haymarketbooks.org/series_collections/4-studies-in-critical-social-sciences.

Series Editor
David Fasenfest (York University)

New Scholarship in Political Economy Book Series

Series Editors
David Fasenfest (York University)
Alfredo Saad-Filho (Queen's University, Belfast)

Editorial Board
Kevin B. Anderson (University of California, Santa Barbara)
Tom Brass (formerly of SPS, University of Cambridge)
Raju Das (York University)
Ben Fine ((emeritus) SOAS University of London)
Jayati Ghosh (Jawaharlal Nehru University)
Elizabeth Hill (University of Sydney)
Dan Krier (Iowa State University)
Lauren Langman (Loyola University Chicago)
Valentine Moghadam (Northeastern University)
David N. Smith (University of Kansas)
Susanne Soederberg (Queen's University)
Aylin Topal (Middle East Technical University)
Fiona Tregenna (University of Johannesburg)
Matt Vidal (Loughborough University London)
Michelle Williams (University of the Witwatersrand)

Extractivism across Production and Social Reproduction

Classes of Labour in Rural Turkey

Coşku Çelik

Haymarket Books
Chicago, IL

First published in 2024 by Brill Academic Publishers, The Netherlands
© 2024 Koninklijke Brill NV, Leiden, The Netherlands

Published in paperback in 2025 by
Haymarket Books
P.O. Box 180165
Chicago, IL 60618
773-583-7884
www.haymarketbooks.org

ISBN: 979-8-88890-570-8

Distributed to the trade in the US through Consortium Book Sales and Distribution (www.cbsd.com) and internationally through Ingram Publisher Services International (www.ingramcontent.com).

This book was published with the generous support of Lannan Foundation, Wallace Action Fund, and the Marguerite Casey Foundation.

Special discounts are available for bulk purchases by organizations and institutions. Please call 773-583-7884 or email info@haymarketbooks.org for more information.

Cover design by Jamie Kerry and Ragina Johnson.

Printed in the United States.

Library of Congress Cataloging-in-Publication data is available.

Contents

Foreword IX
Acknowledgements XII
List of Figures and Tables XIV
Acronyms and Abbreviations XV

1 **Introduction** 1
  1 A Class-Relational Approach to Labour of Extraction under Neoliberalism 4
  2 Introducing the Field 9
  3 The Design and Method of the Fieldwork 10
    3.1 *Semi-structured Interviews* 11
    3.2 *Focus Group Interviews* 12
    3.3 *Participant Observation* 13
  4 Phases of the Fieldwork 14
    4.1 *Phase I (June and July 2015, February 2016)* 14
    4.2 *Phase II (June–September 2016, March 2017)* 15
    4.3 *Phase III (July and August 2018)* 19
  5 Outline of the Book 21

2 **Classes of Extractive Labour across Production and Social Reproduction: Patterns of Dispossession and Class Formation in the Rural Extractive Regions** 24
  1 Proletarianization as Primitive Accumulation 25
  2 Ongoing Primitive Accumulation and Gendered Patterns of Proletarianization: A Marxist Feminist Framework 31
  3 The Development of Capitalism in Agriculture and Dispossession of Small-scale Farmers 38
  4 Rural Class Formation across Production and Social Reproduction 41
  5 Conclusion 44

3 **Extractivism and Labour Control: Reflections of Turkey's 'Coal Rush' in the Underground Coalmines** 45
  1 Controlling and Disciplining the Classes of Extractive Labour: Labour Regime Analysis 45
  2 The Political Economy of Coal Extraction in Neoliberal Turkey 50
    2.1 *A Brief History of Neoliberalism in Turkey* 50

    2.2   Turkey's 'Coal Rush' under the AKP Rule   52
3   Historical Background: Coal Extraction in Soma Before the 2000s   58
4   The Neoliberal Transformation of the Coal Industry in the Soma Coal Basin in the 2000s   61
5   Labour Supply to the Coal Pits of Soma   63
6   Coal Rush Underground: Labour Processes in the Coal Pits of Soma   69
    6.1   *Firms Operating Mines in the Soma Coal Basin*   69
    6.2   *Recruitment Processes and the Informal Subcontractors*   72
    6.3   *The Organization of Work*   74
    6.4   *Coal Rush Underground: Production Pressure*   79
7   Conclusion   82

4 The Social Reproduction of Extractivism: Gendered Patterns of Dispossession and Women's Work in Rural Turkey   84

1   The Production and Social Reproduction of the Classes of Extractive Labour   85
2   The Development of Capitalism in Agriculture in Turkey until the 1980s   89
3   Neoliberalism in Agriculture and Gendered Patterns of Dispossession and Proletarianization in Turkey   91
4   Agrarian Change, Patterns of Dispossession, and Livelihood Diversification in the Soma Coal Basin   95
5   Women's Work in the Soma Coal Basin   105
    5.1   *Labour Processes and Working Conditions of Women in Agriculture*   106
    5.2   *The Social Reproduction of Miner Families: Unpaid Work of Miners' Wives*   111
6   Conclusion   117

5 The Soma Mine Disaster, Labour Control in the Sphere of Social Reproduction, and Moments of Resistance   119

1   Authoritarian Neoliberalism and Extractivism   120
2   The Soma Mine Disaster and Its Prosecution Process   123
3   Local Labour Control and Discipline Strategies   128
4   Local Labour Control and Discipline after the Soma Mine Disaster: Clientelism – Wage Increases – Unemployment   136
5   Moments of Resistance: Attempts for Alternative Unionizations and Local Social Movements in the Basin   143

    5.1   *Anti-coal Resistance in Yırca*   146
    5.2   *Resistance against Redundancy of Miners*   147
6   Conclusion   149

6 Conclusion   152

Postscript: The Condition of Coal Mining and Agricultural Production Amid the Overlapping Crises in Turkey during the 2020s   156

1   Food Crises and Agricultural Production of Small-scale Farmers   158
2   Changing State-Capital-Labour Relations in the Coal Industry   163
3   Conclusion   166

References   167
Index   185

Foreword

This book, as stated by its author, originates from her Ph.D. dissertation, but has subsequently been developed so as to expand its scope and incorporate subsequent developments following her fieldwork into the analysis. It is in some respects unique by bringing the processes of social reproduction in a rural-cum-mining environment into the analysis of extractivism. Dr. Çelik's expertise as a board member of Social Rights Association in Turkey which functioned to improve the social and economic rights of working people also contributed to her evaluation of her field work. The latter in due course enhanced her academic interests beyond labour relations towards exploring patterns of agrarian change in a comparative framework.

It may be beneficial to put the Turkish coal-mining experience in general and the Soma Coal Basin in particular in a comparative framework as they evolved in the context of a radical change in the post-1980 era *both* in the mode of articulation of the Turkish economy with the world economy and in the nature of state-economy relationship prevalent within the social formation. This gains saliency as the neoliberal transitions have transformed the material basis of social reproduction for the countries of the Global South. However, unlike many Latin American countries where several left-wing governments during the so-called Pink Tide, had been engaged with 'redistributive extractivism' so as to finance welfare and employment programmes aimed at reducing poverty, the Turkish experiment of extractivism during the neoliberal transformation especially since the 2000s has had no such counterpart. This contrast is noteworthy as Dr. Çelik reminds its readers, the 'great neoliberal transformation' in the countryside of Turkey has been initiated in the aftermath of the 2001 financial crisis. Thereby, it underlines one of the defining features of the crises in countries such as Turkey, functioning as driving forces of neoliberal transformation.

Nor is it plausible to describe the Turkish experience in terms of 'resource nationalism,' again in contrast to Latin American examples where this concept has been used to characterize a state-led development strategy aimed at recalibrating state-market relations in favour of the former, thus setting in motion the exploitation of natural resources, albeit in collaboration with multinational mining capital. No doubt, there is a need for some clarification here since this particular characterization tends to overlook the fact that neoliberalism as the post-1980 form of capitalism is based on the systematic use of state power to put into effect a hegemonic project of the rule of capital which initiated a series of restructurings of both the state and the capital. Nonetheless, the Turkish experience in extractivism since the turn of the century has not enhanced the role of the state in commodity production with a renewed role for state economic enterprises (SEEs) in contrast to some of the Pink Tide countries. On the contrary, as Dr. Çelik's book highlights, the post-2001 crisis era witnessed a belated flurry of privatization of SEEs in Turkey. The Justice and Development Party (AKP) government which came to power in the wake of the 2001 financial crisis, attempted to make the country an 'investors' paradise' by facilitating the privatizations of the large-scale profitable SEEs through legislative changes that favoured powerful capital groups. However, the neoliberal transformation of the coal industry in the Soma Coal Basin has entailed, as elaborated in detail in the book, 'the transfer of coal extraction to private firms through royalty tenders' whilst the SEE in question TKI was deprived of the necessary means of finance to undertake new investments.

If one of the important contributions of the book to the relevant literature on extractivism is to pursue the latter as a development strategy provided that it is analysed through 'the prism of class struggle' which, in turn, necessitates a focus on 'the peculiarities of labour regimes and labour control strategies.' In this regard, it is important to note that the labour containment strategies put in effect under the AKP rule opted for the market as a mechanism to control and weaken the unions as much as possible so as to achieve the political objective of reversing the political as well as economic gains of the labour movement of the pre-1980 era. Dr. Çelik provides a detailed analysis of the composition of the workforce, the patterns of employment and the ways in which the coal production have been increased in the Soma coal basin with due regard to the political dimension, that is, the relations between the government, coal companies, hometown associations and trade unions. In fact, the book also provides information on how things have changed in this regard in the aftermath of the 2014 coal pit disaster which caused the death of 301 miners.

Yet an equally salient another contribution is squaring the circle, so to speak, by identifying the Soma Coal Basin as a fertile ground for the analysis of the relationship between the rural transformation and the increasing appeal of coal mining for the private capital groups. This has been achieved by combining, on the one hand, the analysis of the transformation of rural environment for the tobacco producers in the wake of the privatization and subsequent closure of cigarette factories by Tekel, one of the pioneering SEEs, dating back to the 1930s, and 'the rush for coal' which propelled extractive investments and resulted in a dramatic rise in demand for miners on the other.

In this context, the transformation of former tobacco producers into miners working in coal pits have been accompanied by the informal employment of women as daily wage workers in capitalist farms which function more often than not on the basis of contract-farming. Yet, the burden that female members of the rural household had to carry would not be limited with their participation in labour market, even though this would not necessarily be reflected in the female labour force participation statistics. They have been equally involved in subsistence farming and variety of unpaid housework which indicated the intensification of their reproductive work.

Indeed, the richness of these different dimensions of the field work and the quality of their analysis is revealed in different chapters of the book in reference to the gendered patterns of social reproduction and proletarianization with a detailed examination of classes of labour as there evolves changing means of rural livelihood in the context of extractivist accumulation. Hence, the book no doubt makes a refreshing contribution to the class analysis in order to develop a better understanding of different modalities of reproduction of labour, quite often without economic and social security in different historically specific contexts,

Galip L. Yalman
16 April 2024

Acknowledgements

The dissertation that lies behind this book was supervised by Galip L. Yalman, who, besides being my mentor, has been a wonderful friend and comrade. His personal and academic support continues to this day. I am so lucky to have you in my life, Galip Hocam! Even though the book is based upon my Ph.D. dissertation (Çelik, 2019), the framework was further developed during my time in the Department of Politics, Department of Social Science, and the Global Labour Research Centre at York University, Canada, as a postdoctoral fellow and visiting professor between 2019 and 2022. I want to thank Terry Maley and Luann Good Gingrich for their support and assistance during very tough times of the pandemic in a different country. The book has been finalized in Istanbul, where I very recently settled. I want to thank my colleagues, Berkay Ayhan, Sibel Karadağ, Dilek Cindoğlu, Lerna K. Yanık, Mary Lou O'Neil, and Murat Güvenç, for making it easier for me to get used to working at a new institution. I feel fortunate to have the chance to work with you all.

I would like to thank Aylin Topal not only for encouraging me to submit a book proposal for the New Scholarship in Political Economy (NSPE) series but also for her continuous academic and personal support. I also appreciate the assistance of the co-Editor of the NSPE series, David Fasenfest, throughout the writing up of the manuscript.

My friends are always there for me in the ups and downs of my life. I want to express my gratitude to my sisters in soul, Ayça Berna Görmez, Ecehan Balta, Sultan Gürbey, Ayşe Pamuk, Görkem Akgöz, Ezgi Doğru, and Deniz Ay, as well as to Can Irmak Özinanır. I feel extremely lucky to have them in my life!

My special thanks go all my contacts in the Soma Coal Basin, who opened up their houses, became my friends and comrades. I am especially grateful to my comrades from the Social Rights Association for their friendship and support. I would like to express my gratitude to Ali Bülent Erdem for his instructive guidance throughout the fieldwork. I would like to give my utmost gratitude to my family for all their support. I am so lucky to have Pınar Çelik as my sister and best friend. My nephew, Uzay Ateş, is the source of joy in my life. My father always makes me feel comfortable through his endless support and love. Last but not least, this book is dedicated to my brilliant mother, Şerife Çelik. Thank you, annecim, for always believing in me and teaching me how to become a strong woman!

ACKNOWLEDGEMENTS

The original version of this research was submitted to the Middle East Technical University, Department of Political Science and Public Administration as a Ph.D. dissertation in August 2019. Additionally, the earlier versions of Chapter 3 and Chapter 4 were published in *Critical Sociology* (2021, 2023) and the *Journal of Agrarian Change* (2023).

Figures and Tables

Figures

1. Number of miners in the Soma Coal Basin in the 2010s   62
2. Values of crop production in Turkey (1995–2021)   93
3. Tobacco production in the Soma Coal Basin (tons per year) between 2004 and 2020   101
4. Agricultural input price index, 2016–2022   160

Tables

1. Phases of the fieldwork   16
2. Firms operating pits in the Soma Coal Basin (2015–2019)   70
3. The number of mines and miners in the district of Soma (2015–2019)   71
4. Tobacco production in Turkey (2000–2020)   99

Acronyms and Abbreviations

AKP	Justice and Development Party
BNEF	Bloomberg New Energy and Finance World Wide Fund
BSB	Bağımsız Sosyal Bilimciler (Independent Social Scientists)
CFPP	Coal-Fired Power Plant
CHP	Republican People's Party
DevMadenSen	Progressive Mineral Research and Treatment Workers Trade Union of Turkey
DISK	Confederation of Progressive Trade Unions
ELI	Ege Lignite Enterprises
FAO	Food and Agricultural Organization of the United Nations
GDP	Gross Domestic Product
GNP	Gross National Product
GNAFC	Global Network Against Food Crisis
GLI	Western Lignite Enterprises
IMF	International Monetary Fund
LPT	Labour Process Theory
MTA	Mineral Research Exploration Institute
OECD	Organization for Economic Co-operation and Development
SAPS	Structural Adjustment Programs
SEES	State Economic Enterprises
SEM	Soma Eynez Mine
SHD	Social Rights Association
SPO	State Planning Organization
UAC	Union of Agricultural Chambers
Tekel	State Monopoly of Tobacco and Alcoholic Beverages
TKI	Turkish Coal Enterprises
TTK	Turkish Hardcoal Enterprises
TOKI	Housing Development Administration of Turkey
Türk-Iş	Confederation of Turkish Trade Unions
TSBD	Turkish Social Sciences Association
TURKSTAT	Turkish Statistical Institute
WFP	World Food Programme
WTO	World Trade Organization
WWF	World Wide Fund for Nature

CHAPTER 1

Introduction

In many countries of the Global South, rural livelihood has been restructured dramatically because of neoliberal rural development policies such as the rapid decline of state subsidies for small-scale farmers, privatization of agricultural state economic enterprises, rising control of agribusiness firms on agricultural production, and expropriation of rural commons and private farmland for mega-investments in natural resources. This neoliberal restructuring of rural livelihood is characterized by 'accumulation by displacement' (Araghi, 2009b) as it has led to massive dispossession of the rural populations from their means of production and social reproduction and, therefore, has created under-reproduced rural and urban labourers. A significant portion of the dispossessed populations of the agrarian South have migrated to the Global North or the urban centres in their own countries and constituted the most precarious segment of the 'doubly free' urban workforce. Yet, these patterns of dispossession and proletarianization have not been straightforward, and a considerable part of the population in the Global South is still rural. In fact, one of the most crucial impacts of neoliberalism in the countryside has been rural livelihood diversification. Neoliberal rural development policies based upon natural resource extraction are particularly salient in this sense as they indicate the exploitation of nature and the 'unlimited supply of surplus labour' (Veltmeyer, 2013: 81) generated by the neoliberal transformation of agriculture. Therefore, under neoliberalism, extractive capital has confronted rural labour markets in which partly dispossessed households who are forced to diversify their means of livelihood in off-farm play a pivotal role.

Under the Justice and Development Party (AKP) governments, Turkey has been a prime example of these patterns of accumulation and dispossession. The neoliberal agricultural policies, which resulted in the impoverishment, dispossession, and proletarianization of small-scale farmer households, have been accompanied by a renewed interest in mega-investments in natural resource industries (Adaman and Akbulut, 2021; Eren, 2022; Erensü 2018a). On the one hand, these investments led to further dispossession of small-scale agricultural producers because of the expropriation and devastation of farmlands. On the other hand, they constituted employment opportunities for the male members of the rural households. Yet, in many instances, neoliberalism in rural Turkey has not completely detached rural households from land and agricultural production. Agricultural production, in different forms, has been maintained through the super-exploitation of paid and unpaid work of women.

Even though the Structural Adjustments Programs (SAPs) were imposing neoliberal reforms such as the withdrawal of the state's protectionist role in agriculture and restructuring of the agricultural sector following a free market logic since 24 January 1980 Decisions, the 'great neoliberal transformation' (Islamoğlu, 2017) in the countryside of Turkey corresponds to the aftermath of the 2001 financial crisis and the consecutive AKP governments. Withdrawal of the former support system, withdrawal of the subsidized agricultural credit system of the public Agricultural Bank, determination of crop prices by the world stock prices, restructuring of the Union and Agricultural Sales Cooperatives following a market logic, and privatization of agricultural State Economic Enterprises such as the Turkish Sugar Factories Cooperation, General Directorate of the Sugar Factories Cooperation or the State Monopoly of Tobacco and Alcoholic Beverages (Tekel) have been the main transformations in this context. As a result, the share of agriculture in the Gross Domestic Product (GDP) fell drastically. However, it would be wrong to interpret this process as a simple deagrarianization as the value of total agricultural production and the average annual growth rate of the value added per worker have steadily risen. The main transformation, therefore, has been a shift from the former agrarian structure dominated by small-scale farming to an agriculture sector designed following the interests of national and international agribusiness capital. The neoliberal transformation of agriculture in Turkey in collaboration between the state, international organizations such as the International Monetary Fund (IMF), World Bank, and the World Trade Organization (WTO) indicates a process of 'modern enclosures' (Aysu and Kayalıoğlu, 2014: 11), which dispossessed the direct producers not only of their lands but also of the control over production. As a result, modern enclosures in rural Turkey in the 21st century have been manifested in the form of impoverishment, dispossession, and, therefore, proletarianization of small-scale farmers.

Since the early 2000s, neoliberal agricultural policies have been accompanied by an economic development model based on mega-investments in natural resource extraction and construction sectors (cf. Adaman et al., 2019; Adaman and Akbulut, 2021; Arsel et al., 2021). After the 2001 financial crisis, the Turkish economy experienced a growth model depended on continuous foreign capital inflows and increased indebtedness, which generated high levels of current account deficit (cf. Orhangazi, 2020; Orhangazi and Yeldan, 2021). One of the most significant items triggering the current account deficit was the increasing demand of this growth model for power generation, which could not be met by domestic resources and led to dependency on imported energy.

To diminish the dependency on imported energy, private sector investments in domestic resources such as hydroelectricity powerplants and coal have been prioritized in the macro development programs since the mid-2000s and especially the early 2010s. The AKP government has played a central role in the neoliberal reconstruction of natural resource industries and in providing political stability and market predictability for the national and transnational extractive capital. On the one hand, significant incentives have been provided for the extractive capital, such as direct subsidies or ease of environmental clearance. On the other hand, the government has repressed any kind of resistance movements against investments in natural resource industries through authoritarian measures.

This book traces the condition of labour in extractive sectors in the Global South under neoliberalism using a relational approach by paying attention to the mutual and internal relationship between production and social reproduction. Drawing on multi-sited fieldwork conducted in a coal mining region in Western Anatolia, Turkey, between 2015 and 2021, the book examines the class and gender dynamics of patterns of dispossession, labour regimes, local labour control strategies, and moments of struggle in rural extractive regions. The book is built upon my Ph.D. research and the work I developed as a continuation of it. For my Ph.D. research, I conducted three-year fieldwork in the Soma Coal Basin (2015–2017) to analyze the patterns of dispossession, labour processes, and labour control strategies as local reflections of the state-capital-labour-nature relations. Accordingly, I argued that for the analysis of labour regimes and labour control in extractive regions, there is a need to focus on four interrelated dynamics: (i) the strategic significance of the natural resource for global value chains and development policies of the country (i.e. extractive developmentalism), (ii) formation of the local labour market through the dispossession of rural populations and other means of labour supply (such as migration), (iii) the organization of work considering both natural limits and workforce composition, (iv) the use of local political, institutional and community dynamics to discipline the local labour force. During the Ph.D. fieldwork, I observed that patterns of dispossession of the local population and labour regimes in the extractive regions were surrounded by gender relations. Therefore, I revisited the field first in the summer of 2018, then virtually in the summer of 2021 to examine the gendered patterns of dispossession and how labour regimes in the extractive regions are determined by the mutual and internal relationship between development policies, relations of production, and social reproduction. Accordingly, I focused on two main inquiries: (i) how do the neoliberal agricultural policies and privatization of natural resource industries restructure social reproduction in rural areas? (ii) how do the changing imperatives of social reproduction shape labour regimes in the rural extractive regions?

1 A Class-Relational Approach to Labour of Extraction under Neoliberalism

This study adopts a dialectical methodology and philosophy of internal relations, according to which understanding any fact requires understanding the processes and relationships in the broader context within which it arose and developed. By focusing on the relations rather than things as the basis of what is real, the relational method enables us to explore the processes through which a social relation has taken place and the broader interactive context within which it happened. In other words, as stated by Bertell Ollmann, the dialectical method replaces the notion of thing with the notions of process (which contains its history and possible features) and relationship (which contains as part of what it is and its ties with other relations) (Ollmann, 2003: 14). Likewise, the analysis of the capital-labour relation (not only the relations of exploitation but also of control, discipline, and containment) in a particular time and space is internally related to the processes within which a particular group of workers were compelled to sell their labour power to a specific capitalist. For the rural extractive investments, these processes indicate the proletarianization of the peasantry in different forms and patterns in different historical phases and geographies.

A relational approach to class analysis within the Marxist tradition defines class as a historical process and social relationship between the producers and expropriators of surplus value and, therefore, rejects any definition of social class exclusive of its dialectical counterpart (Hobsbawm, 1984; Thompson, 1963; Wood, 1995). The distinguishing feature of the capitalist mode of production is that capitalists own the means of production but not the workers (Jonas, 1996) and that the economic and political controls are separated (Wood, 1995). Therefore, there is a need for the capitalists, as a dominant class, to develop specific labour control, discipline and containment mechanisms. Labour regime analysis allows us to capture the complex, contradictory, and multidimensional nature of capital-labour relations as well as the variety of forms of interrelations between the processes of production and social reproduction (Baglioni and Mezzadri, 2020). In analyzing labour regimes in extractive regions, following the framework suggested by Baglioni et al. (2022: 82), this book pays attention to (i) the processes of production, circulation, social reproduction, and ecology as key sites of capitalist exploitation, (ii) articulation of these processes in particular historical, spatial, and institutional contexts, (iii) the empirical observation of how these processes can be studied operationally.

Therefore, I combine four sets of literature to develop a class-relational approach to labour of extraction. First, I draw on the historical development of the literature on Marxist agrarian political economy, which focuses on the processes of primitive accumulation along with the dispossession and proletarianization of the peasantry. Dispossession and proletarianization of peasantry are complex issues that necessitate attention to how conditions of production and social reproduction of the rural populations are dominated by the operations of capital and the capitalist state (Bernstein, 1977). Capitalism as a system in which direct producers' access to the means of production, to the means of labour, and to the basic conditions of survival is mediated by the market imperative has restructured the conditions of production and social reproduction for the peasantry who 'traditionally reproduce themselves through their own labour' (Bernstein, 1977: 61). The development of capitalism in agriculture has taken different paces and forms in the history of capitalism and across different geographies, which led to different paths of dispossession and proletarianization. As meticulously discussed in the works of Karl Kautsky ([1899] 1988) and Vladimir Lenin ([1899] 1974), the development of capitalism in agriculture differs from that of industry, and even though the dispossession and proletarianization of the peasantry is a necessary historical path of development of capitalism, there is a need to pay attention to the moments of persistence of peasantry. In this respect, it is essential to note that capital may dominate agriculture using various forms of exploitation without necessarily transforming property relations. In the contemporary literature of Marxist agrarian political economy, the development of capitalism in agriculture and the proletarianization of peasantry is analyzed as a process of permanent primitive accumulation by referring to the ongoing strategy of capitalism to dispossess small-scale farmers and to integrate the non-capitalist strata (Luxemburg, [1913] 2003) into capital accumulation process (Çelik, 2023b: 194–195).

Natural resource extraction in the Global South under neoliberalism indicates the exploitation of both nature and the partly dispossessed rural populations generated by the neoliberal transformation of agriculture. Following the Marxist agrarian political economy framework starting from classical Marxism (cf. Kautsky, 1988; Lenin, 1974) till contemporary literature, which largely focuses on the patterns of dispossession and proletarianization of the peasantry in the Global South (cf. Araghi, 1995, 2000, 2009a, 2009b; Bernstein, 2001, 2007, 2010; Wood, 2009). I define dispossession not merely as land dispossession or property transfer. I use it broadly to include different forms of losing non-market access to the means of production and social reproduction, such as land, housing, clean water, food, firewood, and other means of subsistence. The wave of dispossession under neoliberalism has led to massive proletarianization and urbanization. Both the Marxist and non-Marxist literature on the proletarianization of rural populations largely focuses on the shift of labour from agriculture to industry. Even though the history of the Global North confirms this view to a significant extent, in the countries of the Global South, the capacity of capitalist industrialization to absorb the surplus labour created by the development of capitalism in agriculture has been somewhat limited (Razavi, 2003: 16). Therefore, proletarianization in the Global South has not been straightforward, and a considerable part of the population is still rural. Rural livelihood diversification under neoliberalism indicates a process and a relationship within which labouring populations who remained in the countryside develop different survival strategies and coping mechanisms by combining various forms of paid and unpaid work in farm and off-farm jobs and activities.

The partly dispossessed rural populations who are forced to diversify their livelihood have been defined by Bernstein (2010: 73) as classes of labour which indicates a component of workforce who are 'neither dispossessed of all means of reproducing itself nor in possession of sufficient means to reproduce itself.' For the analysis of the labour of extraction, I prefer the term classes of labour over semi-proletarian or de-proletarian because it allows to see the multiplicity of proletarian conditions by viewing the class as a 'plural category in terms of its subdivisions ... and in terms of various axes of inequality embedded within it' (Pattenden, 2016: 22). By this way, it becomes possible to (i) avoid dualities such as urban/rural, agricultural/non-agricultural, landowner/landless, (ii) examine how inequalities and oppressions along the lines of gender, race, ethnicity etc. intersect and are combined with class relations, (iii) take into account different forms of exploitation of labour, among which wage work represents only one.

The second literature I built my analysis upon is the "early social reproduction analysis" (Mezzadri, 2019; 2021) within feminism (cf. Dalla Costa and James, 1972; Federici, 2004; Fortunati, 1995; Mies, 1982, 1986, 1988), which re-interpreted the Marxist concepts and theories of primitive accumulation and labour exploitation by re-defining 'the non-capitalist strata' (Luxemburg, 2003), which is indispensable and free of charge for capital accumulation. Whereas Rosa Luxemburg meant the natural economies of the peasants in Europe, the US, and the colonies, early social reproduction feminism included non-wage work of housewives in the Global North and the unpaid work of the subsistence producers and peasants in the Global South, the majority of whom are also women. Following the early social reproduction analysis, this study addresses the need to overcome the dualistic analyses of production and social reproduction to make a relational class analysis. The distinguishing feature of capitalism is the separation of production from reproduction. Accordingly, commodity production is posited as the essential point of capitalist production through which value is created, whereas social reproduction is posited as natural production outside value relations. Yet, even though reproduction appears as outside of capitalist value relations, it contributes to the creation of value as a crucial and central part of the capitalist cycle (Fortunati, 1995: 8). Therefore, a holistic analysis of class formation in the extractive regions necessitates attention to the central role of women in production and social reproduction of the classes of extractive labour. Instead of simply adding the women's work and woman question, following the methodological warnings of the scholars of the early social reproduction analysis (Mies, 1988; 1998), I attempt to define the classes of extractive women as the producers and reproducers of rural extractive communities and reveal how extractive capital exploits their work.

During the first two phases of my fieldwork in the Soma Coal Basin, I realized the central role of women both as housewives and agricultural producers for extractive developmentalism in the region. Meanwhile, I was reading the international literature on mining communities. For example:

> What the husband earns is too little and really we all have to help out, like my making *salteñas*. Soma women help out by knitting, others sew clothes, others make rugs, other sell things in the street. Some women can't help out and then the situation is really difficult. ... Well, I think that all of this proves how the miner is doubly exploited, no? Because with such a small wage, the woman has to do much more in the home. And really that's unpaid work we're doing for the boss, isn't it? ... [E]ven though the state doesn't recognize what we do in the home, the country benefits from it, because we don't receive a single penny for this work.
>
> A miner's wife in Bolivia, 1978[1]

> The only thing men do is to work in the mine. Everything else is women's responsibility. We do farming, we do shopping, we prepare food box for our husbands. all tasks of childcare, care of our husbands are our responsibility. I think, mining companies make profits thanks to us! My husband just goes to the mine. Well, the only thing I don't do is actually going to the mine myself. The way things are, we may even have to go to the mine

---

1 Barrios de Chungara and Viezzer (1978)

one day! My husband works eight hours a day … But if you are a woman, your work never ends.

<small>A miner's wife in the Soma Coal Basin, 2018</small>

As can be seen in the narratives of two women from different parts of the world and at different times, miners' wives work for the extractive capital without receiving a single penny. This can be the case for women who are responsible for the daily reproduction of workers from different sectors as well. It is significant to underline the peculiarities of the social reproduction of the classes of extractive labour. This necessitates attention to how ecological impacts of the mine investments affect women's access to the means of production and social reproduction, as well as the feminization of agricultural work.

First, mega investments in natural resource industries in the agrarian South have not created male breadwinner/female caregiver form of rural households. As the employment generated by these investments for the male members of the rural households is casual and low-paid, women continue working in agriculture in several forms, such as petty commodity producers, unpaid family workers, agricultural wage workers and subsistence producers. Therefore, women in the classes of extractive labour are not housewives dependent upon their husband's income; instead, they are 'the last guarantors of the survival' (Mies, 1982) of the extractive households. Secondly, mine investments in the countryside transform rural households from small-scale agricultural producer families to miner families, which restructures women's social reproductive roles. As seen in the narratives of the miners' wives from two different continents and centuries, miners' wives work for the mining companies without receiving a single penny. In other words, behind 'every mine there is the hidden work of millions of women, who consume their life reproducing those who work [in the mines]' (Federici, 2021: 12).

Finally, I combine the literature on labour process and labour control with the political economy of natural resource extraction. Accordingly, on the one hand, I use labour process theory and labour control regimes to underline the internal relationship between the workplace level, local dynamics, and national or global operation of capital-labour relations, whereas, on the other hand, I draw on the embeddedness of both extractive labour and capital on the economic landscape. Natural resource extraction as a socioecological and sociopolitical process is highly dependent on the following factors: (i) the strategic significance of the natural resource for global value chains and/or development policies of the country (extractive developmentalism), (ii) formation of the local labour market through dispossession of rural population and other means of labour supply (such as migration), (iii) the organization of work considering both natural limits and workforce composition, (iv) the use of local political, institutional and community dynamics to control and discipline the local labour force. Therefore, in the analysis of labour regimes and labour control, there is a need to take into account how nature sets limits to the organization of work, to the patterns of proletarianization as investments in these regions indicate the enclosure of rural commons and 'accumulation by dispossession' (Harvey, 2003). This necessitates attention to the state-capital-labour-nature relations and how they are reflected at the local scale.

2   Introducing the Field

Soma is a district of the Manisa province in Western Anatolia, where lignite mining and agriculture have historically been the main economic activities. The Soma Coal Basin is a larger territory, which I define by referring not only to the location of the coal mines but also to the labour supply to the mines. The Basin includes the districts of Kırkağaç and Soma (Manisa), Savaştepe (Balıkesir), and Kınık (İzmir) and their surrounding villages.

Exploration of the lignite of Soma dates to the late 19th and early 20th centuries. Several small-scale domestic and foreign firms operated coal mines in Soma until they were transferred to Etibank in 1939. In 1957, Turkish Coal Enterprises (TKI) was established, and the operations of the coalmines of Soma were transferred to the TKI. From 1957 to the mid-2000s, surface mining was the dominant form of coal extraction in Soma (Tamzok, 2014). During this period, the majority of the local populations were not working in the coal pits of the basin as they were engaged in agricultural production, mainly tobacco farming. In the early and mid-2000s, two major transformations initiated the dispossession and proletarianization of the local populations. The first one is the privatization of the State Monopoly of Tobacco and Alcoholic Beverages (Tekel) in the early 2000s, which indicated the loss of state support for the tobacco producer families. Under the conditions of the absence of state support and the loss of income security, it has become impossible for the tobacco farmer families to survive merely by farming, and they have started searching for wage income. In this context, the second transformation in the Basin, which is the neoliberal transformation of coal mining, constituted an employment opportunity for the male members of these families. In 2005, coal extraction was transferred to private firms through royalty tender as part of the coal rush plans of the Justice and Development Party (AKP) governments to overcome the dependency on imported energy by utilizing domestic coal. As a result, private sector investments in the coal pits and coal-fired power plants (CFPPs) of Soma have drastically increased. As the majority of these private mining investments were in the underground mines, the need for coal miners has also increased. Therefore, a significant part of the labour supply to the underground coal pits was met by the newly dispossessed tobacco farmer families. Additionally, having large-scale investments, the Basin has attracted migration of miner families from other mining towns of the country. These patterns of dispossession, proletarianization, and migration have brought a diversity of labour regimes and proletarian conditions across gender, hometown, different degrees of access to land, and different versions of housing.

On May 13, 2014, the worst mine disaster and workplace homicide in the history of the country took place in a coalmine called Soma Eynez Mine (SEM), operated by the Soma Coal Company Incorporated. The disaster killed 301 miners. Between 2015 and 2021, 51 defendants, including the chairs of the coal company, managers and engineers, were prosecuted. An expert report submitted to the board of the Akhisar High Criminal Court in 2016 indicates that the coal rush policies of the AKP governments and production processes in the Soma Coal Company led to this disaster. The reported faulty practices include (i) shortcomings of the basin planning, (ii) defects resulting from the implementation of royalty tender, (iii) insufficient inspections and (iv) deficiencies in relevant legislation on health and safety in coalmines. However, there have been no structural changes in the coal rush policies of the AKP governments. Indeed, there have been other mine disasters in different coal regions of the country since the Soma mine disaster.

3   The Design and Method of the Fieldwork

The fieldwork stretched over six years (2015–2021) and across several villages in three cities of Western Anatolia (Manisa, Balıkesir, and İzmir). Between 2015 and 2017, I conducted semi-structured interviews with miners, local activists, and representatives of local community institutions to gather their reflections and perspectives on Turkey's coal policies in the labour processes and local labour regime in the Basin. During this first phase of the fieldwork, I observed that increasing coal investments and neoliberal agricultural policies had transformed the agrarian structure in the region and the local population's relation to land. Having seen that these transformations were surrounded by gender relations, I revisited the field in the summer of 2018 to analyze women's (miners' wives in particular) productive and reproductive work. I conducted interviews with women farmers and agricultural workers, and using the participant observation method, I spent time with them by joining social meetings such as weddings or fast-breaking meals during Ramadan and helping them with their farm work. Finally, in the summer of 2021, I conducted virtual semi-structured and focus group interviews with local activists and agricultural workers to follow up on ongoing land dispossession and labour regimes of agricultural workers during the pandemic (see Table 1).

In line with the motivation of the research, the aims pursued in the fieldwork are: (i) to investigate the patterns of dispossession and proletarianization in the Soma Coal Basin, (ii) to illustrate the reflections of the changing relationship between the state-capital-labour-nature in the spheres of production and social reproduction. The most proper method to reach these objectives is qualitative research methods because the 'insider' view of a locality gained through qualitative research methods provides the researcher with the opportunity to gather information not only on social relations but also on the way in which individuals and groups attach to and evaluate their everyday lives through their beliefs and meanings (Roberts, 2014: 7). As qualitative research stressed the socially constructed nature of the reality, the researchers can seek to answer the questions on how social experience is created and given meaning (Denzin and Lincoln, 2003). Moreover, qualitative research methods provide the researchers with the flexibility to change or diversify the research scope and/or method and to develop new mechanisms to gather during the fieldwork. As put by Mason (2002: 24), decisions about the design of the research are ongoing and grounded in practice in qualitative research. Accordingly, thinking qualitatively means rejecting a priori design decisions, as qualitative research is essentially exploratory, fluid, and flexible (Mason, 2002: 24):

> Thinking qualitatively means the idea of a research design as a single document which is an entire advance blueprint for a piece of research. It also means rejecting the idea of a priori strategic and design decisions, or that such decisions can and should be made only at the beginning of the research process. This is because qualitative research is characteristically exploratory, fluid and flexible, data-driven and context sensitive. Given that, it would be both inimical and impossible to write an entire advance blueprint.

Utilizing the flexible nature of qualitative research methods, I used diverse methods in accordance with the requisites of the research process, including:

3.1 *Semi-structured Interviews*
Semi-structured interviews sit in between focused and structured methods while utilizing from both. In semi-structured interviews, some questions are

specified prior to the interview, but the interviewer can direct the flow of the interview following the answers of each interviewee. Demographic questions are often fixed, then the researcher structures the rest in advance (May, 2004). During the fieldwork, I conducted semi-structured interviews with miners, agricultural workers, housewives, local activists, representatives of local institutions, and lawyers of the miners who died in the Soma Mine Disaster.

The majority of the semi-structured interviews were conducted with the miners and agricultural workers/producers to listen to their narratives on (i) patterns of rural change and dispossession, (ii) processes of migration to Soma, (iii) labour processes in the coalmines and farms, (iv) conditions of agricultural production in different forms, (v) changing imperatives of social reproduction. In the semi-structured interviews conducted with the miners and agricultural workers, the questions on age, hometown, education level, and years of experience in mining and agriculture were fixed, whereas I designed the rest of the questions during the interviews in accordance with different forms of relation to land and agriculture, types of households, employment status and firm, and political stance. I recorded most of the interviews, whereas I took notes when the interviewees did not give permission for the recording.

Secondly, I conducted semi-structured in-depth interviews with the local activists to gather information on the historical transformation of local social relations. In this context, I interviewed (i) activists who were born in Soma and have been part of oppositional political movements since the 1970s and (ii) current representatives of the oppositional trade unions and other political organizations.

The third group I interviewed was the lawyers of the miners who died in the Soma Mine Disaster to explore (i) the relationship between the labour processes in the mines of Soma and the disaster, (ii) the relationship between the legal framework of coal mining in the country and the Soma Mine Disaster, (iii) how the government and coal companies intervened in the prosecution process of the disaster.

3.2 Focus Group Interviews

The strength of focus group interviews lies in the fact that they provide the researcher with the opportunity to discover the reasons behind the differences of opinions, attitudes, and beliefs within the sample, given that, as a moderator, the researcher is able to 'listen in' the conversation within the sample (Kleiber, 2004: 97). Therefore, the researcher is expected to encourage the participants to talk to one another instead of asking individual questions to each of them

(May, 2004: 137–8). In this way, focus group interviews allow the researcher to gather information that they cannot gather through individual interviews.

During the fieldwork, I conducted six focus group interviews (one online and six in-person). In the first one, I interviewed miners who work in different companies to see the commonalities and differences in labour processes. In the second and third ones, I conducted focus group interviews in two different villages of Savaştepe with miners from different generations having different relations to both mining and agriculture. Then, I conducted two focus group interviews in the summer of 2018 with agricultural worker women who had different degrees of access to land and employment status. Finally, I conducted a virtual focus group interview in the summer of 2021 with agricultural wage worker women. Those women had similar experiences of farm work; having a focus group interview instead of individual interviews was their preference.

3.3 *Participant Observation*

Participant observation is a uniquely interpretive research method that enables the researcher to participate actively in the social world in which people experience, interpret, and understand their environments (Atkinson and Hammersly, 1994: 249). To become a part of and participate in a social setting requires more than 'hanging around' and being accepted by that social setting to a certain degree (May, 2004 173).

Participant observation was my most significant method during the fieldwork for two main reasons. First, during the preparation phase of the fieldwork, the participant observation method provided a significant opportunity to gather general information about local social relations and establish connections for future interviews. Secondly, some people were reluctant to talk in a recorded interview due to the political pressures and strict local labour control and discipline strategies. Therefore, during the home visits or certain social events, they felt more comfortable expressing themselves. Thereby, I attended several local social activities such as:

- Trials of the Prosecution of the Soma Mine Disaster,
- Summer schools of the Social Rights Association,
- Women's workshops organized by the Social Rights Association,
- Meetings and demonstrations in the anniversaries of the Soma Mine Disaster,
- Social meetings such as weddings, fast-breaking meals, and home visits,
- Visiting the agricultural producers at the farms and helping out in certain tasks such as stringing tobacco or irrigating the small yards.

Participating in these events allowed me to observe social relations and interactions such as intra-class conflicts, moments of solidarity, or discussions on political issues. Moreover, observing their daily lives and how they interpret them allowed me to identify the underlying tensions and conflicts embedded in the process of rural change and patterns of proletarianization. Additionally, during the trials of the prosecution of the Soma Mine Disaster, listening to the statements of the miners who survived the disaster and of the wives and mothers of the miners who died allowed me to explore the conditions of miners in the sphere of production and social reproduction.

4 Phases of the Fieldwork

4.1 *Phase I (June and July 2015, February 2016)*

The first phase mainly consists of the preparation stage of the fieldwork. During this period, I tried to get to know the field in order to plan the forthcoming Phases. For this purpose, I started following up the lawsuit blocks of the Soma Mine Disaster in the Akhisar High Criminal Court in June 2015. I used the participant observation method while having conversations with the relatives of the miners who died in the disaster in order to gather information about the demographic profiles of the miner families, the factors that had pushed them to work in the underground mines, their relation to land and agriculture, working and living conditions of miner families, etc. Additionally, by following up the defences of the defendants of the criminal lawsuit who are composed of the owner of the coal company, directors, engineers, shift supervisors and the witness statements of the workers of the coal company who survived from the disaster, I gathered information on the labour regimes in the underground coal pits of the Soma Coal Basin.

Secondly, during this first phase of the fieldwork, I did semi-structured interviews with local activists and prominent people in order to gather information on the historical transformation of the social relations in the Basin. In this context, I conducted interviews with an agricultural engineer, a high school teacher, three lawyers, and one politician. Especially two of the interviewees who were born and grew up in the public housing of the Turkish Coal Enterprises (TKI). These two interviews enabled me to have an opinion on the mining community life during the pre-1980 period.

Finally, in the preparation phase of the fieldwork, I carried out interviews the representatives of the oppositional trade unions and other political and activist organizations. In this context, I did two interviews with the local representatives of the local branch of the Dev-Maden-Sen (Progressive Miners'

Union),[2] a trade union affiliated to the Confederation of Progressive Trade Unions (DISK). Then, I took part in the activities of the local branch of the Social Rights Association (SHD), such as the march they organized for each month anniversary of the disaster, their summer school organized for the children of the miner and farmer families, and workshops with agricultural worker women. I also conducted interviews with the then representatives of the local branches of the political parties such as the Republican People's Party and Nationalist Action Party (MHP). In this part of the first phase, I also had a chance to observe the roles of these political and civil society actors in local social relations.

Finally, I interviewed with three lawyers of the criminal lawsuit of the Soma Mine Disaster who were defending the families of the deceased miners. During these interviews, I gathered information on labour regimes in the underground coal mines-especially regarding production pressure over miners and over the natural limits of the mine- and political interventions on the prosecution process of the disaster.

4.2   Phase II (June–September 2016, March 2017)

During the second phase of the fieldwork, I gathered information on the transformation of agricultural production, labour regimes in the coal pits, local class relations and everyday life, local labour control mechanisms and strategies, and moments of consent and resistance. Between June and September 2016, I rented a flat at the centre of the Soma district to carry out detailed ethnographic research.

During my longest stay in the field, one of the most striking political developments in Turkey's recent history took place. On July 15, 2016, a group associated with the Fethullah Gulen movement[3] within the Turkish army attempted to take over the government. The coup attempt faced strong resistance from the citizens, who took the streets at night in response to President Recep Tayyip Erdogan's call to defend democracy. By the morning of July 16, it was clear that the coup attempt failed. Yet, the government declared a three-month state of emergency on July 21, 2016. The state of emergency was extended every three

---

2 The local branch of the Progressive Miners Union in the Soma Coal Basin was established immediately after the Soma Mine Disaster. First, it attracted the attention of workers, who were unhappy about the precarious working conditions in the coal mines. Yet, it lost its power starting from 2015 and 2016. Detailed information on this union, as well as other alternative unionization attempts, are discussed in Chapter 5.

3 A social and religious movement inspired by the teachings of Fettullah Gülen, a Turkish leader of a religious community named, Fettullah Gülen Cemaati.

TABLE 1 Phases of the fieldwork

Phases	Time period	Aims	Research methods
Phase I	June & July 2015	Choosing the scope of the case study Gathering general information about the basin Preparing the interview questions	Document collection Following up the prosecution process of the Soma Mine Disaster Participant Observation Semi-structured interviews with the local activists
	February 2016	Conducting the pilot interviews Developing the interview questions	
Phase II	June-September 2016 March 2017	Gathering information on: (i) the transformation of the agricultural production in Soma (ii) the production relations in the coal pits (iii) local class relations (iv) labour control mechanisms (v) Moments of consent and of resistance	Following up the prosecution process of the Soma Mine Disaster Participant Observation Semi-structured interviews with the local and migrant miner families, trade union representatives, local politicians Focus group interviews in the village coffeehouses Field diaries
Phase III	July & August 2018	Gathering information of women's productive and reproductive labour	Participatory observation (in the production process in the farms) Focus group interviews Semi-structured Interviews
Phase IV	August 2021	Revisiting the field to observe the ongoing land dispossessions Gathering information on the impact of the Covid-19 pandemic on labour processes	Virtual interviews with local activists, miners, and agricultural workers Focus group interview with agricultural worker women

months for two years until it ended in July 2018. During the state of emergency, authoritarian tendencies of the Justice and Development Party (AKP) government have further deepened through measures including judicial repression strategies and intensifying crackdown on political opposition, public servants, academia, trade unions, media, and other actors of civil society, which were accompanied by the government's ongoing authoritarian neoliberalism (cf: Tansel, 2018; Yılmaz and Turner, 2019). In the Soma Coal Basin, in line with the rest of the country, even before the coup attempts, due to the political and social discomfort under the authoritarian regime and mechanisms of oppression after the crisis management process of the Soma Mine Disaster, it was quite difficult to encourage workers to express their opinions about their working conditions, coal firms, and government freely. After the coup attempt and the declaration of a state of emergency, it had become even more difficult. To cope with these difficulties, I had to develop several strategies to reach out the workers and conduct interviews. One of the most important results of this was the use of the participant observation method actively, especially when workers were reluctant to talk during the recorded interviews.

During the first weeks of Phase II, I attempted to conduct group interviews with the representatives of the Ege Lignite Enterprises (ELI) (local branch of the Turkish Coal Enterprises), coal companies, and the Maden İş trade union, which is in close contact with the companies and the government. First, I called the trade union to ask an appointment for an interview. They wanted to see the questions first and asked me not to include any questions having political content. Then, I emailed the list of questions by eliminating the ones that could have been regarded as politically sensitive and trying to keep the questions purely technical. A couple of hours later, someone from the union called me and told me that given the Soma Coal Basin was politically under the spotlight, they were not in charge of deciding to make an interview and told me to request a permission from the district governor. Given that the trade unions are not institutionally and bureaucratically bounded to the district governors, I could not receive such permission.

Later, I scheduled an appointment with the chair of the Ege Lignite Enterprises (ELI), which is the regional branch of the Turkish Coal Enterprises (TKI). He rejected answering my questions and told me that I was supposed to get official permission from the Ministry of Energy and Natural Resources to conduct business with him and with the coal companies. As I noted right after the meeting in my diaries, his statement was as follows:

> I have no idea how you would use what I tell here. That is why I cannot give an interview. Also, the companies are dependent on us. They

cannot accept an interview without our permission. In the end, we are the licence holders of the mines they operate. Three companies operate mines here. Imbat is the largest one, it has around 6,500 workers. Only the general manager can answer your questions, but he would need our permission. We need to get permission from the Ministry of Energy and Natural Resources.

Then, my Ph.D. supervisor, as the coordinator of my research project, wrote a petition to the Ministry to request permission to conduct interviews with the representatives of the ELI and the coal companies. Yet, the Ministry responded to our request by stating that it was not their responsibility to give such permission. As a result, I could not conduct interviews with the ELI and coal companies. The second important shortcoming is the fact that I could not observe the working conditions in the underground mines as no one was allowed to enter them. Therefore, my findings on the labour process in the underground coal pits are based on the narratives of the miners.

During the Phase II, the fieldwork included interviews and participant observation methods with four group of people: (i) local families who live in the district centre of Soma, (ii) migrant families who live in the district centre of Soma, (iii) local families who live in the district centre of Kınık and Savaştepe, (iv) local families who live in their villages. Migrant families are composed of the residents who migrated to Soma from other mining regions of Turkey, such as Zonguldak and Kütahya, and from towns such as Bartın, Ordu, and Çorum, i.e., towns that historically supplied workers to the hard coal mines of the Zonguldak coalfield.

During the second phase, I conducted the first two groups of the interviews at the district centre of Soma. In order to reach out the interviewees, I used the networks of the Soma branch of the Social Rights Association, as well as the network of the families I met during the trials of the disaster. Using a snowball sampling method, I reached out to other people. This part was more difficult than the interviews I conducted in Kınık, Savaştepe, and in the villages due to the political pressures over the miners within the district of Soma. Most of the miner families were unwilling to do the interviews, or they did not feel comfortable expressing themselves while being recorded. As a result, one third of the interviews I did with them were not recorded. Instead, I took notes during and immediately after the interviews.

Later, I carried out interviews with families who live in Kınık, Savaştepe, and their surrounding villages. They were relatively more comfortable during the interviews compared to the people who lived in Soma, as their lives outside the workplace were more independent from the direct influence of the mining capital. In order to reach out these people, in addition to the use of snowball sampling method, I directly contacted the village representatives (mukhtar), some of whom were also miners, and they helped me schedule interviews with other miner families in their villages.

During the Phase II, in addition to the in-depth interviews, I used participant observation method, especially due to the unwillingness of people to be recorded under the authoritarian political and working environment. By attending wedding ceremonies, fast-breaking meals, home visits, visits to the farms, I spent time with the miner families and gathered information about the relations of production and social reproduction. I

During my stay in the field in the summer of 2016, I could not conduct focus-group interviews with the miners as a woman researcher. In March 2017, I revisited the field with my Ph.D. supervisor, Galip Yalman, and conducted focus group interviews in the coffeehouses. The significance of focus group interviews is that they provide the opportunity for the researcher to observe the communication and discussion between the interviewees. We did the first focus group interview in the Soma district center with three migrant miners from Kütahya who worked at three different coal companies. This allowed us to see the differences and similarities of miners in different companies. The rest of the interviews were held in the coffee houses of the villages, with miners from different generations. These interviews enabled us to discover the changing significance of coal mining and agricultural production across generations and the changing working conditions in the mines, especially the difference between the working conditions in the state-operated mines and private sector mines.

4.3 *Phase III (July and August 2018)*

During my visits to the Soma Coal Basin in the first two phases of the fieldwork to analyze the processes of proletarianization, neoliberal transformation of agriculture and coal extraction, and their impact on local class relations, I observed that women assumed a central role through these processes. I realized it during our conversations with the wives, mothers, or sisters of the miners while I was following up the prosecution process of the Soma Mine Disaster in Akhisar High Criminal Court or during social meetings such as weddings or fast-breaking meals during the Ramadan. Initially, I specified my unit of analysis as miner families but did not realize the essential role of the (changing) gendered division of work and women's role as the reproducers of the labour-power in local social relations. Therefore, I realized that it was essential to extending the scope of my fieldwork in order to unveil the gendered characteristics of rural households and rural labor markets. In fact, in contrast to the political economy frameworks, which consider the domestic structures as taken for granted, feminist political economy frameworks have sought to expose how households are structured in relation to broader social and economic structures (Elson, 1998). In doing so, one needs to overcome the analysis of the rural household as a black box, as a homogenous unit and pay attention to the unequal distribution of resources and power and unpack the ways in which global capitalism has historically integrated women members of the patriarchal households into the global market economy (Mies, 2014; Razavi, 2009). Similarly, in order to make a holistic analysis of the agrarian change, patterns of dispossession and proletarianization, and labour regimes in the rural extractive regions, women's central role in the production and social reproduction of the classes of extractive labour needs to be analyzed.

During the previous phases of the fieldwork, I observed that patterns of proletarianization in the Soma Coal Basin did not necessarily result in a complete detachment of the families from land and agricultural production. Instead, they tended to diversify their livelihoods through men's participation in wage work in the underground coal mines and women's longer stay in agricultural production in various forms, including wage work, petty commodity production, and subsistence farming. Additionally, the heavy working conditions of the miners tend to intensify the work of social reproduction for women.

Therefore, I revisited the field to analyze women's work in agriculture and in the reproduction of labour power, as well as how extractive investments transform imperatives of social reproduction. In the summer of 2018, using the methods of semi-structured interviews, focus group interviews, and participant observation, I analyzed the conditions of agricultural wage work, petty commodity production, subsistence farming, and care work done by miners' wives.

During the third phase of the fieldwork, I visited the Basin in July and August, during the harvest seasons of tobacco and tomato and pepper respectively. During the tobacco harvest in July, I did two focus group interviews with women at one of their homes. The first group was composed of six women, three of whom were migrant women, and the rest were living in their villages. Hearing about their severe conditions in tobacco farming, I joined a group of nine women at the farm in order to observe their working conditions and help them. During the tomato and pepper harvests in August, I conducted two groups of interviews. The first was with women who worked as daily agricultural wage work in large, capitalist farms of the lowland villages, whereas the second was composed of three petty commodity producer women raising tomatoes and peppers in their small farmlands.

There are two important shortcomings of the fieldwork. As I mentioned earlier, the first one is the lack of interviews with the state institutions and coal companies, as my requests were rejected. The second important shortcoming is the fact that I could not observe the working conditions in the underground mines as no one was allowed to enter them. Therefore, my findings on the labour process in the underground coal pits are based on the narratives of the miners.

5   Outline of the Book

The next chapter outlines the theoretical approach of the book by employing the term classes of extractive labour. First, it elaborates on the debates on primitive accumulation and proletarianization in classical Marxist literature by referring to the works of Karl Marx, Fredrich Engels, Vladimir I. Lenin, Karl Kaustky, and Rosa Luxemburg. Then, it underlines the relevance of their concepts for the analysis of 21st-century capitalism by referring to the literature on the permanency of primitive accumulation and the reception of the works of Rosa Luxemburg by the early social reproduction analysis within Marxist Feminism since the 1970s. Finally, it discusses the class-relational approach adopted in the book by unpacking the concept of the classes of extractive labour to analyze the class formation processes in the rural extractive regions across production and social reproduction. The chapter suggests that a relational approach to class formation in rural extractive regions necessitates attention to the patterns of dispossession and proletarianization, along with the changing imperatives of production and social reproduction. Such a holistic analysis helps to unveil the impacts of expropriation of the control over agrarian production, expropriation of rural commons and farmland, as well as the super-exploitation of the classes of extractive labour as workers of the extractive industries, agricultural workers, petty commodity producers, and subsistence producers.

Chapter 3 is the first of the fieldwork-based chapters of the book. It focuses on the state-capital-labour-nature relations in Turkey under the AKP governments and how Turkey's coal rush is reflected in the labour regimes in the underground coal mines of the Soma Coal Basin. The chapter starts by unpacking the literature on extractivism, labour process theory, and labour control. Then, it outlines the political economy of Turkey's coal industry with a particular focus on the post-2001 period. Having clarified the strategic significance of the coal industry for the development policies of the AKP governments, the rest of the chapter discusses the labour processes and labour control strategies at the production unit (underground mines) as reflections of the top-down extractive developmentalism of the AKP governments since the mid-2000s. This last part employs the concept of 'production pressure' to explain the super-exploitation of both labour and nature. In short, combining the literature on extractivism and labour process theory, the chapter unpacks the (i) coal rush policies of the AKP governments, (ii) labour supply to the underground coal pits, (iii) labour processes of miners.

Chapter 4 shifts the focus to the changing imperatives of social reproduction and gendered labour regimes in the rural extractive regions by raising two interrelated questions: how do the extractive investments transform social reproduction in rural areas and how do the changing imperatives of social reproduction affect labour regimes of women in paid and unpaid forms. The chapter begins with an analytical framework for the analysis of the classes of extractive labour by paying attention to women's central role in the patterns of dispossession, proletarianization, and diversification of rural livelihood. It then contextualizes the neoliberal transformation of agricultural policies and the rising significance of extractive investments for the rural development models of the AKP governments by paying a particular attention to their gendered patterns. Finally, it analyzes the impact of rising coal investments in the forms of proletarianization of the local populations, land expropriations, land degradation, and water and air pollution on women's paid and unpaid agricultural work and reproductive work as miners' wives.

Chapter 5 discusses the local labour control and discipline strategies of the state, extractive capital, and local political and community institutions in the Soma Coal Basin before and after the Soma Mine Disaster. It seeks to examine labour control beyond the workplace, in the sphere of social reproduction, and how miner families obey or resist them. Labour control in the extractive regions is particularly important because of the geographical fixity of the natural resources. Due to the strategic significance of the coal industry for the authoritarian neoliberal regime of accumulation in Turkey, extractive capital and the state needs to develop local labour control strategies in the resource rich regions to guarantee the rhythms of investments. The Soma Coal Basin is exclusively of essence because of the experience of a fatal disaster in 2014. The state and the extractive capital needed to develop and implement local labour control and discipline mechanisms through various political, institutional, juridical and cultural mechanisms of coercion and consent. The chapter first clarifies the concept of authoritarian neoliberalism along with its manifestations in Turkey. It then elaborates on the Soma Mine Disaster and its prosecution process. The chapter continues by examining the use of local institutional, political and community networks as labour control mechanisms before and after the disaster. It finally discusses the moments of resistance in the Basin by referring to their strengths and shortcomings.

Finally, in the postscript, a brief analysis of the impact of Turkey's overlapping crises in the 2020s on local labour regimes is added. The empirical data included in the postscript is informed by a revisit to the Soma Coal Basin in May 2024 for a new joint research on the policy implications of just transition on coal miners. In the postscript, some notes on the impact of the food crisis on agricultural production and small-scale farmers' families in the basin and the impact of the ongoing crisis of inflation and currency depreciation on the coal industry are shared.

CHAPTER 2

Classes of Extractive Labour across Production and Social Reproduction: Patterns of Dispossession and Class Formation in the Rural Extractive Regions

This chapter examines the patterns of dispossession of small-scale farmers from the means of production and social reproduction and of proletarianization in the extractive regions at a high level of abstraction to explain how extractive investments transform rural livelihood. The debate on the proletarianization of rural populations, the changing forms of their relations to the means of production and social reproduction, and the role of off-farm rural industries in these processes is complex. This chapter aims to clarify it by separating the discussions. First, the concepts of primitive accumulation and proletarianization are elaborated on by referring to their use in classical Marxist literature and their re-interpretations in the late 20th and early 21st century by contemporary Marxist and Marxist feminist scholars. Secondly, historical waves of the dispossession of the small-scale agricultural producers and the rural class formations in the agrarian South are analyzed. Finally, the class-relational approach adopted in this study is unpacked by employing the term *classes of extractive labour*.

In line with the overall aim of the book to reveal the broader sets of processes and relationships behind the labour supply, labour processes, and diversification of livelihood in rural extractive regions, I argue that it is essential to pay attention to the characteristics and transformations of agrarian structures to understand the class contradiction between the extractive capital and extractive labour. This book adopts a class-relational approach and philosophy of internal relations, according to which understanding any fact requires an understanding of the processes and relationships in the broader historical context within which it arose and developed. The philosophy of internal relations allows us to analyze the social world and its elements through the dialectical method and the process of abstraction (Ollman, 2003: 2). Accordingly, by focusing on the relations instead of things as the basis of what is real, the dialectical method enables the researcher to explore the processes through which a social relationship has taken place and the broader interactive context within which it happened. In other words, as put by Ollman, dialectics, by replacing the notion of "thing" with the notions of "process" (which contains its history and possible futures) and "relation" (which contains as part of what are its ties with other social relations). Ollman explains the central significance of paying attention to primitive accumulation to make a relational analysis as follows (Ollman, 2003: 14):

> In abstracting capital, for example, as a process, Marx is simply including primitive accumulation and the concentration of capital-in sum its real history- as part of what capital is. Abstracting a relation brings its actual ties with labour, commodity, value, capitalists, and workers-or whatever contributes to its appearance or functioning-under the same rubric as its continuing aspects. All the units in which Marx thinks about and studies capitalism are abstracted both as processes and relations. Based on this dialectical conception, Marx's quest-unlike that of his common sense opponents-is never for how a relation gets established (as if it were not already changing) but for the various forms this change assumes and why it may appear to have stopped. Likewise, it is never for how a relation gets established (as if there were no relation there before) but for the various forms it takes and why aspects of an already existing relation may appear to be independent.

Likewise, the analysis of the capital-labour relation (not only of exploitation but also of control, discipline, and containment) in a particular time and space is internally related to the processes and relationships through which the corresponding workers have been compelled to sell their labor power to that particular capitalist. For the rural extractive investments, that process mostly includes the dispossession and proletarianization of small-scale farmers in different forms and degrees, as well as different forms of division of labour across gender, race, caste, etc. under different historical and/or geographical settings. Therefore, the chapter begins by unpacking the Marxist and feminist debates on primitive accumulation and its permanency under different phases of capitalism.

1 Proletarianization as Primitive Accumulation

In Volume I of *Capital*, Karl Marx defined primitive accumulation as the 'historical process of divorcing the producer from the means of production' that 'transforms, on the one hand, the social means of subsistence and production into capital, on the other, the immediate producers into wage-labourers' ([1867] 1995). For Marx, the primitivity of this process stems from its correspondence to a particular historical phase when the mode of production essential for capitalist accumulation had not yet been realized. Hence, primitive accumulation indicates the dispossession of the peasantry from the means of production and the formation of a class of doubly free labourers who 'neither they themselves form part and parcel of the means of production, as in the case of slaves, bondsmen nor do the means of production belong to them, as in the case of peasant-proprietors' (Marx, 1995). Therefore, for Marx, the proletarianization of the peasantry was the essential precondition for capitalist accumulation and '[j]ust as the capitalist mode of production, in general, is based on the expropriation of the conditions of labour from labourers, so does it in agriculture presuppose the expropriation of the rural labourers from the land and their subordination to a capitalist, who carries on agriculture for the sake of profit' ([1867] 1999). Similarly, Engels viewed the proletarianization of the peasantry as the logical consequence of the class differentiation processes in Europe and the small peasantry as the future proletariat (Araghi, 1995: 340). Therefore, the thesis of Marx and Engels on the disappearance of the peasantry is based on the capacity of the development and expansion of capitalism in the countryside to eliminate pre-capitalist relations of production. In the *Peasant Question in France and Germany* ([1867] 1950), Engels mentioned the role of the peasantry within the population, relations of production, and political power by questioning the ways to capture political power in the European countries where capitalism had not yet replaced pre-capitalist social relations. Engels' primary focus is on the political implications of the stark division between the capitalist farmer and wage labourer. Accordingly, the ultimate resolution of the agrarian question was the development of capitalism in agriculture and capitalist relations of production along with the formation of rural populations who are doubly free in the Marxian sense (Akram-Lodhi and Kay, 2009: 7; Byres, 2012: 13).

It was Rosa Luxemburg ([1913] 2003) who first interpreted primitive accumulation as a necessary component of capitalism by associating it with the contradictory logic of capitalist accumulation. Accordingly, the persistence of capitalist accumulation was impossible without the existence of a non-capitalist milieu outside of it. In fact, capital needs labour power and natural resources all over the world for unlimited accumulation. Since the majority of that labour power and natural resources exist in the orbit of pre-capitalist production, capital must expand to obtain ascendency over these territories and social organizations (Luxemburg, 2003: 345–6). By relating primitive accumulation to the contradictory logic of capitalist accumulation, Luxemburg's analysis paved the way for analyzing primitive accumulation as a continuous and necessary element of capitalist accumulation instead of a feature of a particular historical epoch. Similarly, she emphasized the permanency of proletarianization by underlining the formation of the urban and rural proletariat, which indicates 'the continual process by which rural and urban middle strata become proletarian with the decay of peasant economy and of small artisan enterprises, the very process, that is to say of incessant transition from non-capitalist to capitalist conditions of a labour power' (2003: 342).

Therefore, referring to Marx's analysis of primitive accumulation and transformation of peasant production, she had gone beyond Marx by regarding primitive accumulation and the violence inherent in it as an essential and continuous element of capitalism (Luxemburg, 2003 345–6):

> [C]apitalism, in its full maturity also depends, in all respects on non-capitalist strata and social organisations existing side by side with it. ... The interrelations of accumulating capital and non-capitalist forms of production extend over values as well as over material conditions, for constant capital, variable capital and surplus value alike. The non-capitalist mode of production is the given historical setting for this process. Since the accumulation of capital becomes impossible in all points without non-capitalist surroundings, we cannot gain a true picture of it by assuming the exclusive and absolute domination of the capitalist mode of production. ... Capital needs the means of production and the labour power of the whole globe for untrammelled accumulation; it cannot manage without the natural resources and the labour power of all territories. Seeing that the overwhelming majority of resources and labour is still in the orbit of precapitalist production – this being the historical milieu of accumulation – must go all out to obtain ascendancy over these territories and social organizations.

Luxemburg's analysis has paved the way for regarding primitive accumulation as a continuous element of capitalist accumulation instead of a specific feature of a particular historical phase and, therefore, constituted the basis for the contemporary debates on the permanence of primitive accumulation.

When Marx's and Luxemburg's analysis of primitive accumulation are brought together, it is plausible to argue that capitalist production owes its existence to continuously reproducing the process of divorcing the direct producers from the ownership and control of the means of production, i.e. 'expanded proletarianization' (Bonefeld, 2014: 66). As mentioned above, Marx's analysis of primitive accumulation indicates the development of capitalism and transformation of subsistence farmer peasantry into the wage labourers. Similarly, for Engels, the proletarianization of the peasantry was the logical consequence of class differentiation in Europe, and the small peasantry was the future proletariat (Araghi, 1995: 340). Therefore, the Marxist thesis on the disappearance of the peasantry is based upon the capacity of development and expansion of capitalism to eliminate pre-capitalist modes of production. As put by Marx in Volume 3 of the Capital (1999), "Just as the capitalist mode of production in general is based on the expropriation of the conditions of labour from labourers, so does it in agriculture presuppose the expropriation of the rural labourer from the land and their subordination to the capitalist."

In *Peasant Question in France and Germany* (1950) Engels underlined the essential role of the peasantry within the population, relations of production, and political power and questioned the ways to capture in the European countries, where the development of capitalism was an ongoing process, yet, capitalism had not yet replaced pre-capitalist social relations. In this process, Engels mainly focused on the stark division between capitalist farmer and wage labourer as well as the political implications of this relation. Accordingly, the ultimate resolution of the agrarian question was the development of capitalism in agriculture and the full development of the capitalist relations of production, in other words, the formation of the doubly free rural wage workers (Byres, 2012: 13; Akram Lodhi and Kay, 2009: 8).

As defined by Charles Tilly (1979: 1), proletarianization is 'the set of processes which increases the number of people who lack control over the means of production, and who survive by selling their labour power.' These processes include impoverishment, dispossession, commodification of the means of production and subsistence and their concentration in the monopoly of private property (Özuğurlu, 2011: 64), and so find their expression in the concept of primitive accumulation. This process has its roots in the development of capitalism in agriculture. Yet, there is no unique law of agrarian development under capitalism (Akram-Lodhi and Kay, 2009: 10), and historically, there have been various forms and paths of the development of capitalism in agriculture and proletarianization of the direct producers depending on the different trajectories of incorporation into the world economy and rural class structures.

By focusing on the contradictions of these processes, Karl Kautsky ([1899] 1988) and Vladimir Lenin ([1899] 1974) ascertained the relatively more complicated dynamics of capitalist development in agriculture compared to industry and defined peasantry as a combination of different classes and groups who should be defined in their relation to other classes (Aydın, 1986: 133–4; Boratav, 2004: 118–9). Following Marx, they both accepted the fact that the dispossession and proletarianization of the peasantry was the general tendency of capitalist development. Yet, they developed their theses by considering different and complicated experiences of capitalist development in agriculture. Kautsky (1988) defined the development of capitalism in agriculture as the transformation of the peasant into a hired labourer. Yet, for Kautsky, capitalism does not impose a path dependence on agriculture, and the proletarianization of the peasantry is a contradictory and complicated process. Accordingly, as the concentration and centralization eliminated petty commodity production in agriculture, traditional peasantry would be dissolved, and a rural society composed of two classes would be established: rural proletariat and capitalist farmers. Additionally, his definition of the rural proletariat includes petty commodity producers as well as wage workers (Alavi and Shanin, 1988: xv). Therefore, he built his analysis upon the processes through which capital dominates agriculture, transforms property relations, and creates new forms of exploitation. By this way, his work allows us to overcome the duality between the disappearance and persistence of the peasantry by underlining the complementary relationship between small and large farms. As it can be detected from his definition of the rural proletariat, in Kautsky's analysis, petty commodity production in agriculture indicates over-exploitation of peasant labour power (Alavi and Shanin, 1988: xv) and small agricultural firms sell labour power instead of commodities and by this way complement big farms (Aydın, 1986: 138).

The contemporary relevance of Kautsky's work stems from his interpretation of peasant family farms within the capitalist mode of production and their persistence under the domination and exploitation of capital. Therefore, he viewed the peasant sector of the capitalist economy as a source of continuous primitive accumulation (Alavi and Shanin, 1988: xxxii). Kautsky's analysis of the proletarianization of the peasantry does not view complete dispossession and separation from land as a necessary condition of capitalist development by defining the peasants who sell their labour power without being detached from land as part of the rural proletariat. As he put it, "The rural proletariat ... swells the ranks of the proletariat without expropriating the small farmers, without breaking their tie to the land" (Kautsky, 1988: 190). Accordingly, the increasing need for cash income due to the development of commodity relations in agriculture compels peasants to sell their surplus labour. This pressure to earn cash income could result in migration to the cities to work in industry as well as search for peasant supplementary employment in the countryside (1988: 168–9). In fact, Kautsky claimed that partial detachment of the producers from their land could be preferred by the agricultural and industrial bourgeoisie as the partly dispossessed farmers who can meet at least a part of the reproduction needs from their land would accept working for low wages. Accordingly, the fact that capitalists have to assume responsibility for the reproduction costs of fully proletarianized and/or migrant workers sharpens class contradiction. In this sense, by focusing on the market and cash dependency of direct producers for their survival instead of viewing wage relation as a mere form of capitalist development in the countryside, Katsky's analysis allows to overcome the dichotomy between landowning and landless rural proletariat.

Similarly, while regarding the dispossession and proletarianization of small agricultural producers as a historical path of the development of capitalism in agriculture, Lenin (1974) mentioned their persistence and viewed the rising cash dependency of the peasant households as the driving factor behind their search for supplementary income (Lenin, 1974: 42):

> It is forgotten that the "freeing" of one section of the producers from the means of production necessarily presumes the passage of the latter into other hands, their conversion into capital; presumes, consequently, that the new owners of these means of production produce as commodities the products formerly consumed by the producer himself, i.e. expand the home market; that in expanding production the new owners of the means of production present a demand to the market for new implements, raw materials, means of transport, etc., and also for articles of consumption (The enrichment of these new owners naturally presumes an increase in their consumption). It is forgotten that it is by no means the well-being of the producer that is important for the market but his possession of money; the decline in the well-being of the patriarchal peasant, who formerly conducted a mainly natural economy, is quite compatible with an increase in the amount of money in his possession, for the more such a peasant is ruined, the more he is compelled to resort to the sale of his labour-power, and the greater is the share of his (albeit scantier) means of subsistence that he must acquire in the market.

For Lenin, capitalism in agriculture resulted in the differentiation of the peasantry and the formation of new types of rural populations (1974: 173). By criticizing the analyses that interpret rural transformation merely as changing property relations, he argued that property differentiation was only a starting point of the whole process through which the old peasantry ceased to exist and was expelled by new types of rural inhabitants: rural bourgeoisie and rural proletariat. In contrast to the 'too stereotyped an understanding of the theoretical proposition that capitalism requires the free, landless worker,' Lenin underlined different ways through which capitalism penetrates agriculture and defined rural proletariat as: 'Completely landless; but most typically (…) the allotment-holding farm labourer, day labourer, unskilled labourer, building worker or other allotment holding worker' whose defining feature is their 'inability exist without the sale of the labour power (...) and extremely low standard of living' (1974: 177). By including poor peasants who are not landless and maintain cultivating their lands in his definition of the rural proletariat, Lenin put the commodification of labour power, either in the form of wage labour or petty-commodity production, at the centre of his analysis (Akram-Lodhi and Kay, 2009: 12).

The works of Lenin and Kautsky, which focus on the contradictory nature of the development of capitalism in agriculture, along with Luxembourg's conceptualization of primitive accumulation as a continuous characteristic of capitalist accumulation, constitute proper ground for the analysis of the transformation of the peasantry and rural class relations under neoliberalism as they allow to capture (i) permanency of primitive accumulation, (ii) various paths of dispossession and proletarianization, and (ii) multiplicity of proletarian conditions in the agrarian South.

2 Ongoing Primitive Accumulation and Gendered Patterns of Proletarianization: A Marxist Feminist Framework

In the contemporary literature, following Rosa Luxemburg, primitive accumulation has been interpreted as a continuous and necessary component of capitalist accumulation (cf. Bonefeld, 2014; De Angelis, 2001; Glassman, 2006; Harvey, 2003; Perelman, 2000) due to the expansionist nature of capitalist reproduction and to the process of subjection of labour to capital. In other words, the scholars of permanent primitive accumulation regard capitalism's need to continuously dispossess direct producers from the control and ownership of the means of production both as a historical 'prerequisite of capitalism and a compulsory component of capitalist reproduction' (Bonefeld, 2014). Following the statement of Marx in Grundrisse (1973: 460) that what "originally appeared as conditions of its becoming – and hence could not spring from its action as capital – now appears as results of its own realizations," Bonefeld (2011) defined primitive accumulation as a constituent element of capitalist social relations which has exterminated in appearance and re-emerged as a result of its own reproduction. Accordingly, the fact that individuals who are divorced from the ownership of means of production can only survive by selling their labour power to capital – i.e. that capitalist form of organization of social labour presupposes the detachment of the direct producer from the ownership and control of means of production – itself proves that primitive accumulation is a necessary condition for continuous accumulation.

Therefore, 'as a result of its own realization, primitive accumulation is a permanent accumulation' (Bonefeld, 2011: 387).

Additionally, in his analysis of neoliberalism, David Harvey (2003) views accumulation by dispossession as the dominant form of accumulation under neoliberalism, not only through the detachment of direct producers from the means of production and subsistence but also through new means of enclosing commons such as privatization of public services (2003: 149–50). Accordingly, the privatization of social services, such as the right to state pension, welfare, or national healthcare, which were won through years of class struggle, have been among the most salient forms of dispossession of neoliberalism (Harvey, 2003: 149):

> The corporatisation and privatisation of hitherto public assets (such as universities) to say nothing of the wave of privatisation (of water and public utilities of all kinds) that has swept the world indicate a new wave of "enclosing the commons." As in the past, the power of the state is frequently used to force such processes through even against popular will. ... The reversion of common property rights won through years of hard class struggle (the right to state pension, to welfare, to national health care) to the private domain has been one of the most egregious of all policies of dispossession pursued in the name of neoliberal orthodoxy.

Therefore, Harvey explains how the crises of capitalism are solved through accumulation by dispossession by referring to its follow-up quality of primitive accumulation. By releasing a set of assets at a very low cost, capital is able to hold these assets and turn them into a profitable use. In the case of the enclosure movement, this necessitated enclosing and expelling a resident population to create a landless proletariat and releasing the land into the privatized mainstream of capital accumulation. Similarly, privatizations under neoliberalism opened up vast fields for capital to seize upon (Harvey, 2003: 149).

Additionally, the analysis of Massimo De Angelis (2001) goes further by defining primitive accumulation as a permanent component of the class conflict between capital and labour and stressing its function as a political strategy of capital to recreate the conditions of capital accumulation. Accordingly, as the working class struggle is the perpetual factor of capitalist mode of production, capital applies the strategies of primitive accumulation to continuously create and recreate the conditions of accumulation:

> [T]he divorcing embedded in the definition of primitive accumulation can be understood not only as origin of capital vis-à-vis pre-capitalist

social relations, but also as a reassertion of capital's priorities vis-à-vis those social forces that run against this separation. (...) Since for Marx working class struggles are a continuous element of the capitalist relation of production, capital must continuously engage in strategies of primitive accumulation to recreate the 'basis' of accumulation itself. (...) To the extent class conflict creates bottlenecks to the accumulation process in the direction of reducing the distance between producers and means of production, any strategy used to recuperate or reverse this movement of association is entitled with the categorization – consistently with Marx's theory and definition – of primitive accumulation.

Overall, the debate on the permanency of primitive accumulation has shifted the attention of classical Marxist theory to the forms of exploitation beyond wage labour by focusing on the commodification of natural resources, land, urban space, and public services. Yet, the feminist re-interpretation of Rosa Luxemburg's work during the late 1970s and 1980s has been overlooked in these discussions. The reception of Luxemburg by feminist scholars is essential to understand the forms of dispossession under neoliberalism as, besides the privatization of land, air, water, social services, etc., neoliberalism stands for invasion of the ways in which people are forced to reproduce themselves (Soiland, 2016: 187–9). The debate on the permanency of primitive accumulation has been significant for feminist scholars since women, as well as the subsistence producers in the colonies, have been treated as if they were means of production or natural resources such as land, water, or air. According to Maria Mies (1988: 5), women as the means of production for producing the essential commodity for capitalism (i.e. labour power) and land are goods that cannot be produced by capital and control over them is a necessary precondition for any system based on exploitation.

The scholars of early social reproduction analysis re-interpreted Rosa Luxemburg's argument on the capitalism's need for the non-capitalist strata for expanded accumulation by arguing that capitalism had always combined a process of ongoing primitive accumulation based on direct violence and robbery with its process of the "so-called 'capitalist accumulation,' based on the 'scientific' exploitation of the wage workers, by 'economic coercion'" (Mies, 1988: 6). By conceptualizing what Rosa Luxemburg termed non-capitalist strata and milieu, as colonies, Mies (1998) argued that colonies were necessary not only to initiate capital accumulation in the dawn of capitalism (primitive accumulation), but they continue to be essential to keep capital accumulation going (ongoing primitive accumulation and colonization). By the non-capitalist strata, Rosa Luxemburg mainly meant natural economies of the peasants in Europe and the US, as well as in the colonies, whereas scholars of early social reproduction analysis included non-waged work of the Western housewife and the unpaid work of the small peasants and subsistence producers in the colonies, majority of whom are also women. Almost three decades after the publication of *Women: The Last Colony*, Maria Mies explained how the analysis of Rosa Luxemburg helped her, Veronika Bennholdt-Thomsen, and Claudia von Werlhof to gain a better understanding of primitive accumulation to include housework under capitalism as follows (Mies, 2014: 217–8):

> [Housework of women], like that of peasants, the colonies, or other 'non-capitalist milieus' (as Rosa calls them) is available 'free of charge' like nature; unprotected by labour law and contracts and available around the clock, it represents the cheapest and politically most efficient way of reproducing labour-power available to capital. (...) We extended Rosa Luxemburg's analysis to women's work, and in particular to housework under capitalism. It is these workers – along with nature, the colonies, subsistence farmers and many people working in the so-called informal sector the world over – who form the basis of what is called the economy: the articulation of capital and wage-labour. The housewifisation of work was and continues to be the trick by which capital keeps women's work devalued, unorganised and atomised, free to access it all times and to reject it whenever it pleases – at no cost.

Using the metaphor of iceberg, Mies suggested re-conceptualizing the capitalist economy by putting women's and subsistence producers' work at the centre of the analysis. In their re-conceptualization, they rejected simply adding the neglected areas (i.e. women and the subsistence producers) to the existing theories (Mies, 1988: 3) and located the main contradiction of capitalism not between capital and wage labour but between 'all labour – life – and capital' (Von Werlhof, 2007: 15). Accordingly, exploitation of wage labour by capital merely constitutes the tip of the iceberg rising above the water while the whole base of the iceberg under the water, which has been neglected by the dominant theories including Marxism, include women's unpaid housework, caring work, nurturing work, and emotional work along with the work of small peasants and artisans in the subsistence economies of the Global South. Therefore, the hidden/underwater part of the economy includes women, nature, and colonized territories and people who are defined by Mies (1998: 11) as the colonies of white men (i.e. of the Western industrial system).

For Mies, colonization had always been based upon violence and this violence had never been gender neutral. In fact, whereas the relationship between the capitalist and wage-labourer is built upon a legal contract, the relationship between the colonizers and colonies is enforced and stabilized by structural violence (Mies, 1998: 8). Additionally, in her celebrated book *Caliban and the Witch*, Silvia Federici (2004) analyzed witch-hunts in Europe as a form of enclosure which dispossessed women of their roles in society and economy. She differentiated her definition of primitive accumulation from Marx's in two respects. First of all, she suggested an analysis of primitive accumulation beyond the formation of male-waged proletariat and the development of commodity production by referring to a set of changes which transformed women's condition and the production of labour power. These changes include (i) the development of a new sexual division of labour subjugating labour and reproductive functions of women; (ii) the construction of a new patriarchal order based upon the exclusion of women from wage work and their subordination to men; and (iii) the mechanization of the proletarian body and (in the case of women) its transformation into a machine for the production of workers. Secondly, just like Maria Mies, for Federici, that violence was not specific to the primitive accumulation in the dawn of capitalism. Instead, capitalism continuously necessitates the return of the most violent aspects of primitive accumulation. Therefore, for their analysis of ongoing primitive accumulation, there is a need to pay attention to how capitalism depends on and is built upon patriarchal relations (Mies, 1986). As a matter of fact, the scholars of early social reproduction analysis rejected viewing patriarchy as a residuum of feudal relations and viewed capitalism as the latest expression of patriarchy (Von Werlhof, 2007: 24). Accordingly, it would be misleading to view patriarchy as a reflection of the remnant of feudal relations, because under capitalism, women's exploitation and subordination is determined by the mutual accommodation of capitalism and patriarchy.

In this respect, one of the key interventions of the scholars of early social reproduction analysis to Marxism has been the rejection of putting gender relations in the superstructural sphere and considering oppression of women and exploitation of women's unwaged work as subordinate to wage relation. To resolve this, they have underlined the need to overcome the analytical duality between 'oppression' and 'exploitation.' As stated by Mariarosa Dalla Costa and Selma James (1972):

> Since Marx, it has been clear that capital rules and develops through the wage, that is, that the foundation of capitalist society was the wage labour and his or her direct exploitation. What has been neither clear

nor assumed by the organizations of the working class movement is that precisely through the wage has the exploitation of the non-wage labourer been organized. This exploitation has been even more effective because of the lack of a wage hid it. that is, the wage commanded a larger amount of labor than appeared in factory bargaining. Where women are concerned, their labor appears to be a personal service outside or capital. The woman seemed only to be suffering from male chauvinism, being pushed around because capitalism meant general 'injustice' and 'bad and unreasonable behavior'; the few (men) who noticed convinced us that this was 'oppression' but not exploitation.

Therefore, by overcoming the duality between oppression and exploitation, they define exploitation of women in a triple sense: exploitation as human beings by men (not economically), as housewives by capital, and as wage workers. The last form of the exploitation is determined by the former two forms of exploitation (Mies, 1986: 37).

Luxemburg's work has offered a framework to understand why women as unpaid domestic workers, the colonies, and natural resources have to be exploited for the ongoing accumulation. Yet, by defining these so-called non-capitalist settings as integral components of the capitalist system, early social reproduction feminists underlined the need for capitalism to create 'non-capitalist 'islands' within its own interior, which it can then reconquer at a later point, namely in the form of subsistence production' (Soiland, 2016: 193–4). The creation of these non-capitalist islands has been possible because of the dual character of capital (Fortunati, 1995). Accordingly, one of the most essential transformations under capitalism has been the separation of production from reproduction, in which the former *appears* as the creation of value, whereas the latter *appears* as the production of non-value. As commodity production and the relationship between capital and wage labour are posited at the core of capitalist production, reproduction is viewed as natural production. As explained by Leopoldina Fortunati (1995: 8–10), although the separation of production from reproduction *appears* as the separation of value and non-value, reproduction *is* the creation of value but *appears* otherwise. It is this dual character of capital and the positing of reproduction as natural production that enables both production and reproduction to function as the production of value, as capital can exploit two workers with one wage. Therefore, for the continuous accumulation of capital, reproduction must appear as a natural process, as a 'personal service outside of capital' (Dalla Costa and James 1972), and 'by historically separating (and valuing) production and (devaluing) social reproduction ... capital creates the very possibility of exploitation' (Baglioni et al., 2022: 85).

It is also essential to clarify who those 'non-capitalist' producers are and what they really do. Firstly, they constitute the majority: housewives throughout the world, peasants of all sexes, mainly in the Global South who produce for their own subsistence, and the army of male and female marginalized people, most of whom also live in the Global South. Secondly, they are forced to produce goods for their own consumption without receiving payment. Therefore, the structural similarity between a caregiver housewife in the Global North and a peasant producer in the South is the fact that both of their production processes are considered to be outside capitalism proper and characterized as non-capitalist, pre-capitalist or semi-feudal, etc. (Mies, 1986: 128). The scholars of early social reproduction analysis use the term subsistence production to refer to both subsistence farming and housework. As defined by Mies (1982: 3), subsistence production, in its broadest sense, indicates the production of life and, just like subsistence farmers (the majority of whom are women as well), housewives produce use values which are inherent factors of the capitalist mode of production. They underline the fact that the production of use value has its counterpart in exchange value, and women's subsistence work produces exchange value with some delay – when the capitalist appropriates the labour power produced and reproduced by women (Bennholdt-Thomsen, 1982: 244). Therefore, women as the producers and reproducers of the most essential commodity under capitalism, i.e. labour power, 'figure as a subsistence producer in spite of being a commodity producer' (Von Werlhof, 1988 as cited in Mies, 1986: 133). This supposedly non-capitalist work not only guarantees the survival of the households but also provides the capital with the opportunity of expropriating the unpaid reproductive work of women without paying for it (Von Werlhof, 1988: 16). The continuous exploitation of this unpaid work is possible through the historical opportunity that patriarchy has provided for capitalism: the existence of women ready to do this work for free either through patriarchal coercion (domestic violence, rape, etc.) or consent (love, motherhood ideology, faithfulness, etc.) (Acar-Savran and Yaman, 2020: 9).

In her celebrated piece, *No Critique of Capitalism Without a Critique of Patriarchy*, starting from the argument that it is not possible to understand capitalist economy without paying attention to unpaid labour, especially in the form of housework, Claudia von Werlhof (2007) argued that it is not always proletarianization but housewifization of labour that characterizes capitalist development. She furthermore mentioned that even more than the wage labour system, it is the unpaid or non-regular wage labour such as domestic labour, new forms of slavery or precarious labour that define capitalism. These forms of labour are inherently capitalist that, in fact, 'capitalism is not about wage labour but about the cheapest possible forms of commodity production' (Von Werlhof, 2007: 4):

> The objective of capitalism is not the transformation of all labour into wage labour, but the transformation of all labour, all life, and of the planet itself into capital, in other words: into money, commodity, machinery, and the 'command over labour' (Marx). The accumulation of capital does not only happen by exploiting wage labour, but by exploiting all labour, as well as nature and life itself. It is not the 'socialization' of labour by 'free contract' that allows devaluating labour and life and hence accumulating more capital, but it is labour's and life's 'naturalization' and its transformation into a 'natural resource' for exploitation/extraction (its 'natural-resourcization') that do so.

Therefore, capitalism served to increase the subordination of women and of women's invisible labour that while men were being proletarianized (transformed into wage workers), women turned into domestic servants of their husbands (unwaged family labourers). Even when women participate in the wage-labour market, they have been limited both by capitalism and patriarchy. Under the wage labour system, men's control over women's labour has been altered but has not been eliminated; it has been maintained and even deepened through sex-ordered job segregation (Hartmann, 1976:152).

3 The Development of Capitalism in Agriculture and Dispossession of Small-scale Farmers

Primitive accumulation as permanent accumulation is directly related to the development of capitalism in agriculture under different phases of capitalism. It indicates, on the one hand, the detachment of petty producers from the ownership or tenancy of land and, on the other hand, the formation of capitalist producers. However, as warned by Lenin, complete dispossession from land is not a necessary precondition for the development of capitalism in agriculture and the proletarianization of the peasantry. The development of capitalism in agriculture mainly indicates direct producers' loss of non-market access to the means of production and social reproduction. As explained by Ellen Meiksins Wood (2009: 42):

> [T]he critical turning point occurred when producers lost non-market access to the means of production – land itself. The emphasis here is on non-market access, not complete dispossession, because market imperatives were set in motion well before the complete dispossession of direct producers or the complete commodification of the labour-power. Indeed, if anything, the complete dispossession of direct producers was a result more than a cause of these market imperatives.

Market imperatives have taken several forms under different phases of capitalism and brought new forms of dispossession and proletarianization.

In the contemporary Marxist agrarian political economy literature, the transformation of the peasantry, as in the permanency of primitive accumulation debate, is viewed as a permanent strategy of capitalism to dispossess small-scale producers and to articulate non-capitalist settings to capitalist accumulation. By building the analysis of the transformation of agriculture and peasantry upon the relationship between theory and history, scholars of agrarian political economy have analyzed 'the great global enclosure of our time' (Araghi, 2000) as a permanent component of both old and new forms of capital accumulation. It is old in the sense that the need to form labour-power free from the means of production and self-reproduction is endemic to capitalism; it is new in the sense that it represents the culmination of the development of capitalism in agriculture and changes in the composition of labour markets and labour relations (Araghi, 2009a: 120; Friedmann, 2006: 462). Therefore, the proletarianization of the peasantry should be analyzed as a structural tendency and strategy of capitalism, which takes different historical forms, by avoiding the determinist, evolutionist and teleological assumptions of both the disappearance thesis of classical Marxism and the permanence thesis of Chayanovians (Araghi, 2009a: 118).

By interrogating the linear analyses of agricultural modernization, the food regime analysis unveils how key historical contradictions of capital accumulation processes have penetrated and transformed the production, circulation, distribution and consumption of food (cf. Friedmann, 1993; McMichael, 2009). Accordingly, different food regimes reflect different forms of power relations embedded in 'crossscale agrarian transformations' which include 'the exercise of, and subordination to, episodic hegemonic political–economic projects within the state system – embodying changing trade, investment, and financial strategies in the global food system' (McMichael, 2021: 218). In this context, the first food regime (from the 1870s to 1930s) combined colonial tropical imports to Europe with basic grains and livestock imports from settler colonies, whereas the second food regime (from the 1950s to 1970s) gave priority to national regulation and authorized both import controls and export subsidies to manage national agricultural policies (Friedmann, 1993: 31; McMichael, 2009: 141). Even though the integration of farmers into markets, the transformation of peasants into petty-commodity producers and the commodification of subsistence were initiated under the second food regime of post-World War II; this process indicated a 'relative depeasantization' (Araghi, 2009a: 130) as the small-scale farmers of the agrarian South were able to benefit from the protectionist policies such as the price supports, subsidies and financing of agricultural inputs by the state. The Third Food Regime, the corporate food regime since the 1980s, has deepened commodification and institutionalized market and property relations privileging agribusiness 'in the name of production "efficiencies," "free trade," and global "food security" ... [and] institutionalized subsidies for Northern energy-intensive agribusiness production and export of artificially cheapened foodstuffs' (McMichael, 2012: 682) at the expense of both farmers of the Global South and the global food security.

Under the corporate food regime of neoliberalism, the main transformations have been (Araghi, 2009a: 131; Bernstein, 2010: 82–3):

- Withdrawal from the agrarian welfare state through the decline or removal of state subsidies for small-scale farmers, privatization of agricultural state economic enterprises, and decreasing price support schemes,
- Restructuring of global value relations through trade liberalization, which transformed food into a commodity produced and traded for profits,
- The determination of crop and input prices by world market prices,
- The increasing concentration of global corporations in both agri-input and agro-food industries through mergers and acquisitions,
- Restructuring the international division of labour through the financialization and deployment of a global debt regime,
- The deregulation of land markets and the reversal of the land reform policies of the national developmentalist era.
- The combination of the corporate economic power of global corporations with resource-intensive agricultural technologies, which have had a significant ecological impact during the recent decades,
- Rising off-farm investments in the agrarian South, especially in natural resources, construction, and tourism.

These transformations under neoliberalism have resulted in the formation of underreproduced rural populations (Araghi, 2009b) and led to the processes of dispossession of small-scale farmers of the Global South from their lands and, therefore, their proletarianization and increasing market dependency of the small-scale farmers to access means of production and social reproduction.

4   Rural Class Formation across Production and Social Reproduction

Since the 1970s, the question of whether the complete detachment from land is a necessary moment of proletarianization or not arose again. To define the lack of the 'double freedom' of workers in a Marxian sense, concepts such as semi-feudal (Bhaduri, 1973; Byres, 1991) or deproletarian (Brass, 1999; 2010) have been employed. The concept of semi-feudalism is used to indicate the dual means of subsistence under conditions where capitalist relations of production had not yet developed. Accordingly, once the capitalist relations are fully developed, these dual means of subsistence would cease, and workers would become completely free from the ownership of the means of production (Çınar, 2014: 121). In contrast to the semi-feudal approach, Tom Brass (2010) developed his analysis of deproletarianization by arguing that labour-power is unfree not because capitalism is at its beginning but instead because it is mature. Additionally, Brass employed the concepts of *bonded labour* by referring to the condition of unfreedom stemming from bondages such as debt and *unfree labour* by referring to its differentiation from the free labourers who dispose of their labour power. In his analysis, he defined unfreedom in terms of the lack of the second freedom – freedom from the control of a particular employer – in capitalist accumulation. Accordingly, an unfree labourer, 'unlike a free labourer who is able to enter or withdraw from the labour market at will,' is subject to extra-economic coercion and, therefore, lacks the freedom to decide on selling her labour power. This unfreedom does not indicate a pre-capitalist or semi-feudal relationship but a critical aspect of the class conflict between capital and labour in which capital's control over labour increases and the cost of labour decreases. Overall, unfree labour, for Brass, is not only compatible with capitalism but it is also a matter of choice because the deproletarianization of the rural workforce is significant for the class struggle that enables capitalist producers to depoliticize, cheapen, and discipline their workforces (Brass, 2010: 25).

Yet, such definitions of the dual means of subsistence have serious methodological shortcomings in terms of the analysis of both the development of capitalism in agriculture and of class conceptualization. Firstly, there is no pure form or path of development capitalism in the countryside. As put by Jairus Banaji, it is more useful to think of agrarian capitalism 'as a trajectory of forms of subsumption of labour into capital based on the dispossession and control of labour by agrarian classes engaged in farming as a business' (2002: 115). This definition allows us to see the multiplicity of forms of commodification of labour-power beyond wage-labour. Moreover, given that Marx defined the capitalist idea of freedom as fiction and the free labourer as a worker who is 'compelled to sell himself of his own free will,' 'it is possible to argue that no contract is really free because economic coercion is pervasive under capitalism' (Banaji, 2003: 71). In fact, capital is capable of exploiting labour power through various arrangements in different historical circumstances and geographies and defining them within the duality of freedom and unfreedom is mostly quite fluid and ambiguous. Capitalist production can articulate diverse forms of exploitation and ways of organizing labour to produce value, and historical materialism needs to go beyond a motionless paradigm to analyze the complexity of ways in which capitalism works (Banaji, 1977: 88, 2012: 231; Bernstein, 2010: 34).

Secondly, definitions such as semi-feudal, unfree labour, or deproletarianization reflect a particular methodological choice in terms of class analysis. These adjectives derive from the definition of class as a structural location within the social hierarchy. Relational class analysis within Marxism, on the contrary, views class as a historical process and relationship (Wood, 1995) between direct producers and appropriators of surplus value. As long as it is a dialectical relationship formed in the process of expropriation of surplus value, class formation is defined as a happening based on class struggle (Çelik and Erkuş-Öztürk, 2016: 421). By replacing the notion of thing with the notions of process and relationship, relational class analysis paves the way for defining 'what is' as part of the process within which 'it has become that and the broader interactive context in which it is found' (Ollman, 2003: 13). One of the most prominent representatives of the relational approach to class analysis, Edward P. Thompson, claimed that as a historical category, class is derived from the observation of social process over time. Accordingly, the reason why we know about classes is that people have repeatedly behaved in class ways (Thompson, 1978: 147). Therefore, to conceptualize/theorize class, there is a need to pay attention to the class formation processes instead of mapping class locations. The proletarianization of the peasantry, in this sense, indicates the transformation of class relations and class formation processes in the countryside. Therefore, these processes are neither mutually exclusive nor zero-sum. As stated by Araghi (2009a: 138) depeasantization and proletarianization do not indicate 'a completed or self-completing process leading to death of the peasantry. Social classes do not simply end or die; they live and are transformed through social struggles.' Instead, proletarianization indicates 'an ongoing historical process, 'a happening' in Thompson's words' (Araghi, 1995: 359).

In defining the labouring populations in the natural resource extraction regions, I adopt a 'class-relational approach' (Pattenden, 2016) which views the class as a 'plural category in terms of its subdivisions … and in terms of the various axes of inequality embedded within it' Ibid, 22) and highlights 'exploitation and domination and how unequal relations between capitalists and labourers extend beyond the labour process to encompass the entire process of material reproduction' (Ibid, 31). Natural resource extraction in the Global South under neoliberalism indicates the exploitation of both nature and the '"unlimited supply of surplus labour" generated by the capitalist development in agriculture' (Veltmeyer, 2013: 81). In other words, under neoliberalism, extractive capital confronted a rural class structure; the protagonists of which are the (partly) dispossessed farmers whose ownership of the means of production may legally persist, but non-market access to the means of subsistence ceased (Araghi, 2000, 2009a; Veltmeyer and Petras, 2014; Wood, 2009). Extractive capital has both created this (partly) dispossessed rural populations by expropriating private farmland and utilized their process of proletarianization as they have constituted a source of cheap labour force for their investments. Overall, neoliberal agricultural policies and extractive investments together have transformed rural livelihood through the removal of state subsidies for small-scale farmers, privatization of agricultural state economic enterprises, rising control of agribusiness firms on agricultural production, and expropriation of rural commons and private farmland. It has resulted in the dispossession of indigenous communities of peasant farmers from their lands (Veltmeyer, 2013; Veltmeyer and Petras, 2014). This has increased the market dependency of small-scale farmers for their reproduction (Wood, 2009) and a subsistence crisis, as defined by Bernstein (1977) as a 'simple reproduction squeeze.' The simple reproduction squeeze has led to a global wave of depeasantization through displacement of rural populations from their villages (Araghi, 2009a).

Yet, depeasantization in the Global South has not been straightforward, and a considerable part of the population is still rural. Rural populations in the South have developed specific survival strategies, one of the most important being diversifying their income sources through increasing participation of small-scale farmers in wage work in agriculture or rural industries such as construction, tourism or mining. Therefore, the analysis of labour markets and labour regimes in the agrarian South necessitates attention to the 'rural labour beyond the farm, supplied not only by fully 'proletarianized' rural workers who are landless ... but also by marginal farmers or those too poor to farm as a major component of their livelihood and reproduction' (Bernstein, 2010: 110).

Therefore, to define the partly dispossessed labouring populations in the extractive regions of the agrarian South, I use the term *classes of extractive labour,* by referring to Henry Bernstein's (2010) concept of classes of labour to define a component of workforce which is 'neither dispossessed of all means of reproducing itself nor in possession of sufficient means to reproduce itself' (2010: 73). These classes of labour refer to 'the growing numbers who now depend–directly or indirectly–on the sale of their labour power for their daily reproduction' (Panitch and Leys, 2001, as cited in Bernstein 2007). Bernstein (2009: 73) preferred the term classes of labour over semi-proletarian as 'it is less encumbered with the problematic assumptions and associations in both political economy (e.g. functionalist readings of Marx's concept of the reserve army of labour) and political theory and ideology (e.g. constructions of an idealised (Hegelian) collective class subject).'

The term classes of labour offers a methodological opportunity for the analysis of rural workforce in the extractive regions as it allows to (i) overcome dualistic modes of analysis within the workforce such as urban/rural, agricultural/non-agricultural, wage employment/self-employment and land-owning/landless (ii) capture multiplicity of proletarian conditions in the agrarian South along lines of gender, race, generation, caste (Bernstein, 2007; O'Laughlin, 1996; Pattenden, 2018). I argue that the transformation of rural livelihood in the extractive regions is inherently gendered, and a holistic analysis of it necessitates attention to the central role of gender division of labour within the classes of extractive labour. Therefore, the third duality that needs to be overcome for the analysis of extractive labour is between paid (productive) and unpaid (reproductive) work(force).

5   Conclusion

This chapter outlined a relational approach to understanding class relations in rural extractive regions by paying attention to the Marxist feminist conceptualizations of primitive accumulation, dispossession, proletarianization, and class formation. Adopting a relational comprehensive approach elucidates the effects of expropriation not only of land but also of control over the means of production and social reproduction in extractive regions. In this respect, it helps to unveil the holistic transformation of the imperatives of production and social reproduction, including expropriation of the control over agrarian production, expropriation of rural commons and private farmland, super-exploitation of the labour power of the workers of the extractive industries, agricultural workers, petty commodity producers, and housewives in paid and unpaid forms, and expropriation of access to fresh air, clean water, and healthy food. Unpacking these processes, in turn, allows us to suggest concrete alternatives.

CHAPTER 3

Extractivism and Labour Control: Reflections of Turkey's 'Coal Rush' in the Underground Coalmines

The fieldwork-based chapters of this book explore four co-constitutive aspects of class relations in rural Turkey: (i) the political economy of the coal industry and agrarian change in Turkey in the 2000s, (ii) the formation of the rural labour markets through gendered division of labour; (iii) labour processes and labour control in the sphere of production; (iv) labour processes and labour control in the sphere of social reproduction. The focus of this chapter is on how state-capital-labour-nature relations determine labour processes in underground coalmines.

The chapter particularly focuses on the reflections of the coal rush at the workplace level, i.e. at the underground coalmines. The next section briefly revisits the literature on extractivism, labour process theory, and labour control to show that extractive industries necessitate peculiar forms of labour control. Then, I discuss the political economy of Turkey's coal industry from the 2000–01 financial crises onwards. Then, I underline the manifestations of the Justice and Development Party's (AKP) coal rush policy in the labour processes in the coal pits of Soma through super-exploitation of both nature and labour.

1 Controlling and Disciplining the Classes of Extractive Labour: Labour Regime Analysis

In the context of neoliberalism, extractivism–exploitation of hard and energy commodities in their raw state–has become a key development strategy for resource-rich countries across the Global South and the Global North (Ayelazuno, 2014). Within this general trend of mineral extraction, countries develop their extractive-based developmentalism within the limits of structural conditions such as availability and magnitude of resources, institutional arrangements, the level of economic growth etc., whereas the driving force behind the extractive developmentalism varies across countries depending on structural or cyclical needs of the economy such as export-oriented development in Latin America or substitution of the imported energy in Turkey. Yet, development policies in general, extractivism in particular, are not mere reflections of structural conditions. They shape and are shaped by the class relations within the country and locality in question. Therefore, extractivism as a development strategy should be viewed 'upon the prism of class struggle, political conflict, and resource wars' (Veltmeyer and Petras, 2014). As long as extractive investments in the countryside indicate exploitation of nature and the surplus labour generated by the global enclosures, there is a need to analyze the peculiarities of labour regimes and labour control strategies considering the natural factors and workforce composition.

Labour Process Theory (LPT) and the literature on local labour control regimes that link the analysis of workplace to the broader social structures constitute a proper ground for the analysis of labour control in the extractive industries and regions. Accordingly, workplace level (particular use of labour force by a particular firm), local dynamics (use of the local labour markets by the locally located capital) and the global operation of capital-labour relations are internally related moments of the same totality and of each other (Gough, 2003: 27–8). Since the publication of Harry Braverman's (1974) influential work, *Labour and Monopoly Capital*, labour process has been analyzed as a site of class relations within the Marxist literature. Building his analysis upon the division of labour (especially between mental and manual labour), Braverman focused on the degradation and deskilling of work. By criticizing Braverman for reducing labour control to the expropriation of skill, Michael Burawoy, in his celebrated work *Politics of Production* (1985), developed the concept of factory regime to define two dimensions of the politics of production. Accordingly, on the one hand, particular social relations are reproduced in the production process; on the other hand, there are distinctive political and ideological apparatuses of production that regulate production relations alongside the work. Based on these dimensions of the factory regime, Burawoy distinguished between the relations of production and relations in production.

Following Marx, Braverman, and Burawoy, the scholars of LPT analyze the labour process as a manifestation of the fundamental moment of inequality in the social relations of production by arguing that as this unequal exchange between the employer and employee is far from natural, measures have to be taken for the perpetuation of it. The need for labour control arises from the separation of the economic and political controls under capitalism (Wood, 1995) and from the fact that capitalists own the means of production but not the workers (Jonas, 1996: 325). LPT suggests that labour processes require a multidimensional analysis of labour control strategies by paying attention to the broader political economy affecting employer-employee relations. Labour control, therefore, indicates the interplay between labour exploitation (production of surplus value) and disciplining (mechanisms of mitigation and containment) (Baglioni, 2018: 112–3).

Locality is central to the analysis of labour process and labour control because, on the one hand, relations in workplaces face pressures from local structures; on the other hand, workers are reproduced in the local communities. Since labour exploitation and labour control are mutually linked and reinforced, labour control strategies represent different articulations between labour exploitation and disciplining through various mechanisms, including interrelationships among workplaces, family and community institutions, local trade union organizations, employers' associations and local political parties (Jonas, 1996: 334; Rainnie et al., 2010: 299). Labour process and labour control are dependent upon the local reproduction of labour power. Spheres of reproduction in the localities produce socially differentiated labour power in which the work capacities of the people are constructed by their household incomes and those of their neighbourhoods. Moreover, the spheres of reproduction are shaped by local production. Labour process and labour control are directly dependent on the local reproduction of labour power. The reproduction sphere is also strongly shaped by local production. The condition of local employment and its segmentation affects the local relations (in the neighbourhood or at home). The labour process and the reproduction of labour power are internally related, and they form a 'single differentiated structure' (Gough, 2003: 37) that shapes the local labour control regimes. Therefore, investments in localities indicate more than entrepreneurialism. They include the reproduction of local market conditions through various strategies of control and containment, such as the development of locality-based recruitment practices, provisions of employee services outside the workplace, organizations of local consumption opportunities, involvement in local philanthropic, civic, and cultural endeavours, proposing local policies and supporting local candidates for elections, etc. (Jonas, 1996: 334).

The state organizes the capital-labour-nature relation to implement economic policies based on natural resource extraction at the local level. This is directly related to the contradictory role of the capitalist state: on the one hand, its role is to guarantee the continuous accumulation of capital by organizing the power bloc; on the other, it needs to organize the popular consent of the masses (Poulantzas, [1978] 2014: 168–9). In this sense, specialized economic apparatuses of the state often become crucial institutional terrains (Albo, 2013: 25) in extractive regions through day-to-day and long-term interventions. At this point, the significance of the natural resource in question determines the labour process and local labour control strategies. The strategic role of the extractive commodity within global value chains, in the macro development plans of the country, or for the development of the locality has a direct impact on the rhythms of production in the pits and the discipline and containment mechanisms of the local labour power in the mining regions. Following the strategic significance of the resource extracted, various political, institutional, and community dynamics within the locality can be executed. Extractive capital seeks to guarantee economic and social stability in the labour markets by extending its influence over the spheres of reproduction of labour power. This is achieved through various methods of control and containment in the locality, commanding workers a sense of loyalty apart from their material interests in wages.

LPT and labour control regime approaches give the opportunity to explain how examining the relations of exploitation necessitates attention to the broader sets of processes and relationships than those contained within the gates of the workplace, which include the spheres of social reproduction, consumption, exchange, and circulation. Yet, the analysis of the relationship between the labour process and social reproduction needs to capture multiple linkages and interconnections within which production and social reproduction co-constitute each other. The concept of labour regime indicates 'a series of overlapping social processes that, together, shape how workforces with specific characteristics are produced and utilized' (Taylor and Rioux, 2017: 26). Labour regime analysis, therefore, allows to apprehend not only the multidimensional and contradictory nature of capital-labour relationship but also complexity of its interrelations with reproductive processes (Baglioni and Mezzadri, 2020; Mezzadri et al., 2022). As argued by Baglioni et al. (2022), social reproductive spaces are sites where class relations are constantly made, fragmented, and hierarchized. Therefore, labour regime analysis necessitates attention to who reproduces the worker, where and how, and what reproductive costs are assumed by households, the state, or capital. In this context, the household, as the key site of social reproduction within which the labour-power is produced and reproduced, requires particular attention. As explained by Baglioni (2022: 2):

> A focus on households highlights who does what job, under what conditions and trajectories – and *why* – thereby emphasizing how the making of workers transcends the factory, the office or the field: exploitation is simultaneously the generative and culminating act in the relation between capital and labour that builds on a hidden forest of relations crossing workplaces, households and other places/institutions.

As the supplier of labour to the extractive industries, capitalist farms, petty commodity production, subsistence farming, and reproductive work within the household, rural households in the extractive regions play a central role in the rural labour regimes in extractive industries.

Finally, labour control in the extractive regions takes peculiar forms due to the dependency on nature. Natural resource extraction is a socioecological and sociopolitical process indicating the exploitation of both labour and nature. The socioecological and sociopolitical construction of natural resources is inherently relational. On the one hand, resource extraction is determined by the discovery of the resources' new use and exchange values (their commodification); on the other hand, natural resources determine the limits and potential of the labour process (Baglioni and Campling, 2017: 2444–5). Labour regimes in extractive industries are shaped by the way workers and capitalists are differently embedded in the economic landscape. Despite the widespread assumption that capital is geographically more mobile than labour, there are significant limits to the mobility of capital as well (Herod et al., 2007). For extractive capital, dependency on nature is the most essential limit (Bridge, 2008; Fine, 1994). While LPT pays attention to how capitalist labour processes transform nature, there is little research on how nature sets limits to capitalist labour processes. This dimension is specifically significant for extractive industries as natural factors pose both opportunities and constraints for capital accumulation (Baglioni and Campling, 2017). In these sectors, 'nature's contribution to production (...) is not materially reducible to labour of appropriation' (Burkett, 1999: 80). The work has to be organized considering the uncertainties and obstacles related to the natural factors such as the mechanical structure of the mines or fertility of the land. (Burawoy, 1979: 206; Kaup, 2014: 1838). Natural uncertainties affect 'the social indeterminacy of the labour process' and 'material features of the natural resources shape class relations' (Baglioni and Campling, 2017: 2446). Hence, for the analysis of labour regimes in natural resource industries, there is a need to pay attention to (i) what sets of natural obstacles and opportunities capital faces, (ii) how the capital appropriates and transforms nature into commodities, (iii) how are workers deployed in the process as forces of nature themselves (Baglioni et al., 2022: 93).

In Turkey, labour processes and labour control strategies in the coal mining regions are determined by the strategic significance attributed to the coal industry by the consecutive AKP governments.

2 The Political Economy of Coal Extraction in Neoliberal Turkey

2.1 A Brief History of Neoliberalism in Turkey

The launch of the stabilization programme on 24 January 1980 marks the beginning of the transition to neoliberalism in Turkey. Import substitution industrialization was denounced for being the source of balance of payment difficulties and macroeconomic instabilities of the 1970s, and an export-oriented development strategy through the repression of labour costs and through the tax and credit incentives to exporters was adopted (Orhangazi and Yeldan, 2021; Yalman, 2019). The main peculiarity of Turkey's transition to neoliberalism is that it was attempted in a period of complete reorganization of the social and political structure of the country. The military coup of 12 September 1980, first of all, provided the social conditions for the implementation of the stabilization program by silencing any political and social opposition and by banning all political parties and trade unions. Secondly, beyond a three-year change in the political regime, it signified a change in the form of the state, which was institutionalized under the authoritarian 1982 Constitution, and has remained in effect after the return to civilian rule in 1983 (Yalman, 2009: 298).

January 24 stabilization programme was not merely a temporary plan; it was the first step of a series of economic liberalization policies in the 1980s and 1990s. Capital account liberalization in 1989 marks the beginning of 'full liberalization' both in external trade and finance (Eres, 2007). Therefore, Turkey entered the 1990s having a completely open economy with a completely liberalized capital account. In the early 1990s, the Turkish economy witnessed a massive inflow of short-term foreign capital, appreciation of currency, and expansion of import demand. This resulted, in the short term, a growing fiscal deficit of the public sector and a sudden rise of wage costs in the labour markets (Köse and Yeldan, 1998: 51). As an outcome of these neoliberalization attempts, the Turkish economy experienced intermittent financial crises in 1994, 1998, and 2000–1.

In 2001, Turkey experienced one of the most severe crises in its recent history, which took the form of a crisis *in* neoliberalism, not as a crisis *of* neoliberalism. The difference between the two stems from the social and political reactions and alternatives that emerge in response to the crisis (cf. Saad Filho, 2011). In the case of Turkey, the intermittent crises of the 1990s and the 2001 crisis resulted in the entrenchment of neoliberalism rather than weakening its credibility. Wrong policy choices of the politically unstable coalition governments of the 1990s were claimed to be the main reason behind these crises. In the absence of any credible political alternative or organized resistance by the losers of the ongoing neoliberal transformation, the AKP has presented itself as a solution to the crises *in* neoliberalism under the discourse of strong and politically stable government since its first electoral victory in 2002 (Yalman, 2016: 256–7). From the beginning, the AKP governments combined neoliberal developmentalism based on promises such as high growth rates, privatization of state economic enterprises, labour market flexibility, and mega investments in the construction and natural resource industries with Islamic fundamentalism.

When first came to power in 2002, by following a series of economic reforms imposed and supported by the IMF and World Bank, the AKP government lowered the inflation rate and public deficits and achieved a considerable rate and speed of growth. However, according to the scholars of the critical political economy of Turkey (cf. BSB, 2015; Boratav, 2010; Orhangazi, 2020; Orhangazi and Yeldan, 2021; Yeldan and Ünüvar, 2016), the 'macroeconomic success' of the Justice and Development Party governments was built upon and further brought structural fragilities and crisis dynamics. Firstly, the growth performance of the AKP during the 2000s was mainly driven by increased foreign capital inflows and concomitant currency appreciation, and this reflected the increased import dependency in the economy. This, in turn, led to widened current account deficits in the 2000s and 2010s (Orhangazi and Yeldan, 2021: 467). Secondly, the employment generation capacity of this growth had been insufficient and the 2000s was a period of jobless growth in Turkey (Ercan, 2007; Şenses and Koyuncu, 2007; Telli et al., 2006; Yeldan and Ünüvar, 2016). The rate of unemployment jumped from 6.5 percent in 2000 to 10.3 percent after the 2001 financial crisis in 2002. It could not be brought down under 10 percent by the end of 2005 (Telli et al., 2006: 256).

Under the AKP governments, a new labour regime characterized by the exploitation of disciplined, low-cost, and highly precarious labour has been established (Bozkurt-Güngen, 2018). Even though the flexibilization and precarization attempts started with the 12 September military coup, they were institutionalized by the AKP governments through the enactment of a new Labour Law (No. 4857) in their first year in office. The labour regime of the AKP indicates authoritarian flexibilization that 'institutionalizes flexibility in individual labour relations and at the same time demonstrates an authoritarian tendency in terms of collective labour relations' (Çelik, 2015: 623). In this context, the mining sector, in general, and the Soma tragedy, in particular, exemplify not only authoritarian flexibilization but also the reason why the industrial working class has not been visible as the leading force in societal struggles in Turkey (Ercan and Oğuz, 2015: 116).

2.2 Turkey's 'Coal Rush' under the AKP Rule

Turkey's coal rush since the mid-2000s is part of the aim of utilizing domestic resources for power generation to overcome the problem of energy supply security. Energy supply security was first brought into the public policy agenda in Turkey during the global oil crisis of the 1970s, when the share of imported oil in power generation rose from less than 10 percent in the first half of the 1960s to almost 50 percent in the early 1970s. The drastic rise of oil prices, along with the high levels of dependence on imported oil, resulted in a significant energy crisis in Turkey. To overcome the crisis, extraction and utilization of domestic coal was encouraged. In this context, a general Basin Planning was prepared to promote coal extraction in recourse-rich basins of Anatolia, such as Soma, Kütahya, Muğla, Afşin Elbistan, Çayırhan, Bursa Orhaneli, and Sivas Kangal. Starting from the mid 1980s, the share of imported oil in the power generation decreased to around 20 percent. However, during 1990s, policies that prioritized the use of imported energy in power generation were promoted again and it resulted in high rates of imported natural gas and hard coal for power generation (Tamzok, 2016).

From the beginning of the attempts at neoliberal transformation in Turkey in the 1980s, privatizations in general and energy privatizations in particular were on the public policy agenda. Even though the country is one of the first countries in the Global South to announce a large-scale privatization program, its implementation largely failed during the 1980s and 1990s (Zaifer, 2020: 148). In fact, prior to the series of large-scale privatizations in the 2000s, privatizations in Turkey were limited to relatively small and medium public enterprises of the tradable goods sectors (Ercan and Öniş, 2001: 110). It was partly because of the fact that the legal framework for privatizations was established in 1994 under the stabilization programme crafted by the IMF to deal with the economic crisis. Privatization Law No. 4046 was enacted in November 1994, and the Privatization High Council was established as a policymaking body along with the Privatization Administration as an implementation body (Ercan and Öniş, 2001: 117; Zaifer, 2020: 150–151). In this context, the Privatization High Council decides on the privatization of key state economic enterprises as well as on the time periods and methods of privatizations, whereas, Privatization Administration is responsible for executing decisions of the Privatization High Council, implementing the necessary procedures to prepare for privatization, managing the privatization fund, and conducting other activities such as advertisement, promotion, and public relations to enhance the stability of the state economic enterprises (Zaifer, 2022: 57). Still, there were still salient obstacles to accelerate privatization process. The reluctance of certain fractions of big capital, opposition within the parliament and government, and popular resistance from different segments of the society were the main obstacles in that respect (cf. Angın and Bedirhanoğlu, 2012; Ercan and Öniş, 2001; Öniş, 2011; Zaifer, 2020; 2022). In contrast, privatizations turned into a central accumulation strategy for Turkish capitalism in the aftermath of the 2001 economic crisis. In line with the general timing and pace of privatizations in the country, the first efforts to privatize (to liberalize, as put by the proponents of neoliberal transformation) were initiated in the 1980s, which mainly took the form of encouraging public-private partnerships such as Build-Operate-Transfer, Transfer of Operational Rights, or Transfer of Autoproducer Rights. The first attempt at the privatization of electricity production was the enactment of Law No. 3096 on the Authorization of Enterprises other than Turkish Electricity Enterprise to Transmit, Distribute, and Trade Electricity in 1984. The purpose of the law, as stated in the first article was to regulate the assignment of electricity generation, transmission, distribution, and trading tasks to domestic and foreign companies with the status of capital companies subject to private law provisions other than the Turkish Electricity Authority. this law was followed by a series of attempts to enable the acceleration of privatizations in the country in the 1990s, such as Law No. 3996 on Build Operate Transfer and Law No. 4283 on Build Operate. Additionally, the amendment of the article 47 of the Constitution in 1999 marks a significant milestone to accelerate privatizations in the country. In this context, article 47 titled "Nationalization" was amended as "Nationalization and Privatization" and regulations defining the authorization for privatization were added. Therefore, in 1999, energy privatizations, which were prevented because of legal restrictions gained a constitutional framework (Erensü et al., 2016: 13).

In 2001, Electricity Market Law No. 4628 was enacted to create a market reform. As defined in the first article, the main objective of the law was the establishment of a financially strong, efficient, transparent electricity market subject to a private law. In the context of this law, Energy Market Regulatory Agency was established to regulate and supervise the electricity, natural gas, oil, and coal markets in the country by ensuring fair competition, consumer protection, and efficient operation of the energy sector. Since came to power in 2002, the AKP governments have not only embraced the framework established by the Electricity Market Law but also encouraged all fractions of power bloc to invest in the energy sector. In order to do so, the governments have passed a number of legislations to complete and strengthen the energy reform based on liberalization and marketization (Erensü et al. 2016: 13; Erensü, 2017: 126:9).

In 2002, when AKP first came to power, 68 percent of the total installed capacity was operated by the public sector, and 32 were operated by the private sector. In 2014, this percentage was reversed to 21.5 percent in the public sector and 68.5 percent in the private sector. This was directly reflected in the power generation within this twelve-year period, and the share of the public sector in installed capacity fell from 62 percent in 2002 to 28.1 percent at the end of 2014 (Pamir, 2015: 397). As stated in the Electricity Market and Supply Security Strategy Document prepared by the State Planning Organization (SPO) in 2008:

> The fundamental aim of restructuring based on liberalization in the electricity sector is to create an investment environment that will ensure the necessary investments for supply security and to reflect the gains obtained through improved efficiency in the sector, facilitated by the competitive environment, to the customers.

Yet, contrary to this expectation, rising private sector investments in the electricity market resulted in the increasing use of imported natural gas and imported coal in power generation, which deepened the problem of energy supply security and current account deficit.

As mentioned above, during the 2000s, the Turkish economy experienced substantial growth, but as this growth was based on capital inflows, it generated high levels of current account deficit. The AKP governments deemed energy imports as one of the main reasons behind this deficit, as over half of the energy demand had been met by energy imports since the early 2000s (Kaygusuz et al., 2015). In 2012, 75 percent of the total energy demand, 93 percent of oil, and 99 percent of natural gas were imported by Russia (Acar et al., 2015). To diminish the dependency on imported energy, domestic resources such as coal and renewables have been prioritized. Yet, exploration of renewable resources has been limited to hydropower and a few wind generation projects. Despite their limited contribution to the electricity generation of the country (Erensü, 2017: 130), private sector investments in small hydroelectric power plants have been encouraged by the AKP governments. As a result, several firms from various sectors entered the hydropower market (Islar, 2012: 382–383). Still, as much greater renewable energy is necessary to replace the same quantity of fossil-fuelled capacity (Acar et al., 2015), hydropower investments have not constituted an alternative to coal-fired electricity production. In fact, to utilize domestic lignite in electricity generation, the government enacted the coal rush plan and declared 2012 as the 'year of coal.'

Policy programs since the mid-2010s, such as The Tenth Development Plan's Action Plan for Energy Program Based on Domestic Resources (2014–2018), the National Energy and Mining Policy declared in 2017, and the Eleventh Development Plan (2018–2022), prioritized the coal industry. Moreover, in

2012, the government enacted the Decree on State Aids in Investments, in which investments in the exploration and extraction of coal along with the construction of coal-fired power plants (CFPPs) were deemed 'priority investments' and received high amounts of investments (Acar et al., 2015; Acar and Yeldan, 2016: 2; Acar et al., 2018; Oil Change International, 2014). Measurable incentives to the coal industry reached US$ 730 million in 2013, including direct transfers, subsidies for exploration of coal reserves, improvements of CFPPs, and coal aid to poor families. The first group of subsidies are provided for the exploration of coal through the government sponsored campaigns of coal exploration undertaken bu the Mineral Research and Exploration Institute (MTA) and the Turkish Coal Enterprises starting in 2005. In this context, coal reserves increased by 50 percent. Still, government spending for the exploration of coal increased further, and it rose from 10 million US dollars in 2010 to 25 million US dollars in 2014 (Oil Change International, 2014).

The second group of subsidies is producer subsidies in the form of investment incentives, privatizations, and loan guarantees. In 2012, the Decree on State Aids in Investments was enacted, and coal projects were declared as prior investments. Yet, measurable incentives underestimate the total subsidy as they do not cover incentives such as investment guarantees, ease of access to credit, exemptions from value-added tax, import duties, and environmental impact assessments (Acar and Yeldan, 2016: 2). Furthermore, as shown in the calculations of Acar et al. (2015), Bloomberg New Energy and Finance and World Wide Fund for Nature (BNEF and WWF, 2014), and Oil Change International (2014), privatizations and royalty tender constitute the most significant incentives for the industry. As a result of this strong state support in various forms, the installed capacity of CFPPs has increased by 77 percent between 2014 and 2015 (Cardoso and Turhan, 2018: 402). Despite its rapid growth, domestic production of hard coal and lignite contributed only 37 percent of the total primary energy supply in 2015. Similarly, as of 2015, the country has been generating around 38 percent of its electricity from imported natural gas and 30 percent from coal. Additionally, the majority of the CFPPs use coal imported from the US, Ukraine, Canada, Australia, Russia, and Colombia (Acar et al., 2018: 101: 107).

Despite the replacement of state-led projects by private sector investments, the successive AKP governments have assumed a pivotal role both in reconstructing the energy and construction sectors and in transforming its top-down developmentalism into base support (Adaman and Akbulut, 2021; Akbulut, 2019; Arsel et al., 2015; Erensü, 2018a). Firstly, privatizations in general and energy privatizations in particular have been supported by all fractions of the power bloc during the AKP period. Large-scale privatizations in Turkey correspond to the AKP governments, and since the early 2000s, privatizations have been central to the accumulation strategies of all fractions of the power bloc (Zaifer, 2018: 819).[1] Despite the tension between the AKP and big capital groups whose class formation dates back to the Early Republican era, they both supported and benefited from the large-scale privatizations during the AKP governments. Energy privatizations, in particular, have created significant investment opportunities for them. Overall, 82 of the 100 richest businesspeople have invested in energy, according to 2014 numbers (Erensü, 2018b).

Even though the privatization of coal extraction has reflected the general path of privatizations in the country in terms of state-capital-labour relations, it has taken a peculiar form in terms of property relations. Although the state owns the vast majority of the country's coal mines, about 90 percent of the active pits have been privatized through royalty tender from 2002 onwards (Makhijani, 2014).[2] In the royalty tender, the management of coal mines is transferred to private firms; the firms, in turn, pay royalties to the state and provide coal to Turkey's state-owned Electricity Generation Company (EÜAŞ). It should be noted that, albeit limited, there were private sector investments in coal mines before the initiation of royalty tender. The distinguishing feature of privatization through the royalty tender for state-capital-labour relations is the guarantee of purchase provided by the state as the sole customer of coal. Besides, there is no legal restriction for the firms to produce more than the minimum amount specified in the contracts, and Turkish Coal Enterprises (TKI) buys all the coal extracted (Ersoy, 2015; TBB, 2014; TSBD, 2016). Therefore, to make profits, coal companies tend to accelerate production by extracting the maximum possible amount of coal at minimum costs. In this context, on the one hand, the coal industry has attracted the attention of big capital groups; on the other hand, for the newly emerging Anatolian bourgeoisie, energy and coal investments have been profoundly important in their process of conglomeration since the mid-2000s.

Secondly, the employment creation potential of extractive industries has been significant for state-capital-labour relations under AKP rule. The 2000s were characterized by the jobless growth of the Turkish economy on the one hand; impoverishment, dispossession and proletarianization of small

---

1 Fractions of power bloc in Turkey are (i) big bourgeoisie whose class formation dates back to the early Republican Period, (ii) Anatolian bourgeoisie who have actively been supported by the AKP governments and established conglomerates since the early 2000s; (iii) foreign capital (cf. Zaifer, 2018; 2020).
2 Currently, there are two state-owned coal enterprises in Turkey, namely, Turkish Coal Enterprises (TKI) and Turkish Hard Coal Enterprises (TTK). The TTK oversees the hard coal mines, whereas the TKI controls lignite mines.

agricultural producers due to the neoliberal transformation of agriculture on the other. The deepening of neoliberalism in agriculture corresponds to the aftermath of the 2000–2001 crises and the AKP governments. The main transformations in this context have been the withdrawal of the former support system and of subsidized agricultural credit system; the determination of prices by world stock prices; restructuring of Union and Agricultural Sales Cooperatives; control of the seed sector by transnational monopolies; and privatization of the agricultural State Economic Enterprises (SEEs) (Günaydın, 2009: 178; BSB, 2015: 96–7). As a result, the former agricultural structure dominated by small-scale farming has been transformed and agriculture has become a profitable sector for the agribusiness capital (see Chapter 4). In this context, many small-scale farmers migrated to urban centres and become the most precarious segment of the urban workforce. However, almost a quarter of Turkey's population is still rural. As a result of the neoliberal transformation of agriculture, small-scale producers have been developing various survival strategies in the countryside, such as wage work in tourism, construction or mining. In this context, extractive investments in the countryside have been regarded as an opportunity both by the rural population and by the precarious urban force. Therefore, they constituted a significant consent-making mechanism for the AKP government. This has especially worked for the legitimization of underground coal mining investments because, as a labour-intensive sector, it promises high numbers of employment in the countryside, as in the case of Soma. In terms of the policy outcomes, it is possible to argue that coal rush of the AKP policies largely failed in terms of its predefined goals in terms of both overcoming the energy supply security and the problem of current account deficit and generating employment. First of all, even though the primary objective of the coal rush policies of the AKP governments has been the aim of utilizing domestic coal to overcome the problem of energy supply security. As shown by Acar and Kızılkaya (2021), the share of coal and lignite mining in GDP decreased from 0.14 percent in the early 2000s to 0.08 percent in 2018, and its share in total value added fell to 0.2 percent. Meanwhile, coal imports increased drastically and reached over 3.7 billion USD in 2019. The export-to-import ratio fell from 2.38 percent in 2008 to 0.15 percent in 2019. In 2019, Turkey's top import sources were Colombia, Russia, Australia, the USA, and Canada. Eventually, the report prepared by Acar and Kızılkaya (2021) shows that Turkey is a net exporter of coal, and the country's imports have increased between 2003 and 2019. Additionally, there has been an increase in the volume of exports as well; however, it fell to 0.15 in 2019.

Secondly, despite the coal rush policies of the governments and the discourse of employment generation since the early 2010s, this period witnessed a fall in the number of coal miners in Turkey, the sector accounts for only around 0.3 percent of total employment on average. As of 2021, the coal mining sector employs around 34,000 workers, down from almost 44,000 in 2012 (Ayhan and Çelik, 2024). Even in the five provinces where coal-based economies are significant – Manisa, Muğla, Zonguldak-Bartın, Kahramanmaraş, and Çanakkale – the sector does not account for a substantial portion of employment. For instance, in the Zonguldak Coal Region, where the coal sector has historically been prominent, it contributes only around 4 to 6 percent of the regional employment. In fact, the coal mining sector does not rank among the top ten employment sectors even in these regions. Instead, employment is concentrated in other sectors, particularly in agriculture and animal breeding (Özen and Aşık, 2021). Still, even though coal mining constitutes only a small portion of total employment, the employment generation potential of coal mining is significant for local economies because of two interrelated factors. On the one hand, many coal regions lack economic diversification and viable employment options (Ayhan and Çelik, 2024). On the other hand, many coal regions are under the impact of the neoliberal transformation of agriculture, where employment is still predominantly concentrated in agriculture. Yet, both family farming and wage work in agriculture are predominantly unregistered and informal in Turkey. Therefore, employment in mining mostly constitutes a decent opportunity (see: Çelik, 2023c).

Overall, it is possible to argue that the coal rush policies of the AKP governments are far from achieving its proposed objectives in terms of energy supply security and employment creation. These policies' primary function has been creating an investment opportunity for the different fractions of power bloc in the country. In the Soma Coal Basin, rhythms of investment, organization of work, and local labour control mechanisms are directly shaped by the political and economic significance of the coal industry for the government.

3   Historical Background: Coal Extraction in Soma Before the 2000s

Lignite mining in Soma dates back to the 19th century when the Ottoman government had assigned a research group to Soma for lignite exploration in 1863. Following the exploration of lignite in Soma, its operation was sold by auction to the owners of cotton factories in order to test the quality of lignite coal and explore its similarities to and differences from the hard coal of the Zonguldak Basin. In 1889, a tender was called for the coal of Soma, and in 1890, two families based in İzmir (Hacı Raşit and Mehmet Nuri Efendiler) took the operation of the pit located in Soma. As stated in the terms and conditions of the contract signed between the state and these families, the annual extraction of two thousand tons of coal was expected. Then, the contract was terminated following the death of Hacı Raşit Efendi in 1891. In 1913, a new coal field in the Basin was explored in the Kısrakdere site of Tarhala (Darkale) village and its tenure was given to Osman Efendi (Yorulmaz, 1998: 291–292). The significance of the lignite of Soma had increased during World War I, and the operations of the mine were transferred to a German firm to extract coal to meet the needs of the army. At the end of the war, as per the terms of the Armistice of Mondros, the operation of the mine was transferred to French firms (Ergün: 98–99, 1997; Yorulmaz, 1998). Three years after the establishment of the Republic of Turkey, in 1926, mine operation was transferred back to the domestic firms, and especially during the years of the Great Depression, the coal needs of the İzmir province were met by the lignite of Soma.

Overall, the mines of Soma had been operated by several small-scale domestic and foreign firms until they were transferred to a state bank named Etibank in 1939. Following the transfer of mine operation to the state, lignite extraction in Soma rose drastically along with hard coal of the Zonguldak Basin in the context of the aim of utilizing domestic resources. As a result, the country's lignite production rose from less than 100 thousand tons in 1937 to more than 1 million tons in 1948, around a quarter of which was extracted in the Soma Basin. Additionally, the share of the state-owned banks rose to 69 percent in 1939 and to 81 percent in 1945. In the mid-1950s, lignite extraction in Soma was prioritized, and local social life was planned to meet the needs of the miners' families. In the context of the Marshall Plan, 300 personnel houses, a hospital, a library, a movie theatre, a clubhouse, a guesthouse, sports courts and a primary school were built (Tamzok, 2014).

Previously, the dominant form of lignite production in Soma was underground mining, whereas surface mining had gained significance in the mid-1950s. In 1957, a new state economic enterprise, Turkish Coal Enterprises (TKI), was established, and the operation of the pits of Soma was transferred from Etibank to the TKI. As a result, coal production rose around ten times in the following decade and reached 1 million tons in 1966. Meanwhile, the first CFPP was installed in the Basin (Tamzok, 2014).

As mentioned earlier, in the 1970s, amid the global oil crisis, the concept of energy supply security had been brought into the policy agenda for the first time in Turkey due to the country's dependency on imported oil. Therefore, to overcome the energy shortage stemming from the rise of oil prices from 1973 onwards, the Turkish government prioritized utilizing domestic coal reserves. In 1978, Law No. 2172 on the Mines Operated by the State was enacted, and the operations of all the coal pits across the country were transferred to the TKI.

As stated by the retired or relatively older miners during the interviews, all the pits in Soma were operated by the TKI between 1979 and 1990s. Meanwhile, TKI prepared the General Basin Planning, according to which the Soma Coal Basin was separated from the Western Lignite Enterprises (Garp Linyit İşletmeleri, GLI) and became an independent coal region under the control of newly established Ege Lignite Enterprises (ELI). In this context, a new CFPP (B powerplant) was installed in the early 1980s, and annual coal production of around twelve million tons was promised (Ergün 1997).

In the 1980s and 1990s, surface mining was still the dominant form of coal extraction in the Basin, and the number of deadly mine disasters was quite limited. Between 1982 and 2004, when the extraction amount rose from 2 million to more than 12 million tons, the number of miners who lost their lives was 26 (Tamzok, 2014). As a matter of fact, miners who had worked in the state-operated mines before the 2000s frequently mentioned better health and safety measures of these mines. For example, a retired miner who had worked both in the state-operated mines and in the private firms after his retirement and whose son died in the Soma massacre compared their working conditions as follows:

> I mean, in our days, work safety was prioritized. In principle ... Production was secondary. Workers' health and safety came first. You go to work in the morning, and shift supervisors come. They say, have a nice working day; your safety comes first. ... Let the production be low, but something bad should not happen to you. This is the distinguishing feature of public mining, I think. There was no 'go on, go on!' 'rush rush rush' when we had state-operated firms. The company is the total opposite! Fortification is not so important, and worker's health and safety is not so important. Extract more coal! That is all!

Until the 2000s, the majority of the miners were not from the villages of the basin, as the rural population was engaged in agricultural production and did not prefer to work in the mines (see Chapter 4).

Back then, the majority of the miners used to live in the personnel houses built in the 1950s. The personnel houses were located in the neighborhood named Maden, a relatively high altitude and isolated neighborhood. Both the civil servants and miners of the TKI used to live in that neighborhood where they had social clubs, markets, a bakery, a movie theatre, a healthcare center, a school, etc. Therefore, their lives were segregated from the local population. Then, during the 1970s and 1980s, as the amount of extraction rose, two more personnel houses closer to the town centre were built. They also had social facilities of their own. Therefore, until the mid-2000s, miners used to live like closed communities.

4 The Neoliberal Transformation of the Coal Industry in the Soma Coal Basin in the 2000s

The neoliberal transformation of the coal industry in the basin has been through privatizations, conglomerations, and the coal rush. Initial attempts for the privatization of coal extraction in Soma date back to 1995 when B plant was brought to the privatization agenda. Yet, much like many other privatization attempts in Turkey in the 1990s, it was unsuccessful. Meanwhile, reserves of surface mining were draining, and the need for installing underground sites to maintain coal extraction was clear. Yet, TKI could not allocate the necessary budget for investment in the underground pits as there was no external credit available, and hiring of new personnel was not allowed. As a result, the production cost of the TKI rose drastically, and it started to transfer certain tasks to private companies. In 2001, TKI prepared a new development plan, and the annual expected amount of coal extraction was determined as 10.6 million tons (Tamzok, 2014).

The transfer of coal extraction to private firms through royalty tender began in 2005. Since then, the lignite of Soma has been a significant part of Turkey's domestic energy production as its lignite has higher calorific values compared to other coalfields in the country (Düzgün and Yaylacı, 2016). Therefore, large-scale private investments in Soma have been encouraged by the state. The amount of coal extracted by the TKI declined from 8.5 million tons in 2004 to 2.9 million tons in 2012, whereas the extraction by private firms rose from 58,000 tons to 11.7 million tons within the same period. This increase in the share of private sector production was accompanied by a shift towards underground mining. The amount of coal extracted from underground mining rose from 300,000 tons in 2004 to around 11.7 million tons in 2013 (Tamzok, 2014). As production in underground mining is more labour-intensive, the number of miners increased significantly (see Figure 1).

Yet, it should be noted that the Soma Basin, different from Zonguldak, for example, had not experienced long-term state-operated mining. The only time when all the pits of Soma were operated by TKI was the decade following the enactment of Law No. 2162 on Mines Operated by the State in 1978, thereunder operations of all the mines across the country were transferred to the state. Prior to its enactment and during the 1990s, there were small-scale private firms operating mines in Soma. Two of these firms were Soma Coal Company

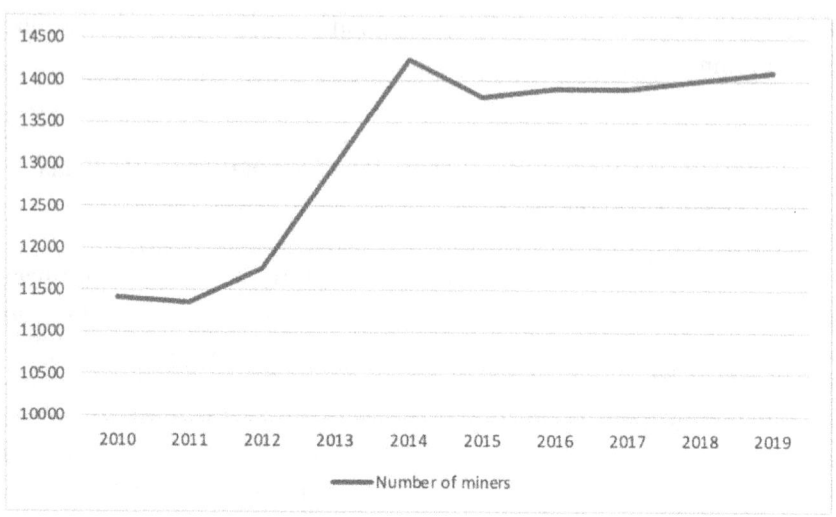

FIGURE 1   Number of miners in the Soma Coal Basin in the 2010s
SOURCE: SOMA MUNICIPALITY STRATEGIC PLAN

and Imbat Mining, which, from 2005 onwards, have become the leading firms operating large pits in the Basin. Therefore, the main transformation since 2005 is the initiation of royalty tender and expansion of coal extraction through private firms. As royalty tender constitutes the most significant component of coal subsidies of the Turkish governments to the coal investors, especially due to the guarantee of purchase provided by TKI regardless of the amount, coal companies tend to extract higher amounts of coal than the amount stated in the royalty contracts.

From 2005 onwards, the guarantee of purchase has been accompanied by several measures for the reduction of the cost of production. For example, the Chairperson of the Executive Board of Soma Holding, Alp Gürkan, in an interview before the Soma Mine Disaster, explained the improvement of Soma Coal Enterprises and conglomeration with their ability to reduce the cost of coal production from 2005 onwards:

> When the TKI was extracting coal in Soma, the cost of extraction per ton was around 130–140 US dollar. We promised to diminish this cost to 23.80 US dollars. Neither our company nor others would invest in this sector unless we knew we would make huge profits.

This reduction in the cost of production has been accompanied by a significant rise in the amount of coal extraction. According to the calculations in the report on the Soma Mine Disaster prepared by the Boğaziçi University Soma Research Group, from 2004 to 2013, through the royalty tender, coal production increased by 13 times, from around 1 million tons in 2004 to approximately 13 million tons in 2013.

5 Labour Supply to the Coal Pits of Soma

Increasing coal investments, along with the shift from surface mining to labour-intensive underground mining, resulted in a dramatic rise in demand for miners in the Basin. Labour supply to the coal pits of Soma since the mid-2000s has taken two forms: dispossession and proletarianization of the local population as a result of the neoliberal transformation of agriculture and migration from other mining towns of Turkey. As it is detailly elaborated on in the next chapter, the local population in the surrounding villages of Soma was mainly engaged in tobacco farming until the mid-2000s, and the income generated from tobacco farming was sufficient for the survival of their families. The sale of the tobacco factories owned by the state economic enterprise (SEE) named Tekel (State Monopoly of Tobacco and Alcoholic Beverages) to international tobacco corporations during the early 2000s resulted in the impoverishment of tobacco farmers. The immediate impact of this privatization was the elimination of former support purchases of the state – especially the guarantee of purchase for the tobacco producers provided by the Tekel. As a result of the elimination of the state support, many families quitted tobacco farming, whereas for those who have maintained tobacco farming, wage-income to subsidize the income by tobacco farming and/or to finance tobacco farming has become necessary (see Chapter 4). As the privatization of coal production and opening up of the new underground coal pits coincided with the dispossession of tobacco farmers, the mid-2000s witnessed a wave of proletarianization in the Basin. As stated in an interview by a former tobacco producer miner:

> Most of the local people working in the mine now were the families living from tobacco in the past. But, the dissolution of agriculture here by the government. ... The dissolution started from the end of 1990s. First, quota was imposed on tobacco farming. For example, we were producing tobacco as much as we could before the implementation of the quota. Then, they imposed the quota in the late 1990s. They limited the amount that families could produce. This did not cover the survival costs of the families. They started to look for alternatives means of income. Other alternative in our villages ... Our villages are all mountain villages. Olive,

tobacco ... These are the only things that we can grow on barren land. People had to orient towards the mine as a means of living because olive cultivation necessitates a long term effort. If you decide it now, you can have the products in ten years ... Therefore, the only option for us was mining. The story of mining started in 2005 in our village. It was very rare. There were few people working in the mine before this. Now, we have all become miners. This was not the case before the 2000s.

One of the most significant transformations of the early and mid 2000s was the expansion of the borders of the Soma Coal Basin beyond the district of Soma. In this study, I define the Basin by referring to the labour supply to the mines, instead of location of the pits. Therefore, the Soma Coal Basin contains Kırkağaç and Soma districts of Manisa, Kınık district of İzmir, and Savaştepe district of Balıkesir and their surrounding villages where dispossessed and impoverished tobacco farmers started to work in the underground mines since the early 2000s (see Chapter 4).

The second means of labour supply was the migration of families from other mining towns in the mid-2000s, as Soma, which had large-scale investments, provided better employment opportunities. In fact, most migrant workers mentioned relatively more secure conditions in Soma compared to their hometowns. Migration from Zonguldak, Bartın, Ordu, and Çorum is due to the diminishing investments in Zonguldak and the existence of relatively smaller or even informal coal pits. Zonguldak is a province of more than 600,000 population at the Western Black Sea coast in Turkey. Zonguldak Coal Basin had historically been the single most important mining centre since the Ottoman Empire, which attracted migrant workers from nearby towns such as Bartın, Ordu, and Çorum. Since the 1980s, Zonguldak has been experiencing a gradual deindustrialization. In the late 1980s, the government announced its intention to close down the coal mines completely. Miners' response to it was a massive strike in 1990 and a huge march from Zonguldak to Ankara in the winter of 1990–1991. As a result, the government had to drop its plans to close down the entire basin. Yet, it started to phase out coal extraction in the Basin through practices such as early retirement, halting recruitments, and suspending new investments. This phasing-out policy was followed by all subsequent governments, and currently, the pits of Zonguldak are closed down, privatized, or operate informally (Şengül and Aytekin, 2012: 156).

Before the privatizations and the phasing out of coal extraction, Zonguldak had a long history of state-operated mining. Royalty tender in Zonguldak started in the 2000s. Since then, there has been an out-migration trend from Zonguldak. As expressed in the interviews, the main reason behind the migration from Zonguldak to Soma is the relatively more stable and secure working conditions in Soma compared to Zonguldak's small-scale or illegal pits. Relatively more precarious conditions of mining in Zonguldak and familiarity with mining as their 'father's occupation' have been the main impulse of their migration to Soma. For example, as stated by a miner from Zonguldak:

> There are illegal pits rather than corporate companies in Zonguldak. I mean a day-long ... There are even families who sell their gardens through royalty. Zonguldak is not a city where great investments are made now. It is worn out now. People are in trouble, people are migrating to other cities. There are people coming to Manisa and extracting coal in mine pits even though they have coal in their hometown. We can understand the situation from this ... Why did these people leave there and come here to extract coal? We have a miner identity recognized from the past. We start out by saying if I can't do this job in Zonguldak, I would either go to Ankara or Edirne Keşan neighborhood or go to Soma ... Another point is that uneducated people try to guarantee one particular thing in life: early retirement. Since we always think about concern for the future, we automatically think that without concern how we would physically get exhausted: I will complete my insurance period in 13 years, and complete my registry in 20 years. If I start this job when I am 20 years old, I will be retired in my 40. What do we do? We prepare ourselves for this in some way. We think we guarantee ourselves but diseases and disorders that would arise after 40 years old.

Firms investing in Soma are larger than the ones in Zonguldak and Kütahya. Additionally, they receive a purchase guarantee from the state. There are no problems such as irregular payment of wages or unregistered employment. Even considering the fatal disaster, the institutionalized structure of the firms makes working in Soma relatively secure, as a miner who was formerly working in an illegal pit in Zonguldak states:

> The good side of Soma ... Firstly money and the weekly leave. And there is no trouble. Only the state-operated mines implement the laws orderly in Zonguldak. If I say with an estimated figure, Turkish Hardcoal Enterprises (Türkiye Taş Kömürü İşletmeleri, TTK) closes every year at a loss of one thousand liras. We do not suffer such trouble here. Because the firms are large, production is high ... Wages are not delayed. The worker is contented. Of course, at the same time all works are state guaranteed here. The state directly purchases coal once it is extracted. For example, we

had a director in Zonguldak, nobody liked him, but they could not dismiss him. Why? He was well-connected. Companies have difficulty in selling coal there. There are also many illegal pits. You cannot receive your money at present in Zonguldak. Here, you are contented; you know your money will be paid on-time.

It was unexpected to hear that almost all workers from Zonguldak mentioning the relatively more secure conditions of mining in Soma two years after the biggest mine disaster in the country's history. Yet, when I raised questions regarding the disaster, most of the workers stated that in case of a deadly accident in Soma, at least their children would have certain rights. For example, as stated by one of the miners from Zonguldak:

> In an illegal pit, everything is under your responsibility, and the company has no liability at all. Even when you die, you would be responsible. If you die, nobody would know this anyway. Look, families of dead miners have obtained all their rights here in Soma.

As a matter of fact, seven years after this interview, an Afghan miner who was working at one of the illegal mines located in Zonguldak got injured while working. Instead of taking him to hospital, owners of the illegal mine beaten him to death then burned his dead body[3].

One final point to be underlined regarding the miners from Zonguldak is that their relation to land and agriculture is minimum or completely disappeared. Given that the history of mining dates to the Ottoman period, the formation of a mining community in Zonguldak is earlier than that of Soma. Therefore, different from the local miners and miners who migrated from Zonguldak, have mining tradition inherited from earlier generations.

Kütahya, on the other hand, is a city in the inner Aegean Region that has a lignite reserve, especially in the Tavşanlı and Tunçbilek districts, where the General Directorate of the Western Lignite Enterprises (GLI) is located. GLI has been extracting lignite in the Tavşanlı-Tunçbilek basin since the 1940s to be used for the CFPP located in Tunçbilek. A significant part of the miners in Soma are migrant workers from Kütahya, given that investments in Kütahya do not provide sufficient employment opportunities for the local population. Different from the migrant workers from Zonguldak, they have relatively

---

3 Afghan worker's dead body burned after beaten to death to 'prevent' disclosure of illegal mine in Turkey. Available at: https://www.duvarenglish.com/afghan-workers-dead-body-burned-after-beaten-to-death-to-prevent-disclosure-of-illegal-mine-in-turkey-news-63312.

weaker relations to mining and a relatively stronger relation to agricultural production. In other words, before migrating to Soma, most of these families were engaged in agriculture. For example, as stated by a retired miner who migrated from Kütahya in 1988 to work in a private coal company in Soma stated that they were also engaged in agricultural production in Kütahya, but they still migrated to Soma given that it was harder to find employment in the state-operated mines of Kütahya:

> Our village is Balıköy located in Kütahya. We lived on farming when we were in the village, then we saw that number of our children increase from one to two, two to three ... We came here, to the mine ... There is also a mine in Kütahya, but there are no private firms there. We could not start a job there. Actually, we had everything, our bullock donkey there.

Migration from Kütahya to Soma has a relatively longer history when compared to Zonguldak. Therefore, families who migrated after the initiation of royalty tender used their family networks to be employed in the pits of Soma. Moreover, miners who migrated in the 2000s, mostly had similar reasons to work in the mines with the local population. As they could not receive sufficient income from agriculture back in their hometowns, they tried to find employment opportunities in coal mining, and given that the investments in Kütahya were insufficient to provide enough employment opportunities for the local population, they used their networks in Soma. For example, as stated by a miner who moved to Soma in 2008:

> As the opportunities are limited in the village, we don't have an occupation ... We thought we could at least work registered here in Soma. We could not find it in Kütahya. We have many kith and kin, relatives here. We came here thanks to them. We have been working nonstop since that time.

Different from the miners from Zonguldak, miners from Kütahya-especially ones who migrated in the 2000s-does not have mining experience in their hometown. Instead, they started to work in the mines in Soma.

Studies on migrant labour underline the relatively more precarious conditions of social reproduction and the higher level of cash dependency of migrant workers (cf. Burawoy 1976; Ferguson and McNally 2015, Wright, 2006). As I discuss in the next chapter, different conditions of social reproduction between migrant and local families stem from different levels of their relations to land and agriculture. Accordingly, the conditions of social reproduction for the migrant workers are much more dependent upon wage income received from mining, whereas local miner households are able to develop certain strategies to lower their cost of social reproduction such as subsistence farming or living in their family houses etc. Migrant families are either completely detached from agriculture or it is limited to women's daily wage employment. Besides, they live in the centre of Soma and pay rent or mortgage. Therefore, migrant miners' dependency on the income they earn from mining is higher compared to the local population, and this dependency makes migrant workers much more obedient to extractive capital. During the interviews, migrant families frequently mentioned their disadvantageous conditions stemming from detachment from their lands and their villages. For example, one of the woman interviewees from Kütahya whose husband and son are both miners explained their precarious conditions of social reproduction due to their lack of access to land as follows:

> For example, I wish my village was closer… I wish we could go to our village more frequently. If my village was closer, I would go there and take care of my own garden. I would make winter storage. Or I could go there before Kurban Bayramı[4], buy a calf and tether it on the yard for two or three months. Then I would sell it during the Kurban Bayramı. If my village was in Savaştepe, I could do all these. But Kütahya is far away.

As for local workers, migrant workers' precarious conditions of social reproduction constituted a significant impediment for the formation of a united worker movement or unionization in the Basin. Accordingly, as migrant workers are more dependent on the cash income received from mining, they were more obedient to the coal companies and to their supervisors in the processes of production, as well as social reproduction. For example, as stated by a miner who lives in a village of Savaştepe:

> We do not pay rent here. We eat what we produce. Or if I say that I need 50 Turkish Liras, there are a lot of people I can ask for. Here, we all know each other. If I run out of my village or the Soma Coal Basin, I would have to rely on a credit card. But we have solidarity here. However, for those let's say from Kütahya, they are all indebted. Then they become the slaves of the mining companies. They even accept doing very dangerous or fatal

---

4 Islamic festival of Eid al-Adha which involves the sacrifice of animals as a symbol of Abraham's willingness to sacrifice his son to God.

tasks if it is ordered by the supervisors. Because they are in debt … People from Zonguldak or Kütahya are like slaves. If, for example, the company tells them you cannot leave the mine and you must work two shifts in a row, they would accept it. They are like puppets. If the sergeant says sit down, they would sit down. If the supervisor says sit down, they would sit down. If you see some people who would resist the production pressure underground, it is us … This is how we are blacklisted all the time. They can tell us 'pack your staff and go' … That is all they can do and this would not kill us. When we arrive in our village, we have our farm, land, animals … We can deal with unemployment and survive without the mines.

In the next section, labour processes and labour control mechanisms developed in the mines of Soma are analyzed by referring to the composition of the local labour market.

6 Coal Rush Underground: Labour Processes in the Coal Pits of Soma

6.1 *Firms Operating Mines in the Soma Coal Basin*

Between 2015 and 2019, there are two open/surface pits operated by the Ege Lignite Enterprises, local branch of the Turkish Coal Enterprises, and four underground pits operated by three private companies. During the fieldwork one underground coal pit was under construction in the Kınık district.[5]

Soma Coal Incorporated, having its headquarters in Istanbul, was established in 1984 by Alp Gürkan and started extracting coal in 1986. During the 1980s and 1990s, Soma Coal Company was a small firm operating coal mines in Soma. Following the initiation of the royalty tender in 2005, the company expanded its investments dramatically. The company also undertook large-scale investments in the construction sector, such as the construction of the biggest business quarter of the country, Spine Tower, in Istanbul.[6] Meanwhile, the Soma Coal Company expanded its investments, and in 2013, it was

---

[5] The findings elaborated on in this Chapter are limited to the time period until 2019. The discussion on the condition of coal mining, firms operating pits, and changing state-capital-labour relations between 2020 and 2024 is discussed in the Postscript. The findings included in the Postscript are based on my last revisit to the Soma Coal Basin on the 10th anniversary of the Soma Mine Disaster, between 13 and 23 May 2024. Given that this revisit was after the original submission of the manuscript of the book, I added the findings of 2024 field as a Postscript.

[6] "He became the boss of a holding company thanks to the coal of the AKP" Available at: https://www.sozcu.com.tr/akpnin-komuru-ile-holding-patronu-oldu-wp511037.

TABLE 2   Firms operating pits in the Soma Coal Basin (2015–2019)

	2010	2011	2012	2013	2014
ELI Open Pits (O. P.) Pits operated by the private firms through the royalty tender	Soma O. P. Deniş O. P. İmbat A.Ş. Eynez Soma Kömürleri A.Ş. Geventepe Soma Kömürleri A.Ş. Uyar Madencilik	Soma O. P. Deniş O. P. İmbat A.Ş. Eynez Soma Kömürleri A.Ş. Geventepe Soma Kömürleri A.Ş. Uyar Madencilik	Soma O. P. Deniş O. P. İmbat A.Ş. Eynez Soma Kömürleri A.Ş. Geventepe Soma Kömürleri A.Ş. Uyar Madencilik Atabacası Soma Kömür A.Ş. Demir Export	Soma O. P. Deniş O. P. İmbat A. Ş. Eynez Soma Kömürleri A.Ş. Geventepe Soma Kömürleri A.Ş. Uyar Madencilik Atabacası Soma Kömür A.Ş. Demir Export Işıklar Soma Kömürleri A.Ş.	Soma O. P. Deniş O. P. İmbat A. Ş. Eynez Soma Kömürleri A.Ş. Atabacası Soma Kömürleri A.Ş. Demir Export Işıklar Soma Kömür A.Ş.

SOURCE: SOMA MUNICIPALITY STRATEGIC PLAN, 2015–2019, HTTPS://WWW.SOMA.BEL.TR/FILES //STRATEJIK%20PLAN%202015-2019.PDF

operating four mine sites in the Basin. First, the Geventepe mine was closed down at the end of 2013 due to the depletion of the coal reserve. Then, the Eynez pit was closed down in May 2014 after the Soma Mine Disaster. The second firm is the Imbat Coal Company, which has its headquarters in Izmir. The company was established in 2002 and operated as a coal marketing firm until 2004, when started coal extraction in Soma. Currently, it is the largest pit and in 2019, almost half of the miners of Soma were employed in the Imbat Coal

TABLE 3   The number of mines and miners in the district of Soma (2015–2019)

	2015	2016	2017	2018	2019
Number of Mines	7	7	7	7	10
Number of Miners	13291	13262	13007	12538	12323

SOURCE: SOMA MUNICIPALITY STRATEGIC PLAN, 2015–2019, HTTPS://WWW.SOMA.BEL.TR/FILES//STRATEJIK%20PLAN%202015-2019.PDF

Company. Both Soma Holding and Imbat Mining used to operate small-scale mines before the initiation of royalty tender. These companies represent the second fraction of the power bloc (Anatolian bourgeoisie) in the Basin, which has close relations with the AKP governments and established conglomerates thanks to the initiation of royalty tender and other government subsidies for the coal industry.

Demir Export Incorporated is an associated company of Koç Holding, the largest investment holding in Turkey. Koç Holding was founded in 1926 by Vehbi Koç, and it is the most significant representative of the big bourgeoisie formed during the early Republic period. The company operates in several sectors, including energy, automative, consumer durables, finance, and information technology. The holding is known for its national as well as global brands and companies, including Arçelik, Tofaş, and Yapı Kredi Bank. Demir Export was established as an associated company of Koç Holding in 1957, and it initially operated in the iron mining industry. Then, the company started the extraction of several minerals, such as silver, gold, and chalcocite. In the Soma Coal Basin, Demir Export took the tender of a coalmine in the Eynez region for 18 years in 2011 and started extracting coal in 2015 following a preparation phase. Despite specific differences in the recruitment and labour processes, representatives of the different fractions of the capital display similar tendencies in terms of production pressure over the pits and over miners. According to the findings of the fieldwork, labour processes in the coal mines of Soma embody the elements of the recruitment process, workload and organization of work, working time, wages, production process, and health and safety measures. I argue that all these elements are directly shaped by the strategic significance of the coal industry for the Turkish economy.

6.2 Recruitment Processes and the Informal Subcontractors

Most of the miners start working in the coal mines by means of an informal subcontracting system that operates through labour intermediaries called *dayıbaşı*. Most of the informal subcontractors are experienced miners who provide workers for the coal companies. I employ the term informal subcontracting to discuss their role in the labour processes, yet, informality here does not indicate unregistered employment. In the coal mines of Soma, all miners are hired as registered employees of coal firms. I use the term subcontractor because it is what the miners call the labour intermediaries, *taşeron* in Turkish. I use the adjective informal to address two features of this system. The first one is the fact that it is different from subcontracting, defined in Turkish Labour Law No. 4857 enacted in 2003 as the transfer of certain services of a company to another firm specialized in those services. However, informal subcontracting in Soma does not take the form of a legally defined relationship between two firms. Instead, it is an informal and illegal relationship between the coal firms and the individual subcontractors. Secondly, the relations in production between the informal subcontractors and the miners working in their teams tend to exceed the formal and legal boundaries of wage work. It includes physical violence, insults, production pressure, etc.

Informal subcontractors first provide workers for the coal companies using their networks based on kinship and hometown. These subcontractors are also hired by the companies as registered wage employees, yet, besides their wages, they receive additional payment for each worker they hire. The informal subcontracting system was essential for the coal companies in the early and mid-2000s when the need for miners rose drastically. It was frequently mentioned that, especially before the Soma Mine Disaster, informal subcontractors were hanging notices in the coffeehouses, bus stops, or parks around the basin and in other mining towns such as Zonguldak and Kütahya to find miners for their teams. Therefore, the informal subcontracting system was initiated when it was difficult for the firms to recruit miners. Yet, this system has been maintained even when the number of people who are willing to work in the underground mines of Soma increased. This is related to the second and equally essential function of informal subcontracting for coal companies: informal subcontractors are expected to guarantee the extraction of the maximum amount of coal by pushing miners. In other words, this system functions as the labour control and oppression mechanism in the underground pits through production pressure. As stated by almost all the interviewees, informal subcontractors poise over the workers, just like the *Azrail* (the angel of death in Islam), to implement production pressure. As stated by an experienced miner:

> In the underground mines, you have to work as teams. You cannot work individually. There is a variety of teams in charge of a variety of tasks. Each team is led by a *dayıbaşı* who is supposed to control the workers and fasten the production. If this system is not used, I argue that production per shift would decrease by two tons. There are three shifts per day. This means firms produce an additional six tons of coal per day thanks to the informal subcontracting system.

As mentioned above, almost all informal subcontractors are experienced miners. Given that the number of experienced miners was quite high in the Basin, I questioned how an experienced miner can become an informal subcontractor. Almost all the interviewees underlined that the only requirement was having a network, and there were no criteria in terms of qualifications. For example, as stated by an experienced miner who refused to become an informal subcontractor: "Any man who collects workers can become an informal subcontractor. There is no other requirement or criteria." Or, as explained by a worker, the recruitment process works as follows:

> Suppose that I am a subcontractor. I go meet the employer and promise to bring certain number of miners. Then, I go collect miners. For example, if a miner who is not working within a subcontracting team receives 1,000 liras, it is told that he would receive 1,100 liras if he works with a team. Additionally, the subcontractor commits the firm to bring 20 workers from his village or from somewhere else. That's all that they do. He does not even go to work. Now, we have an informal subcontractor named Mehmet Ali. His team is composed of 150 workers. He never comes to work. He spends all his time in the coffee houses or somewhere else the whole day. But his income keeps increasing!

Additionally, informal subcontractors receive extra payments for the performance of their team. The commission system is applied through the subcontracting teams. Therefore, besides their wages and the payments made to them for the workers they provided for the firm, they receive commissions. For example, if there are thirty subcontracting teams, the subcontractor of the team extracting the maximum amount of coal is rewarded with the highest premium payment. Therefore, they push the workers to compete against other teams as well. As stated by a miner who no longer works in the mines:

> Well, these men receive regular wages from the firms. There is also a production share they receive from the company. Suppose, that I am

> an informal subcontractor and I am in charge of extraction. How much did my team dig? For example, 2 meters. I receive the allowance for the 2 meters ... I receive extra payment for that besides the wage and the amount I receive per worker I provided for the company. I receive lots of subcontracting money without working. The only thing I do is to go down the mine once a day, storm around, and swear a blue treak at people.

Overall, even though the informal subcontracting system constitutes a significant cost burden for the firms, according to the statements of the miners and union representatives, companies make significant profits thanks to the subcontractors. As a matter of fact, almost all the interviewees stated that it would be impossible to achieve high levels of productivity through formal employment relations. Accordingly, production pressure implemented through informal relations constituted a significant mechanism of achieving productivity and controlling workers. As explained by a miner:

> Why do the firms prefer informal subcontracting? Shift supervisors or directors cannot follow up the production process. The pits are very large, the number of workers is quite high ... So, what can they do? Informal subcontracting comes into play. The firms find informal subcontractors to control the workforce. Under certain circumstances, the informal subcontractor can hit or swear to the miners. A university graduate engineer or shift supervisor cannot do these.

6.3 The Organization of Work

During the first two phases of the fieldwork, I asked questions regarding the organization of work and workplace hierarchy in order to understand the specificities of the labor process in the underground coal mines. Given that labour process and working conditions may be experienced in a different manner by workers who work at the different levels of the technical division of labour, the analysis of *relations in production* along with the relations of production is necessary. As put by Burawoy (1979: 15), relations of production are "always combined with a corresponding set of relations into which men and women enter as they confront nature, as they transform raw materials into objects of their imagination," and this relation constituted the labour process. Such definition of the labour process as the relations in production embodies the relations in which workers enter during the production process both between each other and also with the management.⁷

The first division of labour underlined during the interviews was among the different technical units, which were listed as follows: mechanical unit, coal conveyor unit, safety unit, preparation unit, and production unit. The rest of the units are based on specializations such as electric installation, health and safety provision, and transmission of extracted coal.

A lot of workers used the metaphor of a town or neighborhood to explain the plan of underground pit. For example:

> Think about this town as a forty-floor mine. Main streets, alleys ... For example, if home is a production panel, corridors would be conveyor and the rooms would be production units.

Coal is extracted in the production units named *ayak* where the subcontracting teams work. The work hierarchy within a production unit was explained as: unskilled worker, substitute, foreman, sergeant, and informal subcontractor. Above all units, there are shift supervisors and principal engineers. As expressed by an interviewee who worked as a foreman:

> Well, I am a foreman, my immediate supervisor is sergeant. At the bottom, there is the unskilled worker, then comes the substitute, there is the foreman above the substitute, then the sergeant. Well, the sergeant always stands over me. Suppose than, as a foreman when we need to bore a tunnel by task is to bore 30–35 holes or maximum 60 holes with a gun. My task is to bore this hole, when do I need the substitute at my back? Some frames will be placed there. What is needed for the frame? Three pieces of TH iron is necessary for a frame. Here it is, studding, brushing, gamma ... The task of them, namely those behind me, is to prepare this

---

7   The information I gathered regarding the relations in production and technical division of labour is quite limited for three reasons. First, I could not empirically observe the labour processes in the underground coal mines because I was not allowed to enter the mines. As mentioned in the Introduction, my findings on labour processes are built upon the narratives of miners. Secondly, during the main phases of the fieldwork, I could not conduct interviews with the managers or employers. I could have meetings with them for the first time in May 2024, therefore, the analysis of their narratives is included in the Postscript. Finally, due to the sharp division of labour in technical and informal sense, most of the interviewees did not have sufficient knowledge on the operation the whole production process in the underground mines. Their knowledge is mostly limited to the unit and subcontracting team they work within.

stuff in back of me. Suppose, we are working here, there is no material at the pit, they were not sent from the ground ... They say you should find somewhere underground. The man, namely the substitute, goes out from there, heads for the Bus Station, he cannot find and comes back. Then he goes to Government Office from there, he cannot also find there and comes back. He covers the distance till the station bridge, he has to bring and the materials from there to here on-time. Beside, all these ways are inclined. It is not a flat area like the ground. There are ups and downs, you need to pass through mud and water (...) Unskilled worker also goes with the substitute to learn the issue. Newly recruited workers are called as unskilled worker. He learns about the materials and the job he is doing by going and returning with the substitute. One day he will be a substitute. The shift supervisor controls us and informs his supervisor. Just like, today this work has been done or not done or there is such danger etc.

Each sergeant also has a team for which they are responsible. In some cases, it was argued that an informal subcontracting team is composed of teams of sergeants, and sergeants may also provide workers to the informal subcontractors. As mentioned by a retired miner, sergeants may be defined as the "subcontractors of the informal subcontractors." Yet, they mainly underlined their difference from the informal subcontractors by putting that sergeant work with their teams in the underground pits whereas informal subcontractors never work. For example, as stated by an unemployed miner from Kınık who was a sergeant before:

> I was sergeant, I had my own team. But was also working underground. Informal subcontractors never work. Even when they visit the pits, it is impossible to see them working. They yell at their team, even swear. Then, they leave the pit.

Finally, another group of underground miners oversees portage. Especially in the sections of the pits where mechanized conveyors are not installed, extracted coal is carried by portage workers. They do not work in the production units but carry the coal extracted in these units. Mostly, portage workers stated that mechanized conveyors were not installed in the sharp slope sections of the pits, and for example, "a 60-kilogram man may carry around 100 kilograms of coal" in these sections.

Within such an organization of work hierarchy, there are three eight-hour shifts per day: day shift (8 am – 4 pm), evening shift (4 pm – 12 am), and night shift (12 am – 8 am). Therefore, coal extraction literally never stops. Miners of each shift reach to their production units through conveyor bents. Most of the miners I talked to used the metaphor "like slaves," while expressing the way they are transported to the underground production units, such as "think about the movies in which slaves are transported all together. It is exactly how miners go to the production units every day." In order to understand their daily working routines and workloads, I asked the miners to explain their average days, An example from a miner who works on a day shift was as follows:

> If I work on a day shift, I have to wake up at 5:30 am, have breakfast and leave home at around 6:15 and take the personnel bus at 6:30. I arrive at the workplace at around 7 am, wear my overalls and start going down the mine at around 7–7:15 am. I take the instructions from the sergeant. Then I concentrate on my work. I do whatever I am told to do. At around 3:45, I start going out slowly. Then, I can be on the ground at around 4:30. Normally, it takes around half an hour, but it depends on where you work. Sometimes, I do not even have a chance to wash my hands and face; I can hardly catch the personnel bus. Then I arrive at home, take a shower, have dinner at around 8 pm. What can I do after that time? I cannot go to a coffee house for example. Or I cannot take my wife and children out. I have to sleep and rest. I get extremely tired during the day. And, you know, it is dangerous work; I have to take a good rest.

Meanwhile, they do not have a lunch break. They have lunch when they have an opportunity to take a short break. Their lunch boxes are prepared by their wives at home. Almost all the miners I talked to mentioned that the maximum time that they could spend for lunch was a half an hour, and it was controlled by the sergeants.

Within this hierarchical and horizontal organization of work, several formal and informal labour control mechanisms were mentioned by the miners. Yet, for a recently dispossessed rural population as well as for the miner workers who were not able to survive in their hometowns, despite the fatal working conditions in the underground mines, mining was regarded as an "opportunity" to "earn their bread." For example, one of the retired miners who lives in a mountain village of Soma used the following words to describe his appreciation to an informal subcontractor:

> A miner who used to work at a state-operated mine has become an informal subcontractor. He made us peasants, breadwinners. Thanks to him, young residents of our village are still working. Young families can earn

> their bread thanks to him. May god bless them. Peasants have finally started to earn decent money and have social insurance.

As can be seen in the quotation above, the reason why local populations regard rising mine investments as an opportunity is related to the social rights, including regular wage income, social insurance, and early retirement.

As it is elaborated on in the next chapter, neoliberal transformation of agriculture led to the commodification of means of subsistence and increasing market and cash dependency, which resulted in massive proletarianization in the Basin. Rising cash dependency along with the relatively more precarious, unstable, and informal characteristics of other employment opportunities such as wage work in agriculture or construction has made mining the most secure income generating sector in the Basin. Similarly, for the migrant families, mining provides a secure employment opportunity compared to the small-scale or illegal mines in their hometowns, such as Zonguldak, Kütahya or Bartın. In the Soma Coal Basin, all the miners are registered and receive their payments regularly each month. Furthermore, wage levels are quite tempting both for the local and migrant miners.

Miners frequently specified two significant material benefits of mining. The first and most important factor that makes mining the most attractive employment opportunity in the region is the wage levels of the underground coal mines. In September 2014, Additional Article 9 was added to the Mining Law No. 3213. Accordingly, in workplaces where lignite and hard coal are extracted, the wage amount to be paid to workers who work underground cannot be less than twice the minimum wage determined in accordance with Article 39 of Labour Law No. 4857. Therefore, the minimum wage that unskilled workers in the underground coal mines receive is twice the minimum wage in the country. The second benefit underlined by the miners was the early retirement of underground miners. In Turkey, workers employed in underground mines are qualified for retirement once they complete 4 thousand working days, regardless of their ages. Therefore, average retirement age is around 40 for the miners. For example, as explained by a miner from Zonguldak:

> We came to work in Soma and extract coal in Soma. Well, we have this miner identity inherited from our families in Zonguldak. But the mines of Zonguldak are mostly small-scale or even illegal. The employment is not registered, there is no social insurance. If you search another job, in another sector ... Well, uneducated people always try to guarantee one single thing: early retirement. It is because of our anxiety for the future. You calculate it: my insurance premium is completed in 20 years. And

> I started working when I was 20. I will be retired at the age of 40. We try to guarantee our future. But still ... What we miss is the occupational diseases of mining.

Similarly, for the local workers whose families are still engaged in agricultural production, decent wage levels, as well as early retirement, are seen as a means to finance agricultural production. For example, as explained by a miner from the village of Savaştepe whose wife is engaged in farming and animal breeding:

> The brighter side of mining has been. Once you complete 4 thousand working days, you are retired when you are 39 or 40. Then, I can maintain my other works, such as farming and animal breeding. I will have the retirement bonus, retirement pension and other benefits. I can finance farming and even extend it. For example, if I buy an oil grove following my retirement, I can do olive farming with my children, my wife ... Our life is relatively more comfortable than our counterparts in other sectors. My income is quite higher than the minimum wage, I will be retired next year.

Similarly, unemployed miners whose contracts were terminated after the Soma Mine Disaster were complaining about losing their right for an early retirement. As underlined by a worker who started working at a factory in Izmir following his dismissal from mining:

> When they fired us, I was 39 years old. There were around 500 days left for my retirement ... Now I work at a factory and I will have to work until the age of 55 to get retired. I lost the opportunity of early retirement. If I could have continued in mining, I would be retired by now.

6.4   *Coal Rush Underground: Production Pressure*

To define the organization of work in the underground pits of Soma, miners use the term 'production pressure' to indicate the super-exploitation of both nature and labour. In other words, they use the term in terms of both pushing the natural limits of the pits and the workers to produce more with the aim of extracting the maximum possible amount of coal per shift. As discussed earlier in this chapter, in mining, work is organized to adapt to natural factors. In the Soma Coal Basin, production pressure includes disregarding natural limits, and coal extraction exceeds the mechanical capacity of the pits. This was explicitly exemplified in the 2009 report on the Soma Eynez Mine (SEM), the pit in which the Soma Mine Disaster happened. Between 2006 and

2009, SEM was operated by another coal firm, Park Teknik Incorporated. In 2009, the firm applied for the termination of the royalty tender and reported the mechanical constraints, such as frequent fires and irreparable safety concerns stemming from the original design of the mine. Despite this report, the TKI transferred the operation of SEM to the Soma Coal Company. While Park Teknik Incorporated had extracted less than one million tons of coal between 2006 and 2009 (despite the agreement on 1.5 million tons of annual extraction), the TKI and Soma Coal Company signed a royalty tender for extraction of 14.1 tons of coal in 7 years (Düzgün and Leveson, 2018: 43). Despite the natural limits underlined in the report, the Soma Coal Company increased the production using conventional and semi-mechanized mining techniques. As these systems necessitate a labour-intensive organization of work, the employment of a high number of workers in each shift has further increased the risk of deadly mine disasters. In 2014, the outcome of this production pressure was the death of 301 miners.

Meanwhile, Demir Export Incorporated, which started extracting coal in the Basin at the end of 2015, performs fully mechanized mining and employs relatively fewer miners. From the beginning, the investment of Demir Export was appreciated for its fully mechanized mining and higher standards of health and safety. However, in its first year of operation, six miners were poisoned due to a methane leak, and it was realized that the ventilation did not work properly during a power outage due to compressor failure. Additionally, since then, there have been a couple of deadly mine disaster of injuries of miners in the same pit. As explained by an experienced miner, it was due to the pressure of the mechanized system over the pit. These examples clearly show that nature, i.e. the mechanical structure of the basin and the pits, puts significant pressure on the production process and exceeding the natural limits results in deadly mine disasters and injuries of miners. Yet, firms tend to neglect work and safety measures and risk the lives of miners by exceeding the natural limits and the state overlooks this for the sake of its coal rush policy.

Production pressure over the miners indicates the top-down relations in production to guarantee extraction of the maximum possible amount of coal despite geological limits. In mining, natural uncertainties bring two opposed forms of work organization: independent working groups with decision-making power as well as disciplining and hierarchical methods. In both cases, despite mechanization, labour power controlled and disciplined by wages are the effective forms of work organization (Burawoy, 1979: 207). In the Soma Coal Basin, these seemingly opposed forms of work organization operate complementarily. On the one hand, the organization of work is strictly hierarchical, and the rhythm of production is intensified through production pressure on the miners within this hierarchical structure. On the other hand, miners are divided into subcontracting teams through informal subcontractors who function as underground discipline mechanisms of the coal companies.

As mentioned earlier, the initial role of the informal subcontractors is to provide workers for the firms using their networks based on kinship and hometown. The firms hire the contractors as registered and waged employees, and they also receive additional payments for each recruited worker. Even though the original aim of this system was related to the miner shortage in the initial years of royalty tender, it has been maintained since the system guarantees the extraction of the maximum possible amount of coal. It is the duty of informal subcontractors to apply production pressure on the miners. As one of the interviewees explains:

> They need informal subcontracting because a shift supervisor, cannot oppress the workers that much. The informal subcontractor assigns the sergeant to control the workers for eight hours. The sergeant is at the disposal of the informal subcontractor. ... They control us for eight hours! They even control us during the lunch break. If it takes more than half an hour, they start to ask 'why are you late' or 'it has been forty minutes.' A shift supervisor cannot control you during the whole shift. They do not work at all! We were eighty miners in the production unit; there were four sergeants controlling us. Keep extracting! If there is no extraction even for a minute. ... Keep extracting the company will go bankrupt!

Similarly:

> Subcontractors are like sticks for the workers for further extraction ... Go on, go on ... Rush, rush! They do not have any other function. They are assigned to oppress the workers for the extraction of the intended amount of coal!.

As mentioned in the previous section, commission system is employed through the informal subcontracting teams. According to the miners, this system fosters competition among the subcontracting teams as the team extracting the highest amount of coal is rewarded with the highest level of premium payment. As expressed both during the interviews and during the witness statemtnes in the trials of the Soma Mine Disaster, production pressure may include physical violence, swear words, and insults. For example, as stated by an unemployed miner:

> I saw a miner who was hit by the informal subcontractor just because he took a rest for two minutes. Even their most decent statements include swear words and insults.

Sergeants also have their teams for which they are responsible. During the interviews, it was frequently mentioned that sergeants may also provide workers for the informal subcontracting teams. As narrated by a retired miner, sergeants function as 'sub-subcontractors.' Yet, they mainly identified their difference from the informal subcontractors by underlining that sergeants worked with their teams in the underground mines, whereas informal subcontractors did not work at all. For example, as stated by an unemployed miner who used to be a sergeant:

> I was a sergeant But I was working with my team … Informal subcontractors never work. Even when they visit the mine, it is impossible to see them working. They yell at their team, even sweat. Then they leave.

There are several formal and informal control mechanisms and pressures over miners in the underground mines. However, for a rural population in the process of dispossession and for the migrant workers who are not able to survive in their hometowns, despite the fatal working conditions, mining is considered as an 'opportunity' to 'earn their bread.' For example, a former tobacco producer who lives in one of the mountain villages located in the Basin expressed his gratitude to the informal subcontractor who hired his son as follows:

> One of the miners who used to work for the TKI has become an informal subcontractor. He made the peasants of out village, real breadwinners. Thanks to him … Young people of our village earn their bread thanks to him. God bless them. villagers started to earn money and acquired social insurance.

7   Conclusion

In this Chapter, I have argued that labour processes and organization of work in the extractive industries are determined by state-capital-labour-nature relations. Combining the literature on extractivism and LPT, I have paid attention to (i) the coal rush policies of the AKP governments, (ii) the labour supply to the coal pits of Soma, (iii) labour processes in the coalmines. I have argued that the organization of work around production pressure over nature and miners is a direct reflection of the strategic significance of the coal industry for the AKP governments, particularly for overcoming energy dependency by utilizing domestic coal. Additionally, I have mentioned the need to focus on the mutual and internal relationship between the imperatives of production and social reproduction. In the next chapter, social reproduction in the Soma Coal Basin is elaborated on by referring to the gendered patterns of proletarianization and dispossession and women's productive and reproductive work in the Basin.

CHAPTER 4

The Social Reproduction of Extractivism: Gendered Patterns of Dispossession and Women's Work in Rural Turkey

In this chapter, I argue that rural change and patterns of dispossession and proletarianization in the rural extractive regions are inherently gendered, and women assume a central role in the production and social reproduction of the classes of extractive labour. In contrast to the analyses of rural change and resource extraction, which largely focus on women's role in resistance movements organized against investments in natural resources, I seek to unveil the inherently gendered character of the transformation of rural livelihood in resource extraction regions. To do so, I refer to the 'miners' wives' as the producers and reproducers of the classes of extractive labour amid the commodification and diversification of rural livelihood. Therefore, in contrast to the representation of women as 'shadowy figures' (Mercier and Gier, 2007) of the extractive communities, I define the classes of extractive women as the producers and reproducers of these communities and reveal the ways in which extractive capital exploits women's work as miners' wives.

Firstly, mega-investments in natural resource industries in the agrarian South have not created male breadwinner/female caregiver form of rural households. As the employment generated by these investments for the male members of the rural households is usually casual and low-paid, women continue working in agriculture in several forms, such as petty commodity producers, unpaid family workers, agricultural wage workers and subsistence producers. Therefore, these women are not housewives who are completely dependent upon their husbands' income, rather, they are the 'last guarantors of the survival' (Mies, 1982) of the extractive households. Secondly, mine investments in the countryside transform rural households from small-scale farmer families to miner families, which restructures women's social reproductive roles. The imperatives of social reproduction, and especially unpaid reproductive work, also determine the conditions for women in participating in wage work. By universalizing the housewife ideology, capitalist patriarchy has defined women's unpaid work as an activity (not as work) and paid work as supplementary work to support the male breadwinner of the family. This mystification has promoted the super-exploitation of women's unpaid work as invisible and justified low wages and extremely precarious conditions in their paid work (Mies, 1986: 119–20). As explained by Federici (2021: 18):

> [A]s the history of the runaway shop demonstrates, a reserve of wageless labor both in the 'underdeveloped' countries and in the metropoles has allowed capital to move away from those areas where labor had made itself too expensive, undermining the power that workers in these areas had achieved. Whenever capital could not run to the 'Third World,' it opened the gates of the factories to women, blacks, and youth or migrants from the 'Third World.' It is no accident, in fact, that while capital is based on waged labor more than half of the world's population is still unwaged. Wagelessness and underdevelopment are essential elements of capitalist planning, nationally and internationally. They are powerful means to make workers compete on the national and international labor market and make us believe that our interests are different and contradictory.

This chapter begins with an analytical framework for the holistic analysis of the classes of extractive labour in the agrarian South by paying attention to women's central role in the patterns of disposession, proletarianization and rural livelihood diversification. It then outlines the gendered patterns of agrarian change in Turkey and then the reflections of coal rush and rural change of Turkey in the Soma Coal Basin in the 2000s. Finally, I analyze women's paid and unpaid agricultural work and reproductive work as miners' wives.

1 The Production and Social Reproduction of the Classes of Extractive Labour

The social reproduction of the rural populations under different phases of capitalism and the question of how the conditions of production and social reproduction of the peasant households are determined by the operations of capital and of the state (Bernstein, 1977) require particular attention (cf. Çelik, 2023b). Capitalism as a system in which the direct producers' access to the means of production, to the means of labour, and to the basic conditions of their survival and self-reproduction are mediated by the market (Wood, 2009) has restructured the 'imperatives of social reproduction' (Mezzadri et al., 2022; Stevano, 2022) for the peasantry who traditionally 'reproduce themselves through their own labour' (Bernstein, 1977: 61). For Bernstein (2010: 4), the development of capitalism in agriculture has changed the social character of small-scale farming in two respects. First of all, it has led to the commodification of subsistence by transforming peasants into petty commodity producers who are obliged to produce their living through integration into broader social divisions of labour and markets. Secondly, petty-commodity producers are subject to class differentiation, which has led to the class formation of the classes of small-scale capitalist farmers, petty commodity producers, and wage workers. I employ the term *classes of extractive labour* by referring to Henry Bernstein's concept of classes of labour, which allows to capture the multiplicity of proletarian conditions along axes of gender, ethnicity, caste and overcome dualities such as rural/urban, agricultural/non-agricultural, wage employment/self-employment/, landowning/landless households, and productive/reproductive work (see Chapter 2).

Firstly, what is observed in the agrarian South under neoliberalism is rural livelihood diversification (Bernstein, 2001, 2010; Ellis, 1998; Johnson, 2004; O'Laughlin, 1996). This diversification indicates changes in class relations and divisions of labour within the rural labour markets and rural households. To analyze this 'non-dualistic agrarian structure of great complexity' (O'Laughlin, 1996: 4) under neoliberalism, one needs to take various forms of access to land, differentiation within rural labour markets, and household division of labour into account. To begin with, there is a complex structure of land ownership and landlessness. These different forms and degrees of access to land include households with established use rights to adequate land, households whose access to land is limited to contract farming or subsistence farming, landless squatters, and tenants with temporary use rights (O'Laughlin, 1996: 4–5). Additionally, there are intra-class inequalities and fragmentations within (rural) local labour markets along the lines of gender, ethnicity, generation, and caste that co-constitute class relations (Mezzadri, 2016; Stevano, 2022). National and transnational capital often strategically use these fragmented local structures at their disposal to minimize labour costs (Mezzadri, 2010: 128). As the next sections illustrate based on the analysis of rural labour regimes in Western Anatolia, one of the most striking elements of this differentiation is the migrant workers.

Livelihood diversification is also a strategy for rural households that are unable to meet the conditions of social reproduction (Razavi, 2003, 2009), which do not necessarily lead to class transitions (Stevano, 2022: 1852). Therefore, the analysis of rural livelihood diversification necessitates a redefinition of the rural households by overcoming the neoclassical interpretations of household as a black box. The transformation of rural production systems, commercialization of agrarian economies, commodification of the means of production and social reproduction, and rural class differentiation have taken place along with gender differences and gender division of work within rural households

(Razavi, 2009: 203). In this respect, livelihood diversification corresponds to survival strategies and coping mechanisms (Aydın, 2002) characterized by the use of household labour reserve (Özuğurlu, 2011) through gender division of work. Labour supplied to global production networks, rural industries, capitalist farms, petty commodity production, subsistence farming, and reproductive work within the household are some of the ways in which this gendered labour reserve is directed (Baglioni, 2022). Deepening subsistence crises have encouraged rural men to search for off-farm work either by seasonally migrating to urban centres or rural industries. Rising extractive investments have constituted an opportunity for rural households to diversify income sources without migrating to city centres. However, as the employment generated by extractive industries is precarious, informal, or low-wage, wage income is predominantly insufficient for households' reproduction. Therefore, the proletarianization of male members of the rural households in extractive regions of the Global South has not created a male breadwinner/female caregiver form of proletarian households. Instead, their reproduction is possible primarily through a combination of various forms of waged and unwaged activities. Thus, women in the rural extractive regions 'are not housewives dependent on the income of their husbands; they are in fact the last guarantors of the survival of the family through various types of work and services' (Mies, 1982: 4).

Secondly, as extractive industries offer employment for the male workforce, proletarianization in the extractive regions has primarily been in the form of men's moving out of agriculture and women remaining at the farm or moving out much slower, leading to the feminization of agriculture (Deere, 2005; Katz, 2003; Pattnaik et al., 2018; Pattnaik and Lahiri-Dutt, 2020; Radel et al., 2012). Feminization of agriculture does not merely indicate a quantitative increase in women's participation in agricultural production. Instead, it indicates the intensification of exploitation of women's labour while lacking control over production. According to Shiva (2014, 2016), Structural Adjustment Programmes (SAPs) have aimed to replace women and subsistence producers by promoting agribusiness corporations as the main providers of food, therefore marginalizing the domestic food economies in which women play a pivotal role. This indicates the masculinization of modern, commercial, and capital-intensive agriculture and the feminization of traditional agricultural production that feeds the rural poor. Therefore, neoliberalism in the countryside indicates, on the one hand, the masculinization of the markets, control over production, and farm management and, on the other hand, feminization of agricultural labour through increasing exploitation of women as low-waged and/or unpaid workers (Harriss-White, 2005). As stated by Shiva (2016: 109–110):

By splitting the agricultural economy into a cash-mediated masculinised sector, and a subsistence, food-producing feminised sector, capitalist patriarchy simultaneously increases the work burden and marginalisation of women. The cash economy draws men away from basic food production, thus increasing women's workload for producing subsistence.

Finally, extractive investments in rural areas transform women's reproductive work as subsistence producers. Following the scholars of early social reproduction analysis, I use the term subsistence production to refer to both subsistence farming and women's unpaid housework. Therefore, women's reproductive work in the classes of extractive labour consists of subsistence farming to subsidize the wages of men (in this case, miners) and housework for the daily and generational reproduction of labour power. As discussed earlier, for the scholars of early social reproduction analysis (Dalla Costa and James, 1972; Federici, 2004; Mies, 1986, 1988), the blind spot (Von Werlhof, 1988) of the mainstream and Marxist political economy was the inability to conceive the centrality of social reproduction and women's unpaid reproductive work for capitalism (Federici, 2012). However, 'capitalist accumulation still draws its life-blood for its continuous volarisation from waged as well as unwaged labour' (Dalla Costa 1995: 7). Therefore, the main contradiction of capitalism is not between capital and wage labour but between 'all labour– life– and capital' (Von Werlhof, 2007: 3). Drawing on Rosa Luxemburg's ([1913] 2003) emphasis on capitalism's need for non-capitalist strata for the persistence of accumulation, they analyzed how the exploitation of women's unpaid work is related to the global accumulation of capital (Federici, 2014; Mies, 1988; Von Werlhof, 1988). Accordingly, the supposedly non-capitalist work within the household does not only guarantee the survival of the household but also provides the capital with the opportunity of expropriating the unpaid reproductive work of women without paying for it (Von Werlhof, 1988: 16). The continuous exploitation of this unpaid work is possible through the historical opportunity that patriarchy has provided for capitalism: the existence of women ready to do this work for free either by patriarchal oppression (domestic violence, rape, coercion, etc.) or consent (love, motherhood ideology, faithfulness, etc.) (Acar-Savran and Yaman, 2020: 9). Furthermore, unpaid reproductive work determines the conditions for participating in wage work for women. By universalizing the housewife ideology, capitalist patriarchy has defined women's unpaid work as an activity (not as work) and paid work as supplementary work to support the male breadwinner of the family. This mystification promotes the super-exploitation of women's unpaid work as invisible and justifies low wages and extremely precarious conditions in their paid work (Mies, 1986: 119–120).

Extractive investments transform rural women's subsistence production both as farmers and as housewives. Firstly, factors such as the expropriation of smallholder farmland for extractive investments and the ecological impacts of these investments, such as biodiversity loss, water pollution, and soil deterioration, limit women's access to the means of subsistence (Lahiri-Dutt, 2015; Lozeva and Marinova, 2010; Lutz-Ley and Buechler, 2020; Scheyvens and Lagisa, 1998). Therefore, extractive investments trigger a shift from subsistence to market and cash-dependent forms of rural livelihood. This leaves rural women who have been 'the subsistence farmers of the planet' (Federici, 2004) at the mercy of the market. In most cases, the impact of extractive investments on farming is accompanied by the neoliberal transformation of agricultural production mentioned above. As a result, women in the extractive regions are forced into marginalized forms of wage labour in agricultural or non-agricultural sectors (Bhanumathi, 2002). Secondly, as extractive investments, especially mining, mostly absorb the male workforce, they transform women's reproductive work within the family as well. The reproduction of miners who work in fatally dangerous conditions indicates super-exploitation of miners' wives' unpaid work both physically and emotionally. Historically, as seen in many examples, extractive capital prefers married miners to guarantee their productivity thanks to the stabilizing impact of women's unpaid work within the family for the daily reproduction of miners (Erwiza, 2002; Lozeva and Marinova, 2010; Parpart, 1983). Therefore, instead of viewing women as passive victims of the highly masculinized mining communities, there is a need to focus on women's central role in the production and social reproduction of extractive communities and how extractive capital benefits from it (Lahiri-Dutt, 2015; Mercier and Gier, 2007).

2 The Development of Capitalism in Agriculture in Turkey until the 1980s

In the late 19th and early 20th centuries, the Ottoman Empire witnessed an export-led agricultural growth and commercialization. Yet, the structure of agriculture largely remained dominated by small peasant households and non-commodified family labour. The existence of large holdings was limited to the Kurdish south-east region and some fertile plants in the Southern and Western parts of Anatolia, such as Çukurova and Söke plains. Even though the use of seasonal wage labour started in these regions where large holdings existed, commercial production was also mainly based on small family farms (Pamuk, 2008, as cited in Bozkurt-Güngen, 2017). Similarly, in the 1920s, following the foundation of the Republic of Turkey, agricultural policies of the new regime were built upon the establishment of export-oriented agriculture through strong state support for the large landowners. Therefore, there was no structural change in agriculture and rural class relations in the early years of the Republic.

Throughout the early years of the Republic, the dominant economic activity in the country was agriculture, which largely took the form of subsistence peasant farming instead of a capitalist agriculture. Just like the late Ottoman period, market-oriented agricultural production and cash-cropping were limited to Western and Southern Anatolia, whereas the majority of the country's agricultural activities were characterized by subsistence farming built upon family labour. (Oral, et al. 2015: 71). Once the effects of the 1929 Great Depression reached the country, new taxes were imposed by the single party government, which led to the discontent of peasants. 1930s are marked by the policies of etatism and protectionism in Turkey. In line with this, there were several attempts to achieve an agricultural development, such as the establishment of an institutional structure which would guarantee price stability, establishment of agricultural state economic enterprises such as Turkish Sugar Factories and Soil Products Office, or subsidies for agricultural research and product diversification (Oyan, 2015: 112). Yet, the only portion of the rural population who could benefit from these protectionist measures were large landowners. Especially due to the significant tax burden, rural populations' discontent from the single party governments was obvious. During the Second World War (1939–1945), unrest in the countryside of Turkey peaked. To prevent the threat of shortages and hunger in the cities, the military officials forcible seized the products from peasants at prices below the market value. Along with the further increase of taxes, these provoked the poor peasantry's hatred towards the single-party government. Meanwhile, large landowners who had strong connections with local and central authorities were able to remain immune from these measures, smuggling their products into the cities and selling them at extortionate prices (Gürel, 2014: 320–321). Therefore, the period between the early republican period and post second world war marks the process of capital accumulation for large landowners and impoverishment for smallholder peasant families.

Today's agrarian structure in Turkey has its roots in the international division of labour formed in the postwar period when the Bretton Woods System was accepted. In the context of this international division of labor between developed and underdeveloped countries, the former was in charge of industrial production, whereas the latter were expected to provide agricultural commodities and raw materials. Similarly, Turkey's inclusion in the Marshall Plan in

1948 gave the country the role of supplying food and raw materials to European countries. In this context, the state adopted an agriculture-based development strategy to achieve rapid modernization and mechanization of agriculture (Yıldırmaz, 2009: 71–73; Bor, 2014: 91). Despite the country's inclusion in the international division of labour and commodification of agriculture since the mid-1940s, small-scale farmers had made significant gains from state subsidies and the provision of infrastructure in Turkey until the 1980s. The Marshall Aid intensified the state support for small-scale farmers to ensure higher productivity, price stability, and increased exports by implementing state-declared floor prices, input subsidies and subsidized credits.

Starting from the 1950s, as a result of the introduction of mechanization and an increasing number of tractors, migration from rural areas to cities began due to developments such as urbanization, improvement of transportation and railroads, and industrialization. Consequently, the shift of labour from agriculture to industry and services began in the 1950s. While the share of agricultural employment in total employment declined only around 10 percent within the 25-year period prior to 1950, it continued to decrease by 10 percent each decade after 1950. Yet, this did not lead to a dramatic decrease in the share of agriculture in the GDP; instead, the 1950s was a period of extensive production, which was marked by a drastic increase in the cultivated area as well as the amount of wheat production (Oyan, 2015: 113).

Furthermore, one of the main premises of import substitution developmentalism of the 1960s was the complementarity of agricultural and industrial development. To achieve this, the state maintained active support for the small-scale farmers (Aydın, 2010: 153). Thus, farmers enjoyed considerable income and social security and remained substantially immune to market fluctuations (Keyder and Yenal, 2011: 64). It is possible to argue that, the protectionism, which was intended initially in the 1930s were actually realized in the 1960s. In fact, in 1976, agricultural support purchases of the state constituted around 23.67 percent of the gross agricultural product and 6.36 percent of the Gross National Product (GNP) (Somel, 2021). As a result of such strong state support, the number of cultivators rose significantly from less than 1000 in 1948 to 8000 in 1967 and more than 130,000 in 1980 (Gürel, 2011: 202).

3   Neoliberalism in Agriculture and Gendered Patterns of Dispossession and Proletarianization in Turkey

In the early 1980s, the SAP reforms brought into the agenda transformations such as the state's withdrawal from its protectionist role in input subsidies, implementation of minimum price and guarantee of purchase for several crops. Whereas the market dependency in agricultural production was limited to input and product markets and farmers as petty commodity producers were able to control the production process until the 1980s, restructuring attempts from the 1980s onwards suggested a shift of the control of both production and marketing processes to the agribusiness capital (Bor, 2014: 104–105). However, the neoliberal transformation of agriculture in Turkey has not been a smooth process.

Gürel (2011: 59–63) discusses the neoliberal transformation of agriculture in Turkey since the 1980s by referring to three sub-periods. The first period (1980–1986) constituted the beginning of neoliberalization attempts under the regime change when the support purchases declined drastically. Accordingly, throughout the 1980s, the share of support purchases in total production volume decreased from 10 percent to 3 percent in wheat, from 71.5 percent to 39.3 percent in tobacco, from 40.4 percent to 7.5 percent in hazelnuts, and from 73 percent to 22.5 percent in cotton. Such a significant decrease in support purchases increased the cost of production for the farmers. The second period (1987–1998) is characterized by political instability. The number of political parties running for elections was quite high, and the coalition governments tended to re-introduce some of the earlier support mechanisms by interfering in price formation and re-introducing subsidies and support prices to farmers because of their political expediency.[1] The third period, the crises of 1999 and 2001 led to the abandonment of the majority of subsidies for the small-scale farmers.

The deepening of neoliberalism in the countryside of Turkey corresponds to the aftermath of the 2000–2001 financial crises and to the AKP governments. The main mechanisms of this neoliberal transformation consist of the withdrawal of the former support system, withdrawal of the subsidized agricultural credit system of the Agricultural Bank, determination of the product prices in accordance with the world stock prices, restructuring of the Union and Agricultural Sales Cooperatives, restructuring the seed sector by shifting the responsibility for controlling and regulating formal seed systems from public authorities to private sector, and the privatization of agricultural state economic enterprises (SEEs) (Değirmenci, 2021; Günaydın, 2009: 178; Nizam and Yenal, 2020: 747). These transformations triggered a drastic decline in

---

[1] The only exception in this respect is the aftermath of the April 5, 1994 stabilization program. In 1994–1995, the number of subsidized products along with the amount of subsidies fell drastically. This led to an unrest of the masses and the coalition government that won the 1996 elections re-introduced agricultural supports.

Turkey's total agricultural production. The share of agriculture in the GDP fell from 23.8 percent in 1978 to 18.9 percent in 1988, to 9.1 percent in 2010 (Gürel, 2014: 352), and to 6.4 percent in 2019 (TURKSTAT, 2020). Yet, the value of total agricultural production has risen steadily (see Figure 2). Therefore, despite the dramatic fall of the share of agriculture in the GDP, it would be wrong to claim that neoliberalism has created a simple deagrarianization in Turkey. Instead, neoliberalism has resulted in a shift from a smallholder-based to an agribusiness-based agrarian structure in Turkey (Gürel et al., 2019: 465), and agriculture has become a profitable sector for national and international agribusiness capital.

Therefore, the impact of neoliberal agricultural policies has been manifested in the countryside of Turkey as impoverishment, dispossession and, therefore, the proletarianization of small-scale farmer families. In some cases, the dispossession of small-scale farmers has taken the form of land expropriation for off-farm investments, whereas in many instances, they have merely lost control over production on their own lands. Between 2000 and 2012, almost 7 million people left the countryside and migrated to the urban centers (BSB, 2015: 104), and the share of the rural population fell from almost 70 percent in 1960 to 35 percent in 2000 and 23 percent in 2019 (World Bank, 2020). Under the simple reproduction squeeze stemming from the decline of state support, diminishing availability of affordable credit mechanisms, and rising production costs relative to farm incomes, small-scale farmer families who remained

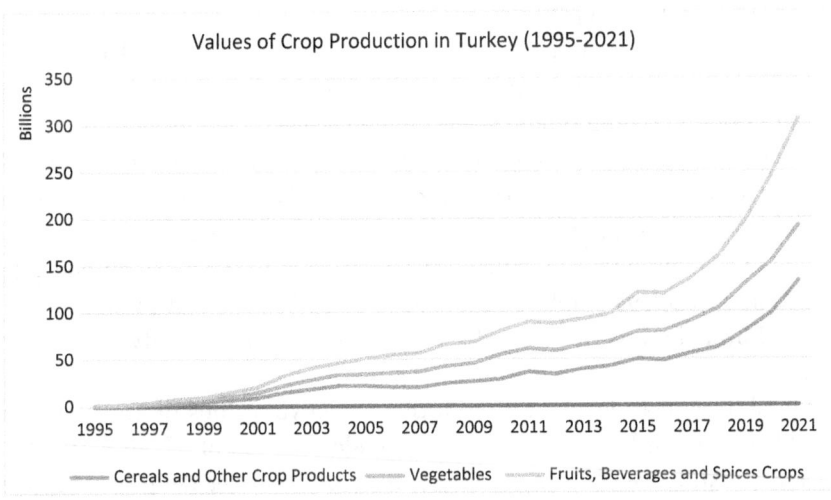

FIGURE 2   Values of crop production in Turkey (1995–2021)
SOURCE: TURKSTAT

in the countryside tended to diversify their income sources in farm and off-farm works as a survival strategy (Aydın, 2002; Çelik, 2021; Keyder and Yenal, 2011). As explained by Keyder and Yenal (2011: 58)

> Structural adjustment and market liberalisation policies have played a fundamental role in intensifying the struggle for viable livelihoods one result of which has been the re-orientation of rural dwellers toward income diversification outside of agriculture. The gradual liberalization of agricultural markets and dwindling state support to agricultural producers have contributed to the decline in agricultural revenues and led rural dwellers to search for complementary resources of income generating activities. This process was, to a large degree, aided by the development of alternative sources of employment in the countryside, thanks to the growth, especially, of the tourism and construction sectors. Thus, migration to large cities by the younger members of rural households has largely been avoided. (…) Younger members of poorer households with limited land availability are more eager to engage in contemporary, seasonal or preferably permanent off-farm employment, but in the vicinity of their villages. In most cases, those with off-farm jobs continue to reside in the village.

One of the most significant means to diversify livelihood for the rural populations is contract farming. In contract farming, farmers transfer control over the production process to agribusiness firms and maintain the production on their own land by using their own family labour and means of production. In the absence of the former state subsidies, framers may prefer contract farming due to the purchase guarantee, and in this way, agribusiness firms or supermarkets exploit the agricultural producers as "hidden proletarians" in their own land. On the other hand, by avoiding the direct control of production, they get rid of the cost of socially necessary wages for the survival of the whole family (Çelik, 2021: 124). Therefore, it can be argued that contract farming is the implementation of subcontracting in agriculture and transforms the small farmers into subcontract workers employed on their own land. The direct producers lose control over the production and solely possess simple property rights (Bor, 2014: 116–7).

Rural livelihood diversification in the extractive regions of Turkey under neoliberalism has been based upon the gender division of labour within the classes of extractive labour. Following Bernstein's expanded definition, I define classes of extractive labour in Turkey beyond wage work to include petty commodity producers in the process of the dispossession, family farmers, agricultural workers, seasonal (migrant) agricultural workers and wage workers of the extractive investments. Firstly, the growth of natural resource industries has constituted a salient 'employment opportunity' for the young male members of the recently dispossessed families (Adaman et al., 2019; Çelik, 2023a). Instead of a complete detachment from land and agriculture, these households have maintained agricultural production through the paid or unpaid work of women in one or more of the following forms: wage work, petty commodity production and subsistence production. Secondly, therefore, these investments absorbed the male workforce of the classes of extractive labour and have led to the feminization of agricultural work. According to 2017 data of TURKSTAT, the share of agricultural employment constitutes 19.5 percent of total employment: 28.7 percent in women's and 15.5 percent in men's total employment (TURKSTAT, 2017). In addition, self-employed, unpaid family workers constitute the majority of the agricultural workforce in Turkey. According to the data from 2019, the share of unpaid family workers is 88% in the agricultural workforce and 76 percent of these unpaid family workers are women (Kocabicak, 2022: 108).

However, official statistics on paid and unpaid employment in agriculture do not clearly reflect the real conditions of the rural workforce in general and, in particular, women's agricultural work. Firstly, the majority of wage agricultural workers in Turkey are employed in big capitalist or small-scale farms as informal and unregistered workers. Additionally, small-scale farming is predominantly an unregistered economic activity in Turkey. According to the statement of the Union of Agricultural Chambers (UAC, 2021), the estimated rate of women (paid and unpaid) agricultural workers who are not included in the social security system is 94.5 percent. Therefore, women's agricultural work in Turkey is invisible in both paid and unpaid forms (Çelik, 2021; Eren, 2019), and to make it visible, it is essential to support quantitative data with qualitative research and the narratives of rural women.

4 Agrarian Change, Patterns of Dispossession, and Livelihood Diversification in the Soma Coal Basin

In 2005, as part of Turkey's coal rush policies to overcome dependency on imported energy by utilizing domestic coal, coal extraction in Soma was transferred to private firms through royalty tender (see Chapter 3). Thanks to the guarantee of purchase and high amounts of incentives (Acar et al., 2015) provided by the AKP governments to the coal investors, both big capital groups and the newly emerging bourgeoisie during the AKP governments have invested in the coal industry. This was directly reflected in Soma since the initiation of royalty tender in 2005 and private sector investments in the underground coal pits have drastically increased. As a result of rising investments in the underground coal pits where labour-intensive coal extraction techniques are used, the need for coal miners has also increased.

The number of miners in Soma rose from around 4 thousand in 2000 (Tamzok, 2014) to more than 14 thousand in 2014. There have been two means of labour supply to the coal pits of Soma. Having large-scale investments, Soma has been a migration destination for miner families across Turkey since the initiation of royalty tender. Firms investing in Soma are larger and have a purchase guarantee. Therefore, in contrast to the small-scale or illegal mining companies in other mining towns, wage levels are relatively high and paid regularly and all the workers are registered (see Chapter 3). The second and main means of labour supply is the proletarianization of local farmer families as a result of the neoliberal transformation of tobacco farming.

Until the 2000s, the population in the villages of the Basin were mainly engaged in agricultural production. Especially the local peasants who owned a certain plot of land did not work in the mines as the income they received from farming was sufficient for the subsistence of the whole family. For example, as stated by one of the miners who work in a private coal company while his wife still takes care of tobacco farming:

> We neither intended to work in the mine nor in the power plant at that time. We were already earning their compensation amount in one harvest. It did not make sense to work in the mine.

As explained by the chairperson of the Trade Union of Tobacco Producers (Tütün-Sen) and secretary general of the Trade Union of Farmers (Çiftçi-Sen), Ali Bülent Erdem, during our interview, during the 1970s, the population of the district of Soma was around 29 thousand, 19 thousand of which were living in the villages. Accordingly, around 4,300 to 4,800 households (around 17–18 thousand people) were producing tobacco, and a considerable number of today's miners were from those families:

> We had already been an agricultural country since the establishment of the Republic. Soma is also an agricultural town. However, the agrarian structure of Soma is rather different than the surrounding regions such as Akhisar or Kınık. There are so large plains in Kınık which are available for irrigated farming. But Soma is one of the towns where the Bakırçay River flows through. The Bakırçay river flows through a narrow valley. That is

why Soma has historically been a tobacco-producer town. Tobacco grows over barren lands and does not need water. Because of the characteristics of the soil, the main crop of Soma is tobacco. The population of Soma was around 29 thousand in the 1970s, 19 thousand of which were living in villages. Around 4,300–4,800 households were engaged in tobacco farming. In order to calculate tobacco production, you should consider at least a four-people family because tobacco farming is very demanding and it necessitates the work of the whole family. Therefore, nearly 17–18 thousand people were rural people who earned their living by tobacco farming at that time.

Until the mid-1990s, small-scale tobacco producers in rural Turkey had made significant gains because of the strong state support, especially the guarantee of purchase provided by the State Monopoly of Tobacco and Alcoholic Beverages (Tekel) and the possibility of producing high amounts of tobacco. In 1990, the number of tobacco producer households in Turkey was 521,952, the total area under cultivation was 320,236 ha and the total amount of production was 296,008 t (Önder, 2022).

As underlined in the quotation from the chairperson of the Trade Union of Tobacco Producers as well, tobacco farming was done by the whole family until the 2000s. It was mainly because of the fact that tobacco farming is a quite labour intensive and time-consuming form of agricultural production and it takes around 11 months at intervals. Additionally, given that the income generated by tobacco farming was sufficient for the survival of the household, they did not need to diversify their sources of income. Therefore, the whole family was engaged in tobacco production until the 2000s and instead of shuttling between the tobacco farms and their villages, they were moving to farms for a four-month period during summer and stay in shelter tents. Therefore, the landowning families did not work as agricultural wage workers, and their need for wage workers was quite limited. An average landowning family, for example, did farming jobs through the use of all labour power potential within the household. For example, as explained by a miner who was formerly a tobacco producer:

> For example, we were producing 4–4.5 tons of tobacco per year. All by ourselves ... I mean all the families who had land could do this. I even know some families producing 8 tons per year, and we were not employing any workers. We had our own family. I mean my elder sisters, siblings ... We were producing tobacco with my uncles anyway. So, we did not need workers. Our conditions were well indeed. That's to say, I do not

know how much 70 cl Yeni rakı is now, but ... When we used to stay in the village, tobacco price was equal to the price of "big rakı. 1l." I mean, we were making good money. Tobacco farmers could buy a new tractor with the annual income received by tobacco farming.

On the other hand, during my visits to the higher-altitude mountain villages not possessing large arable land, interviewees stated that they had always been agricultural workers as almost all the villagers were landless. Still, they also mentioned relatively better conditions for agricultural wage workers before the 2000s. For example, during a focus group interview at a mukhtar's[2] home in a mountain village of Kınık, an agricultural worker mentioned that:

> We have always been agricultural workers ... We, the whole village, live by working at tobacco farms. Before, you could not find a single person if you visited our village in the daytime. Everyone was at the farms. They still go, though ... But it is not worth anything now. Our people were always poor and still poor. No one has their own land in our village. Look, there is no available land around. People cannot even find a decent area to build a house. (...) But working as a daily wage worker was better in the past. The tobacco prices were higher before. And we were paid better. Then once the quote was imposed ... Then the state support ended ... Even the producer cannot survive now, what can he pay for us.

In 2000, the number of tobacco producer households rose to 583,400, whereas the area of cultivation dropped to 237,700 ha and the total amount of production dropped to 208,000 t (Aydın, 2010: 172). The reason behind this change was the implementation of quotas for production, the first transformation in tobacco farming. Previously, under the Law (no.196) on Supporting Farmers' Tobacco Markets enacted in 1961 and the Tobacco Law (no.1177) enacted in 1969, Tekel used to purchase all tobacco produced annually. In time, the problem of overproduction had begun, and the quotas were initiated to curb tobacco production (Ertürk-Keskin and Yaman, 2013: 422).

The second and main transformation has been the privatization of Tekel. The privatization of Tekel was a protracted process and the state support for the tobacco producers phased out from 1998 onwards. In the aftermath of the 2000–2001 financial crises, the then coalition government pushed the Tobacco Law (no.4733) in July 2001 in accordance with the impositions of the

---

2 Head officer of villages and neighborhoods in Turkey.

TABLE 4   Tobacco production in Turkey (2000–2020)

Years	Cultivated area (hectares)	Production amount (tons)
2000	2,377,000	208000
2001	1988000	152500
2002	1994000	161300
2003	1837000	150100
2004	1927100	133913
2005	1853420	135247
2006	1461669	98137
2007	1449041	74584
2008	1468741	93403
2009	1161433	81053
2010	813335	53018
2011	766575	45435
2012	1076984	73285
2013	1330733	93158
2014	992615	74696
2015	919691	67990
2016	925048	74238
2017	995287	93666
2018	935031	75276
2019	882362	68224
2020	884659	79081

SOURCE: AYDIN, 2010 (2000–2003); TURKSTAT (2004–2021)

IMF and World Bank to open Turkish markets for transnational corporations. First, the then-president of the Republic vetoed the Law on the grounds that it would have a harmful impact on tobacco producers. Then, the government resubmitted the bill to the president and the Law was enacted in 2002 given that the president could not veto the legislation twice. In the context of this new Tobacco Law, the Tobacco and Alcohol Market Regulatory Authority was established as the absolute regulatory power over the market and the regulatory power of Tekel was dismantled. The cigarette factories of Tekel were sold to Japan Tobacco International in 2003 and then to British American Tobacco in 2008 (Ertürk Keskin and Yaman, 2013: 428; Yalman and Topal, 2017: 453).

The immediate impact of the Tobacco Law and privatization of tobacco factories on tobacco farmers has been the elimination of former support purchases. As frequently mentioned by the (former) producers during the interviews, they felt the 'absence of state support' and lost income security. For example, as stated by one of the former tobacco producers who started to work in the underground mines when he was 46 years old (in 2005):

> When you don't have state support, you cultivate your land with fear. Peasants are always afraid and feel oppressed anyway … We always worry, wondering if we will earn from what we do. And without the state support behind us … We had no choice but to become miners.

Another impact of the elimination of Tekel's regulatory role has been that the price of tobacco started to be determined by international tobacco corporations and, therefore, there was a drastic decline in product prices (Aydın, 2010: 172) and a continuous rise of input prices. For example, as stated by an unemployed miner who lived in a mountain village of Kınık in 2016:

> Now, you pay 10 liras for a pack of cigarettes, but a kilo of tobacco is 13 liras. A kilo of tobacco means 50 packs of cigarettes. A kilo of tobacco was equal to the price of 70 cl rakı in the past. 70 cl rakı is 80 liras now. If you produce 500 kilos of tobacco, it would have meant 40 thousand liras. Now, it worths almost nothing.

Under this reproduction squeeze, many households had to quit tobacco farming in the 2000s. Between 2000 and 2021, the area under cultivation fell from 2,377,000 to 686,606 ha, whereas the annual production amount dropped from 208,000 to 73,000 t in Turkey (see Table 4). Similarly, in the Soma Basin, the annual production fell from 7891 t in 2004 to 1447 t in 2020 (see Figure 3).

As explained in the previous Chapter, one of the most significant transformations of the early and mid 2000s was the re-demarcation of the Soma Coal Basin beyond the district of Soma. In this study, I define the Basin by referring to the labour supply to the mines, instead of location of the pits. Therefore, the Soma Coal Basin contains Kırkağaç and Soma districts of Manisa, Kınık district of İzmir, and Savaştepe district of Balıkesir and their surrounding villages where dispossessed and impoverished tobacco farmers started to work in the underground mines since the early 2000s. Households from the villages of Savaştepe, Kırkağaç, and Soma have similar relations to land and agriculture,

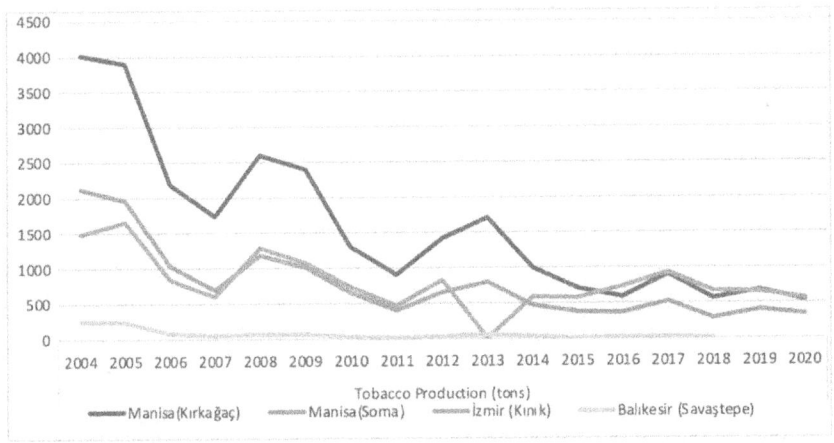

FIGURE 3   Tobacco production in the Soma Coal Basin (tons per year) between 2004 and 2020

and, therefore, the historical transformation of their relation to agriculture and patterns of proletarianization have been similar. Peasants of these villages have historically earned their living from tobacco farming either as family farmers or agricultural wage workers. Currently, as a result of the neoliberal transformation of agriculture in general and tobacco farming in particular, as detailly discussed in the next chapter, income they receive from farming is no longer sufficient for the survival of their families. They either gave up agricultural production and started to work in the mines, or, more commonly, diversified their livelihood in different forms of agricultural production and mining.

In Kınık, on the other hand, the neoliberal transformation of agriculture has taken a much more diversified path. Roughly, there has been an explicit the differentiation between the landowners of lowland villages and mountain villages. In the lowland villages of Kınık, where the land is much more fertile, it was possible for the families to change their products and do irrigated farming. Landowners of these villages tend to continue agricultural production and generate a considerable income from contract farming. Therefore, they do not prefer to work in the mines. They are called rich farmers because they have made significant gains from irrigated farming due to the contracts they have made with canning factories or supermarkets. Mostly, miners' wives are employed as unregistered daily wage workers for these farmers (see Chapter 4). The second part of Kınık consists of mountain villages where residents have had similar patterns of dispossession and proletarianization as the residents of Soma, Kırkağaç, and Savaştepe. Mainly, the fact that the state abandoned its protective role for the tobacco farmer families led to the conditions of "simple reproduction squeeze" (Bernstein, 1977) as a result of the continuous rise of input prices and fall of product prices. Therefore, peasants of these mountain villages are mainly (former) tobacco farmers whose male members started to work in the mines after the neoliberal transformation of the tobacco industry.

As an outcome of the neoliberal transformation in tobacco farming and the increasing investments in the underground coal pits of the Soma Coal Basin, male members of the (former) tobacco farmer families started work in the mines (Çelik, 2017, 2023a). However, it would be wrong to claim that the proletarianization of local tobacco farmer households indicated an elimination of agrarian relations in the Soma Coal Basin. Instead, what I observed during my fieldwork was rural livelihood diversification through gender division of labour in paid and unpaid works. Male members of the families have started to work in the mines, whereas women maintained agricultural activities in several forms, including agricultural wage work, petty commodity production or subsistence production. For example, as stated by a miner from Kınık:

> Now, we keep the tobacco farming at the least. My wife is working … Our relatives work with her, we pay them daily money. I mean my wife works with them. We do tobacco farming as contract farmers but it does not yield anymore. The merchants make the contract on US dollars. Without even asking the farmers. Actually, we even quarreled last year. Its yield is low, really, very low … It is a bit better this year. But still … In the end, tobacco is a very demanding plant. My wife works as a daily wage worker as well, but tobacco takes much of her time.

Women's labour processes in these forms are directly related to the product composition change in the region. In line with the rest of the Global South, the product composition in Turkey has shifted from traditional crops (staple food products) to the products prioritized by agribusiness and supermarkets (Aydın, 2022; McMichael, 1997; McMichael and Myhre, 1991). For example, since 2001, the total area under cultivation has decreased by 12 percent in Turkey. The cultivated area for cereals, legumes and oleaginous seeds has decreased by around 3 percent –29 percent, whereas the cultivated area for different fruits has increased by around 51 percent (Aydın, 2022). In the surrounding farming regions of the Soma Coal Basin, tobacco production has diminished, whereas the production of commercial crops such as tomatoes (both for tomato paste and table tomato), olives (for olive oil) and corn (silage) has increased. The total amount of tomato production in İzmir has almost tripled from 2005 (605,207 t) to 2020 (1,658,277 t), whereas the total amount of olive production has more than tripled in Manisa during the same period (from 104,750 t in 2004 to 345,269 t in 2020). The most dramatic increase in all these three cities has been seen in silage production (from a total production of 1,588,533 t in 2004 to 5,650,375 t in 2020). All the women I interviewed worked as daily wage workers in big capitalist farms at which these commercial crops are produced.

Another factor determining the agrarian change in the region has been the dispossession of private farmlands for mines, coal-fired power plants (CFPP) and highway constructions. Land expropriations for off-farm investments in the Global South limit classes of labour's access to rural commons (such as land, water and firewood) and lead to intensification of reproductive work of classes of rural women. This, in turn, affects women's labour force participation (Naudi and Rao, 2018; Rao, 2018). During the last decade, land expropriation and dispossession have intensively taken place particularly in three villages in the Soma Coal Basin (Elmadere, Kınık; Deniş and Yırca, Soma). In Elmadere, construction of a new underground coal mine and CFPP started in 2014, and it has been extracting coal since 2020. This investment, which led to both the expropriation of private farmlands and the eviction of the residents of Elmadere from their villages, has dramatically shifted the patterns of production and social reproduction. On the one hand, the villagers' access to land and agriculture has become limited to the agricultural wage work of women because they had to sell their farmlands. Yet, women in Elmadere were engaged in both tobacco production and subsistence farming until the expropriations. On the other hand, they had to move to the town centre of Kınık, lost access to land as a means of subsistence and became more dependent on the wage income men received from mining for the survival of the household. As stated by a miner from Elmadere who currently works in this mine:

> The income from tobacco is almost nothing now. ... I wouldn't have sold my land, but my father sold it. It was voluntary, to be honest. But I understand. ... It is a dryland, you can't simply grow another crop. So, my father thought at least we could buy a house in Kınık with that money. Now we live in Kınık. But my mother and my wife still work on farms as daily workers.

Or, as stated by a woman who moved to the centre of Kınık after the land expropriations:

> Our village has almost disappeared. There are only a few families left who did not sell their lands, but they are completely surrounded by the constructions now. I think they will have to leave Elmadere once the

production starts. There'll be no village left. How can you even breathe when there's a power-plant at doorstep? It's no longer a village, it's a mine site now ... Now, we live in Kınık. I still go to the farm every day (as a wage worker). But I can no longer grow my own tomatoes, eggplants, peppers.

In Yırca, in April 2014, the then Council of Ministers decided on an urgent expropriation of olive groves for CFPP construction. In contrast to the case of Elmadere, the CFPP construction plan faced strong resistance from the residents of Yırca (see Chapter 5). As a result, in November 2014, the Council of State adopted a motion for a stay of execution. Leaders of the movement in Yırca were women, and they defined their main motivation as preventing the condemnation to the coal industry like other villages of the Basin. As stated by a woman during the resistance: '[miners] died in the mine for once, we would die slowly' (Tuncer, 2016) because of the ecological impact of the CFPP. In 2018, when I interviewed the neighborhood representative of Yırca, he stated that the number of miner households in Yırca was very limited, and the main means of living was still olive farming. Eventually, the coal company relocated the CFPP construction to a nearby village called Deniş in the Basin. As stated by the Chair of Farmers' Union in our virtual interview in 2021: 'Once the urgent expropriation in Yırca was cancelled, the company sold the farmlands of five villages. The dwellers of those villages accepted selling their lands because they couldn't make money from tobacco farming.'

The difference between the cases of Yırca and Elmadere and Deniş is directly related to the impoverishment of tobacco producers. As the main agricultural activity in Yırca is olive farming and farmers can still earn their living from it, they could organize a strong resistance against the expropriation of their land for coal investments. Tobacco producers, however, could not survive by cultivating their lands, and as defined by a miner, they had to choose from 'dying from hunger or dying in the mines' or dying due to the ecological impacts of coal.

Finally, coal investments in the Soma Coal Basin have had a detrimental impact on land and water in the region. The Soma Coal Basin is located in close proximity to the Bakırçay River, which flows through the Manisa and İzmir provinces and irrigates the farmlands of the lowland villages of the Basin. Rising underground and surface mine constructions have resulted in pollution of groundwater supplies that feed the Bakırçay River. Moreover, the coal-washing facilities in Soma directly pollute the river (Gacal and Stauffer, 2018). Pollution of the Bakırçay River causes not only fertility loss and land degradation but also rising costs of agricultural production. As emphasized by several interviewees, they had to start using drilling water for irrigation because of the water pollution that has also dramatically increased the cost of production.

5   Women's Work in the Soma Coal Basin

The neoliberal transformation of coal mining and agricultural production in the Soma Coal Basin have led to livelihood diversification and rural social differentiation that created three groups of working women within the miner families: local women who live in their villages, local women who live in town centres, and migrant women. Their work is determined by the mutual and internal relationship between the production and social reproduction. On the hand, 'the imperatives of social reproduction' (Mezzadri et al., 2022; Stevano, 2022) shape their working conditions and differentiation among them, and, on the other hand, changing labour relations of both women in agriculture and men in mining has restructured social reproduction. Women's work in the Soma Coal Basin includes the following forms: (unpaid) subsistence farming, (unpaid) family farming (petty commodity production), agricultural wage work and (unpaid) reproductive work at home. For example, as stated by a woman who does not possess land:

> Well, we start working in April and we continue until January. We work nonstop until January, until new year … We do tomato planting, pepper planting, oil … We also hoe the plants … There is no work we do not do! For example, we plant tomatoes, do this (tobacco farming), then comes cotton. I hoe cotton, when I finish hoeing cotton, then I start picking tomatoes. When the tomato harvest ends, then it comes to pepper. Peppers grow up later, at the end of August. We work on pepper farms until late September. It is time to go to Akhisar plain … Oil starts in September lasts for two or three months.

As can be seen in the quotation above, almost all women workers in the basin work during the planting, irrigation, and harvest processes of each product at different times of the year. For example, a woman who grows tobacco on her family's land works as a daily wage worker during the harvest seasons of tomato, pepper, and olive as well.

The most essential factor that determines the conditions of these women in the relations of production and social reproduction is the different forms and degrees of their access to land. Local women who live in their villages are engaged in all forms of paid and unpaid agricultural work, including subsistence farming, whereas local women who have moved to the town centers because of the land expropriations in their villages have relatively more limited access to land as a means of social reproduction as they cannot produce for their own consumption. As for migrant women, access to land and agriculture is limited to informal wage work in large capitalist farms located in lowland villages.

5.1   Labour Processes and Working Conditions of Women in Agriculture

Because of the simple reproduction squeeze of local households stemming from the neoliberal transformation of family farming and from the extremely precarious conditions of social reproduction of the migrant households, not only have men proletarianized in the mines but women have also been proletarianized on their own land or in large capitalist farms. Women's work in agriculture as unpaid family farmers on their own land or as tenants of a small plot of land is as extremely precarious as wage workers of petty commodity producers or capitalist farmers.

Although tobacco production has dropped drastically in the Basin, there is still a considerable number of families who maintain tobacco farming either on their own land or by tenancy. Rural livelihood diversification under neoliberalism in the Global South has come to increasingly depend on wage income as a means to invest in agriculture and cattle (O'Laughlin, 2009: 193). Similarly, in Soma, some miner families maintain petty commodity production and animal husbandry through the unpaid work of women and finance the cost of production from the wage income men receive from mining. On the one hand, households in the mountain villages who lack off-farm income cannot finance the costs of production, such as input, tenancy and wages of daily workers, whereas miner families use the regular wage income for production costs. On the other hand, households who own large and fertile land in the lowland villages have shifted to irrigated farming to produce more profitable crops such as tomatoes or pepper. These families do not prefer working in the mines as they make considerable gains from contract farming. Therefore, the majority of the current tobacco farmers are miners' wives who live in their villages. Yet, the feminization of tobacco farming in Soma has indicated increasing exploitation of women's work, whereas male members of the households (miners) take care of the management part, such as signing the contracts with tobacco dealers or marketing the products.

Baglioni (2023: 26–7) underlines that a focus on the material aspects of the labour process includes the conception of the labour process as a combination of forces and materials of nature (labour, raw materials, and instruments and conditions of production). In the case of food and agriculture, "distance and durability" (Friedmann, 1992) of crops along with the characteristics of soil constitute significant natural restrictions for the interlinks between the processes of production, circulation, distribution, and consumption of food and other crops. Even though food and agriculture have been globalized to a significant extent under the corporate food regime of neoliberalism, the biophysical nature that acts upon products directly or indirectly has affected the production, circulation and trade of certain crops (Freidberg, 2001). Therefore, there is a need to consider how nature informs the production, circulation, distribution, and consumption of agricultural products. For tobacco farming, the interrelationship between two factors affected the labor processes of tobacco farmer families. On the one hand, factors such as the fact that tobacco is cultivated in dry and barren land and that tobacco farming leads to land degradation (Ali et al. 2023) make it difficult for the farmers to change their products. On the other hand, tobacco farming is quite labour-intensive, which necessitates the work of either the whole household or hiring wage workers. As underlined by an agricultural engineer in Soma during our interview:

> Well, tobacco has some specific characteristics; it is not like other products. It grows on barren lands, and it is done almost in the form of a craft. Namely, you must spend eleven months to produce tobacco. You have to cultivate seeds and seedlings; you have to plant, harvest, press tobacco, and then bale tobacco. You have to store them and deliver them when the companies ask for the product. You have to assume full responsibility, and this is a very hard labour. They earn when the whole family works. Additionally, once they quit, they have no chance to return back. If you give up tobacco, you cannot cultivate anything on these lands. Any other product does not grow on lands where tobacco was made. But irrigated farming on a plain is not like this. Now, Kınık Plain is a very fertile plain with large lands. The farmers there have hope; I could not earn from tomatoes this year, so I should plant corn and earn from corn next year. They do not prefer mining. Those who prefer mining are usually former tobacco farmers. People who do irrigated farming do not usually work in the mines. But, wives of those miners go to these farms to work as daily wage workers.

As a labour-intensive work, tobacco farming takes around 11 months of the year. It has several phases, such as seed growing, plant seeding, stringing and packaging. As explained detailly by a tobacco producer woman:

> First, they have seedlings. Then, they are planted, hoed with machines. At least four months are spent at the plain. After that ... Tobacco is very

demanding, you see. Then, you saw us today, we go to harvesting, rape tobacco, bring the harvested product and string. This part takes at least a month. Then, they are pressed in November. This job takes around eleven months.

During the fieldwork, I helped women during the reaping and stringing period. They wake up at 3 a.m. and arrive at the farm at 4 a.m. They immediately start reaping until their half-hour breakfast break at 9 a.m., and then they keep reaping until 12 p.m. They string the reaped tobacco until 3:30 p.m. (either at the farm or at the yard of the employer woman's house). The daily wage of tobacco workers are extremely low and they work without social insurance. Employer women also work under the same conditions as daily wage workers but as unpaid family workers. Their husbands receive the annual income once they sell the products. As stated by a woman who produced tobacco as a tenant in the summer of 2018:

> Now a kilo of tobacco is around 17 liras. Depending on its quality … If it got dry badly, it decreases to 10 liras. We already pay 70 liras for daily workers. Then how much do we earn? For example, last year I made 15 thousand liras expense, I received 27 thousand liras. The cost includes workers' payments, land tenure (lease of farm) money … If I also attempted to give insurance, I would have nothing remained. Everything about this job is extremely expensive … On the other hand, if I don't do this and work as a wage worker the whole summer, I would earn 6 thousand on my own. At least when I take this trouble, we earn 12–15 thousand. Besides, we receive this as lump sum. Here, they call me boss. Have you ever seen a boss like me?.

Almost all women interviewed during tobacco production have underlined that tobacco production is a "female work," and even before the massive proletarianization of men in the mines, women had been in charge of most of the work other than portage and contract. The reaping and stringing processes are defined as female work as they have similarities with handicrafts, such as stitching, and it necessitates patience. For example, as stated by one of the interviewees:

> No other worker can do the work that we do. For example, our husbands could not do what we are doing even though they did not work in the mine. They can never do tobacco, especially. Tobacco is a feminine work. Because it is difficult, it demands patience. Men are more impatient.

> Women are more patient. This is surely a sort of work that can be done by women. Look, this is something like handcraft. Women are more skilled in this. (Laughing) Look, how many you have even strung ... This is the case not just because they have started working in the mine now; this has always been that way. For example, how was it happening? Men were engaging the fire bar. They were not harvesting tobacco by leaning furiously. If there were some who did harvesting, they were not even ten percent. Men were engaging the fire bar and laying out tobacco to dry.

In the surrounding villages of the Basin, some families are engaging in small-scale irrigated farming or stock farming. These families cannot make contracts. Instead, they sell the product to the dealers after the harvest. Similar to the tobacco farmers, they finance the cost of production with the wage received from mining. And, likewise, in these families, it is women who are engaged in farming and animal breeding as unpaid family workers. As stated by a miner living in a village of Savaştepe:

> Animal breeding is my wife's responsibility, she looks after the animals. What do I do? I bring their feeds such as hay bale, fodder ... But the maintenance work formally belongs to my wife. Well, sometimes ... Of necessity. Sometimes she may be ill or have a thing to do, then I go there. But my wife looks after the animals in general, I do not.

In the lowland villages of the region, capitalist farmers who own large plots of land produce several crops, including tomatoes, peppers, fruits and vegetables and corn/silage by making contracts with canning factories, sauce factories, feed factories or supermarkets. The most widespread form of agricultural work in the Basin is daily wage work on these capitalist farms, and it includes all groups of women (women who live in their villages and in the towns and migrant women). All the women I interviewed were working as unregistered workers. Labour intermediaries collected daily workers for these farms, directly received the payment of their teams from the farmers and paid daily workers. In large capitalist farms, labour processes are very different from small-scale tobacco farms. In large farms, a high number of workers work as teams of labour intermediaries and the majority of women I interviewed mentioned mistreatment of labour intermediaries on the farm. During the virtual interviews conducted in the summer of 2021, a relatively new labour regime in silage and sunflower farming was mentioned. Accordingly, big global seed companies started to sign contracts with capitalist farmers and instead of employing unregistered workers via labour intermediaries, they recruited workers via private employment agencies. Therefore, on these farms, workers are registered and have short-term social insurance (around 10–15 days). However, the same women continue working informally in the farming of other products after the silage harvest.

Almost all the migrant women explained why they work as daily wage workers by referring to the indebtedness of their families. For example, as stated by a woman from Zonguldak:

> We bought a house, we are paying mortgage. My husband's wage is not sufficient. I have to work as an agricultural worker. I work no matter what the product is. I am going for corn silage now; then tobacco will start, then tomatoes, olives.

Following the collective redundancy of miners in 2014 (see Chapter 5) and increasing male unemployment in the Basin, unemployed miners also started to work as daily wage workers of the large capitalist farms. Yet, still the vast majority of agricultural workers are women. Just like the division of work between men and women in the family farming, they mentioned a gender division of work in these capitalist farms as well. Accordingly, whereas men were in charge of "man handling" part of the work such as portage, tasks such as reaping or planting are considered as feminine. For example, as explained by a woman whose husband is an unemployed miner and works together with her:

> Men cannot stand doing what we do. They pull the baskets, pack the boxes once we finish reaping … Men do not want to lean all the time, under the sun.

During the tomato harvest, workers wake up at 5 am, prepare their meal (breakfast and lunch both for themselves and for their husbands to eat in the mine) they eat in the farm and arrive in the farm at 7 am and start working. They give two breaks for breakfast and for lunch and they arrive back at home at 7 pm.

Mostly, women workers take their children with them to the farm because they cannot leave them at home alone and especially children older than nine or ten years old are set to work. For example:

> I have to go with my kids. 12 year-old child is going to work, just think! For example, you saw how it was hot yesterday, it was about 45 degrees. It was also moist. We pick tomatoes all day along for 50 liras under 45 degree temperature. We have a hope if we can send our children to school, if we can cover school expenses … But a 10 year old, 12 year old children go to

work I mean. For example, my son is 13 years old, he is carrying baskets. Just think; he is doing porterage. A 13 year-old child! A 13 year-old child is doing porterage from 7 a.m. till 6 p.m.

From the beginning of the COVID-19 pandemic in 2020, farming was deemed essential work in Turkey. Therefore, even under the curfews imposed by the Turkish government until the summer of 2021, agricultural workers had exemptions. The workers I interviewed virtually mentioned their fear of being infected, especially during the first weeks of the pandemic. For example, as stated by a woman:

> Even during the curfews, we went to farms every day. We could not stay at home even a single day. And there were no Covid measures … Especially during the transportation … We were around 20 people in a tractor. No social distancing, no tests … In time, we got used to it. Sometimes I even forget about Covid. We have to go to farm and there are no measures … At least we work outdoors. But my husband is a miner for example, he works at an underground pit having a poor ventilation. He also kept working from the beginning.

5.2 *The Social Reproduction of Miner Families: Unpaid Work of Miners' Wives*

Women's unpaid reproductive work in Soma takes two forms: growing fruits and vegetables or animal breeding for household consumption – subsistence farming – and reproduction of the workers within the household, especially the miners who have extremely severe working conditions. The defining feature of women's work in production and reproduction is, as stated by several women: 'Women in Soma never stop!' For example, a tobacco farmer woman summarized her average day as follows:

> I wake up at 3 a.m. We start picking up workers at 3:30. We arrive at the farm by 4 a.m. and start working immediately. We return back to here (home yard) at 1 p.m. We string tobacco here till 3:30 p.m. Once we string them, we will lay them out to dry outside. Then, I will clean here, I have to water the garden, vegetables. Then, bath time and dinner of children … After I put them to bed, I have to prepare the food to myself and my husband for tomorrow (food they will eat at the workplace). It would be 11:00–11:30 p.m. until I go to bed. Then I will wake up again at 3 a.m. … Our life is very fast … Believe me you cannot follow it. If you want, try just for one day, you would fail.

Another woman described her day during the tomato harvest as follows:

> I work on the farm for eight hours but while trying to prepare my husband's food box, my food box ... I have to wake up at 5 am to prepare them. I leave home at 6 am and come back at 7 pm. This is just the time for coming back home from work. If we consider the work we do at home, in thr garden ... It would be impossible to calculate. It would count around 7 days and 24 hours.

All the women I talked to attributed a positive meaning to subsistence farming as a legacy of the 'good old days.' These 'good old days' indicated for the local women the time when their life was not market and cash dependent and their husbands had not started working in the mines. For the migrant women, it meant when they lived in their hometowns and had not detached from their land. In the Global South, neoliberalism brought a new social reproduction regime characterized not only by dispossession because of land grabs and simple reproduction squeeze but also by financialization and indebtedness (Fraser, 2017). In the Soma Coal Basin, even before the neoliberalism in agriculture and land grabs for mine investments, local families were not mainly subsistence producers. They were petty commodity producers who produced cash crops to sell either in the market or to the state. Still, the neoliberal transformation of agriculture and coal mining has led to the commodification of means of subsistence through increasing market and cash dependency for social reproduction. According to the narratives of (former) tobacco producers, before the mid-2000s, tobacco farming was done by the whole family as the income they generated from it was sufficient for the subsistence of the household. Moreover, instead of shuttling between the farms and villages, they used to move to the farms for a four-month period every summer and stay in shelter tents. They used to cultivate certain plots of their farms for subsistence production for their immediate needs when they stayed in the farm and for their winter storage. Almost all of them stated that they did not need cash for their daily lives:

> How have we become a part of such system of exploitation? Before we used to go to the farm and eat our tarhana soup all together. We didn't have money but we were happy. We didn't used to need money as we do now anyway. Now they condemned us to money!
>
> We were planting tobacco, for example on ten decare field. On one decare of this, we were planting horse bean, chickpea, lentil, melon, water melon, eggplant etc. Any fruits and vegetables. Then we could dry

our eggplant, pepper, beans for the winter ... We could make our tarhana of curd, tomato and flour. So, we did not need money.

Moreover, local populations whose lands were expropriated for mines or CFPP construction migrated to the centers of the districts. Now, they live in flats, and they cannot maintain subsistence production. Male members of these families have become miners, whereas women continue agriculture as daily wage workers. As explained by a 58-year-old woman whose son died in the Soma mine disaster:

> We had to sell our land. My sons became miners, we (women) kept going to farms for a daily wage because, you know, we sold our own land ... Then my son died in the mine. I still go to farm every day. I don't know how to live without touching the land. The only days I do not go to farm are the ones I come to Akhisar for these trials (of the Soma mine disaster) because I don't want any other mother to lose their sons for the mines.

Scholarly works on migrant labour have shown the relatively more disadvantageous conditions of migrant working-class households and their cash-dependent and higher-cost social reproduction (Burawoy, 1976; Ferguson and McNally, 2015; Wright, 2006). These studies base their analyses on emigrated workers and pay close attention to their lack of or limited access to the social reproductive services provided by the state. In the Soma Coal Basin, the most significant differences between migrant families (who are also citizens of Turkey) and the local ones are the complete detachment of migrant families from their own lands as a means to reproduce their households and extremely financialized patterns of social reproduction. Reproduction and renewal processes of the migrant households are more dependent on wage income, whereas local households are able to develop certain strategies to lower the costs of reproduction such as subsistence production. Migrant households are completely detached from their own lands, and their relation to agriculture is limited to women's daily wage employment in capitalist farms. Moreover, all the migrant miner households live at the centre of the Soma district and pay rent or mortgage. Migrant women repeatedly mentioned their disadvantageous conditions of not being able to produce food to feed their families. Moreover, migrant women mostly stated that they used to engage in farming in their hometowns, at least as subsistence producers, whereas in Soma, they are mostly lonely and isolated in their apartments. Therefore, most of the migrant women experienced the process of housewifization because of the distance from their land.

Finally, the most significant factor transforming women's reproductive labour is the over-exploitation of their unpaid work as miners' wives. During the interviews, almost all the miners underlined their need for the reproductive work of women and the fact that miners tend to get married at young ages because of the need for the stabilizing effect of marriage for their 'dangerous and extremely heavy working conditions.' For example, as stated by a miner:

> Here in Soma, all the miners prefer to get married at younger ages. Someone should deal with your food and care. We get exhausted at the workplace. It is a very dangerous job ... If we cannot eat well, or sleep well we can give rise to a fatal accident.

Despite their need for the stabilizing effect of marriage, they argued that it was unbearable for a miner 'who is mentally depressed enough at work' to take responsibility for marriage and children. For example:

> Mining takes our whole day anyway ... Miner families mentioned this frequently after the massacre,[3] "go on, go on, go on" "rush, rush, rush" I already get perished underground because of this whole "go on, go on, go on" I cannot spare much time to my family, because I kind of want to get rid of any kind of responsibilities or pressures outside the mine. Because if I go somewhere with my family, there is so much responsibility, pressure. For example, my children would want something, my wife would want something ... I mean this pressure totally exhausts us. I want my spare time, by myself, alone ... To feel more relaxed. When I go home soon, my wife will start "we need this, we need that; this should be bought" Just like the sergeant at work! Our sergeant keeps telling "you worked less," "you got off work early" I feel the same pressure at home when my wife asks for something. I feel being pinned down. I mean, the pressure at home makes things more difficult in psychological terms ... As I mentioned, resting time is very short, working conditions are oppressive, the mine is extremely noisy. When a problem arises at home ...

---

3 Some families use the term massacre instead of disaster to indicate the Soma Mine Disaster. Similarly, most of the activist groups call it a massacre. And the slogan, "not an accident but a massacre." In the original version of this work, I also used the term massacre. Yet, I preferred the term the Soma Mine Disaster to indicate the disastrous character of capitalism. (see Chapter 5).

> I mean, I feel being pinned down. So, I spend my time with friends ... In a coffeehouse or something like that.

Therefore, whereas miners do not want to assume any kind of responsibility outside the work, they are in need of the care work of women in order to be productive and physically strong at work. Just like the quotations included in the Introduction Chapter of the book from two different women from two completely different geographies and times, "the only thing men do is to work in the mine" and everything else, including farming, childcare, housework, care of the miners, preparation of the food boxes of miners etc. are women's responsibility and as mining companies benefit from the stabilizing effect of marriage and prefer married miners "that's unpaid work" women "are doing for the boss, isn't it?" Therefore, just like stated in the same quote from a woman in Soma miners work "eight hours a day ... But if you are a woman your work never ends." (see Chapter 1).

Overall, the physical and mental implications of miners' working conditions result in the super-exploitation of women's unpaid reproductive work at home.

> I think being a miner's wife is difficult. Why? Especially in summer time ... Sometimes I go out as soon as my husband comes home. My husband comes from night shift at 1 a.m. and I leave for tobacco at 3 a.m. towards morning. Sometimes I cannot even make his food in time ... This is hard. We have animals, we need to cook food at home, take care of our husbands ... I have to wash his uniforms etc. These stuffs are not done by the company. And you know, his working conditions are very dirty ... At least twice a week, I rub my husband with a coarse bath-glove.

Almost all the women described their husbands' angry, nervous, tense and exhausted moods at home, and its impact on their emotional labour was quite visible. For example, as stated by a woman whose daughter has a mental disability:

> Mine makes men very angry. He wasn't like this before. When he comes here. Oh! He would terrorize. Mining is stressful ... You know, men blow off their anger at home. He will come soon ... He would tell us 'I don't want to hear your voice.' For example, my daughter is a bit ill ... He gets angry if she cries. He says don't cry. He says, look I am stressful, I am depressed ... Every evening is like that.

All kinds of childcare is undertaken by women as a "natural" extension of traditional gender roles. Yet, as mentioned in the previous section, due to women's overload in the processes of production and social reproduction, they are mostly forced to take their children to farms. Therefore, their productive and reproductive work overlaps. Most of the interviewees, openly or implicitly, mentioned that they were experiencing domestic violence.

Consequently, due to their overexploitation in the productive and reproductive work, women almost have no spare time at all. Most of the women mentioned that they work all the time expect for when they are asleep:

> If we count housework as work, we work all the time. We only don't work when we are asleep. We cannot even sleep properly. For example, I went to bed ar 11 pm last night and woke up at 3 am. We generally sleep for three or four hours a day. We do not go to farm only for one day on Fridays.[4] Normally, we should take a rest on our off days. But childcare, housework, shopping, garden, animals … Sometimes we even forget that we are women in such a rush. Such an extent … Believe me.

Overall, during the interviews, women defined their work in two somewhat contradictory ways. Firstly, all the women I interviewed defined their unpaid reproductive work as work. As can be seen in the narratives quoted so far, they include care work, housework, subsistence production, unpaid family farming and agricultural work to explain their working conditions. Moreover, around half of them mentioned that mining companies benefit from their unpaid work by using statements such as 'mining companies make money thanks to us,' and 'normally, washing the uniform overalls should be the company's responsibility. But why would they hire workers to wash them when we do it every day for free' or 'the only thing we don't do is physically going to the mine. The food our husbands eat in the mine, washing their uniform overalls, bathing them … Everything is our responsibility.'

Secondly, however, almost all the women defined themselves as housewives instead of agricultural workers. For example, when I checked the application forms for the summer school organized by the Social Rights Association in 2017, only one of the women I interviewed filled in her occupation as an 'agricultural worker,' whereas all of the others wrote housewife. Yet, during the interviews, when I asked them why they preferred this summer school for their children,

---

4 On Fridays, agricultural workers do not work in Kınık, because there is a district bazaar. They go shopping on Fridays.

they told me that these free summer schools were important opportunities for them because someone takes care of their children while they are working on the farm. At this point it is essential to remember Mies' thesis of how capitalism is built upon the naturalization of women's work as a relationship outside capitalism proper, against the general assumption that with modernization and industrialization, patriarchy as a system of male dominance would disappear (1998: 8):

> [P]atriarchy not only did not disappear in this process, which is identical with the spreading of the modern capitalist world economy, but the ever-expanding process of growth or capital accumulation is based on the maintenance or even recreation of patriarchal or sexist man-woman relations, an asymmetric sexual division of labor within and outside the family, the definition of all women as dependent 'housewives' and of all men as 'breadwinners.' This sexual division of labor is integrated with an international division of labor in which women are manipulated both as 'producer-housewives' and as 'consumer-housewives.'

Similarly, the fact that women in Soma define themselves as housewives not as workers is a clear sign of naturalization not only of women's unpaid work but also of their paid work through patriarchy and housewife ideology. As long as the economic sphere is limited to the relationship between wage labour and capital (tip of the iceberg) by excluding informal work, subsistence peasants' work and housework (larger, underwater part of the iceberg) (Mies, 1998), women who work as unregistered wage workers, petty commodity producers, subsistence farmers, and unpaid reproductive workers are not recognized as workers. Women's agricultural work is defined as a (side) income-generating activity to support the main income earned by their husbands, whereas their reproductive work is seen as 'a personal service outside of capital' (Dalla Costa and James, 1972).

6 Conclusion

Ultimately, the case of Turkey and Soma Coal Basin unpacks key aspects of how neoliberal rural development and resource extraction operate through the gender division of work within rural households and rural labour markets and women's invisible work. In Turkey, neoliberal agricultural policies, together with mega-investments in natural resource industries, have resulted in the dispossession and proletarianization of small-scale farmers. Recently (partly) dispossessed farmers have become the source of cheap labour power for extractive capital and agribusiness capital through gender division of labour. These patterns of accumulation and dispossession have formed the classes of extractive labour whose production and social reproduction are built upon the super-exploitation of women's work

CHAPTER 5

The Soma Mine Disaster, Labour Control in the Sphere of Social Reproduction, and Moments of Resistance

This chapter examines the labour control strategies beyond the workplace in the Soma Coal Basin and how miner families are articulated to or struggle against the authoritarian neoliberal labour regimes. In the previous chapters, I have argued that the analysis of the labour process is internally related to what goes on outside the gates of the workplace, how workers reproduce themselves, and how local labour markets are regulated. Labour control in extractive regions is specifically important due to the spatial fixity of ores (Ellem, 2006, 2016) and, therefore, the inability of extractive capital to relocate investments in times of crisis. In order to sustain its investment in a particular locality, extractive capital needs to develop local labour control strategies by considering the social composition of local labour markets and the peculiar imperatives of social reproduction. Due to the strategic significance of the coal industry for the Turkish economy (see Chapter 3), various political, institutional, and community dynamics are employed as labour control mechanisms to guarantee the rhythms of investments and production in the Soma Coal Basin. As long as the strategic significance of the industry remained the same after a fatal disaster in the basin, it was essential for the government and coal companies to effectively develop and implement local labour control and discipline mechanisms through various political, institutional, and cultural mechanisms of coercion and consent. In this chapter, I argue that the authoritarian neoliberalism of the AKP governments provided the extractive capital with proper conditions to control and discipline the local labour force despite the experience of a fatal disaster.

This chapter consists of five sections. In the first one, the concepts of authoritarian neoliberalism and disaster capitalism are clarified by referring to the experience of Turkey. In the second section, details of the Soma Mine Disaster and its prosecution process are elaborated on. Then, the following section focuses on the local labour control strategies operated through the local institutional, political, and community networks. The third section further analyzes the local labour control strategies by paying attention to the period after the Soma Mine Disaster. The final section examines the moments of resistance in the Basin by referring to their strengths and shortcomings.

1 Authoritarian Neoliberalism and Extractivism

Following the relational approach adopted throughout the research, I follow the definition of neoliberalism as a "material structure of social, economic, and political reproduction underpinned by financialization" (Fine and Saad-Filho, 2016: 2), defining feature of which is "the systematic use of state power to impose (financial) market imperatives" in every aspect of production and social reproduction "that is replicated internationally by 'globalisation'" (Saad-Filho and Johnston, 2005: 3). At the global level, the political hegemony of neoliberalism is built upon the discourse of removal or minimization of the economic roles of the state. Yet, in practice, neoliberalism triggers commodified and financialized forms of social reproduction through the central role assumed by the state. Therefore, under neoliberalism, economic, political, and social roles of the state have radically been transformed rather than being reduced or eliminated (Boffo et al., 2019: 260). Yet, neoliberal transformations, as well as experiences of neoliberalism, have taken various forms across different geographies and decades and in order to capture the heterogeneity of neoliberalism, there is a need to engage with its continuities and discontinuities over time as well as its variation and variegation across space (Jessop, 2019: 344).

Since the global financial crisis of 2008, critical political economy literature has extensively explored the relationship between neoliberalism and authoritarianism by referring to two, albeit similar, distinct concepts. The first one is neoliberal authoritarianism, which refers to the neoliberal type of political authoritarianism, whereas authoritarian neoliberalism addresses an authoritarian shift within neoliberalism (Boffo et al., 2019: 247). In this study, I prefer the term authoritarian neoliberalism over neoliberal authoritarianism as the former helps to avoid ahistorical accounts of different state forms, regimes of capital accumulation, and class relations within neoliberalism. In this way, the term highlights how crises in neoliberalism strengthen the coercive apparatuses and practices of the state to sustain capital accumulation despite its inability to achieve egalitarian distribution of wealth (ibid.: 253). In fact, authoritarian neoliberalisms insulate policy making processes by marginalizing, disciplining and controlling the moments of popular resistance (Tansel, 2017: 3; Bruff and Tansel, 2019: 234).

It is essential to note that the rise of authoritarianism does not reflect a structural shift from the main logic of neither neoliberalism nor capitalism. Despite the use of the concept to address political and economic responses to the crisis in neoliberalism, authoritarianism is endemic to both capitalism in general and neoliberalism in particular. As mentioned by referring to Poulantzas' concept of the contradictory role of the capitalist state in Chapter 3, the capitalist state has to guarantee continuous accumulation of capital and organizing the power bloc and disorganizing the masses; on the other hand, it needs to organize the popular consent of the masses. To achieve these complementary yet contradictory responsibilities, the capitalist state necessarily shows authoritarian tendencies.

In order to ensure the ongoing reproduction of class relations, the capitalist state has to apply coercive powers (Ayers and Saad-Filho, 2015: 599), and as long as democracy is confined within the limits of bourgeois liberalism under capitalism, the realms of oppression and coercion are essential for the ongoing accumulation of capital (Wood, 1995: 234). As such, policies and institutional arrangements of the capitalist state represent the relation of domination and exploitation between classes (Bruff, 2014: 119). Secondly, under neoliberalism, it has become even more vital for the capitalist state to maintain its contradictory role due to the more dramatic forms of economic repression and social discipline imposed upon the classes of labour. In fact, neoliberalism has further strengthened the authoritarian tendencies of governments in transforming pre-existing public institutions and policies into market-oriented forms (Yalman et al., 2023). The inability of neoliberal projects to receive popular consent stems from the fact that "they have little to offer to large segments of the population other than deterioration of their living and working conditions" (Bozkurt-Güngen 2018: 220). As pointed out by Tansel (2017: 4) "authoritarian neoliberalism does not conjure policies to solve specific problems (e.g. fiscal deficit, the lack of affordable housing, failing public services), but it does so increasingly to 'discipline' those who confront such policies and 'perpetuate' the underlying conditions that give rise to these predicaments." Overall, two key limitations of neoliberalism necessarily led to authoritarian tendencies. On the one hand, the neoliberal project remains rooted in class interests and agendas of capitalist classes; on the other hand, its economic perspectives on addressing societal issues falls short of meeting the essential needs and expectations of the most marginalized groups, such as job creation, basic conditions of social reproduction, provision of public services, ecological justice, etc. (Arsel et al., 2021: 263).

Authoritarian neoliberalism in many countries has developed the trend of "strong leaders" whose political projects combine "neoliberal restoration with majoritarian appeal and is based on large electoral victories" (Sinha, 2021: 321), as exemplified in cases of India, Brazil, Turkey, etc. For instance, by presenting themselves as a solution to the crisis in neoliberalism, strong leaders such as Narendra Modi in India or Recep Tayyip Erdoğan in Turkey, combined radical neoliberal programs such as high growth rates, credit rankings, mega-investments in the construction sector and natural resource industries with nationalism and religious fundamentalism (cf. Sinha 2021; Arsel et al. 2021; Adaman and Akbulut 2021; Yalman 2016, 2021). Yet, while presenting themselves as a solution to the crisis in neoliberalism, authoritarian neoliberal leaders have not aimed at resolving major problems affecting the lives of the masses, such as unemployment, precarious work, poverty, and lack of sufficient public services.

Neoliberal extractivism has largely been built upon using authoritarian measures in the Global South. In fact, even though the majority of extractive sectors have been privatized in the context of neoliberalism, the central and local apparatuses of the state remained as powerful agents of extractive developmentalism (Kumar, 2022) (see Chapter 3). In this context, the role of the central and local economic apparatuses of the state has shifted from being the main investor to the main facilitator of investments (Rao, 2018: 267). As long as extractive developmentalism is built upon accumulation by dispossession (Harvey, 2003) and accumulation by displacement (Araghi, 2009b), and expropriation of non-market means of production and social reproduction, the use of force is a necessary precondition for it. Therefore, authoritarian political regimes play a pivotal role in providing political stability and market predictability for the national and transnational extractive capital. On the one hand, they provide incentives to the extractive capital, such as direct subsidies or ease of environmental clearance. On the other hand, they repress any kind of resistance against investments in natural resource industries by using authoritarian measures. As aptly put by Kumbamu (2020: 164–5):

> [I]n the age of neoliberalism, although capital, technology, and commodities can flow across space and time without any barriers, they certainly need political "stability" and market "predictability" in the places where they finally reach … The state plays an authoritarian role in creating conditions for the endless accumulation of capital, in which exclusion (or dispossession) and extraction operate dialectically.

One essential point to be underlined in terms of the extractive capital's need for authoritarian conditions is related to moments of (mine) disasters. Coal mining has historically been associated with fatal disasters. In the original version of this work, I used the term massacre instead of accident or disaster to define the Soma Mine Disaster. I did not use the term accident because it veils the responsibility of the coal company and the deficiencies stemming from the macro coal policies that have led to the death of 301 miners. On the other hand, I did not prefer the term disaster as it could have implied natural incidents. I preferred the term massacre over others in order to underline the fact that it was an outcome of systemic neglect of the Soma Coal Company regarding health and safety for the objective of the extraction of the maximum amount of coal through the labour-intensive production methods and the deficiencies of the macro coal policies permitting the companies to neglect these measures and implement production pressure. Even though it is quite clear that the Soma Mine Disaster is neither natural nor discrete from the structural problems embedded in the coal industry, I ended up using the term disaster in order to address the fact that disasters are neither natural nor breaks or deviations from the normal flow of capitalism but direct products of it. In fact, capitalism not only turns disasters into opportunities for further accumulation of capital (Klein, 2007) but also produces and relies upon them (Benlisoy, 2021). Therefore, in order to show that the Soma Mine Disaster is an outcome of the characteristics of capitalist relations of exploitation in the coal industry and it did not lead to a structural change in these relations, I ended up with the term disaster over massacre. As exemplified in the rest of this Chapter, authoritarian neoliberalism in Turkey granted secure conditions of accumulation for the extractive capital even after a fatal disaster by using different mechanisms of coercion and consent.

2   The Soma Mine Disaster and Its Prosecution Process

On May 13, 2014, the worst mine disaster and workplace homicide in the history of Turkey, which killed 301 miners, took place at an underground coal mine operated by the Soma Coal Company. The disaster occurred when a fire spread in the galleries when a wall collapsed and exposed self-burning coal. When the severity of the situation was realized, a rescue operation was organized. Yet, it was ineffective for several reasons, including lack of proper air circulation, the employment of a high number of miners in each shift, lack of safe rooms for miners to take refuge in during emergencies, and insufficient guidelines for evacuation in case of an emergency (Adaman et al., 2019: 521–2). The then Prime Minister of Turkey, Erdoğan, referred to miners of 19th century England to explain the disaster and employed the Islamic term *fitrat* to underline that such tragedies are inherent in mining and, therefore, inevitable.

The prosecution process of the disaster lasted between 2015 and 2021, during which 51 defendants, including the chairs of the company, managers, and engineers, were prosecuted. As indicated in the expert report submitted to the board of the Akhisar High Criminal Court in 2016, the coal policies of the governments and production processes in the Soma Coal Company were the reasons behind the disaster. Coal policies and relevant state institutions were deemed responsible for (i) shortcomings of the basin planning, such as the mismatch between the amount of coal extraction and the mechanical structure of the basin, (ii) defects stemming from the implementation of royalty tender, (iii) insufficient inspections by the relevant state institutions, and (iv) deficiencies in relevant legislation on health and safety in coal mines. The company, on the other hand, was blamed for the shortcomings in the ventilation system, worker training, use and quality of gas masks, and, most significantly, extraction of coal beyond the mechanical capacity of the pit. The prosecution resulted in the punishment of 14 defendants – including the chair of the company – and exculpation of the remaining 37 defendants. For the families and lawyers of the death miners, these punishments were far from being lawful. Similarly, the Supreme Court reversed the ruling by saying that the ruling should not have been in accordance with reckless homicide but eventual intent. Then, the prosecution process was relaunched. Yet, in 2002, the final ruling remained as it was in 2018. Families and their lawyers frequently mentioned that the Soma Mine Disaster was investigated as it was a 'traffic accident' or a 'natural disaster.' They insistently underlined that what happened in Soma was 'not an accident but a massacre' and considering the massacre as the 'fate of miners' was not acceptable. Accordingly, they have argued that the Soma Mine Disaster was a result of the systemic neglect of the Soma Coal Company, the representatives of the relevant state institutions, and the 'collaborator' trade union named Maden İş for the objective of extracting the maximum amount of coal by pushing both the miners and the mechanical capacity of the pit.

As discussed in Chapter 3, the coal industry and the objective of utilizing domestic coal for power generation have strategic importance for the Turkish economy, as dependency on imported energy is among the most significant reasons behind the high levels of current account deficit. Even after this fatal disaster, the Ministry of Energy and Natural Resources announced the objective of quadrupling coal-fired power plants (CFPPs) by 2020 (Adaman et al., 2019: 525). The Soma Mine Disaster and its prosecution had turned into a challenging barrier, given that the final rule would have affected the coal industry and coal policies as a whole. The role of the authoritarian neoliberal state was influential during the legal process, especially in the form of interventions in the legal process. For instance, on the last day of the trial blogs of January 2017, the attorney general declared that his opinion on the final rule was ready and that he would announce it following a ten-minute break. Yet, after the break, he did not give his opinion by claiming that he needed more time to reorganize his opinion. He did not give an opinion over the following fourteen months. Meanwhile, in the summer of 2017, the Council and Judges

Prosecutors enacted a Decree, which, among other things, changed the judge of the Soma Mine Disaster. Families and lawyers of the death miners protested this change for two reasons. First, it was the initial judge who had a good grasp of the case, saw the underground pit, and knew the exact place where each miner died. Therefore, he should have been the one to give the final ruling. Secondly, the newly appointed judge was known for his widely criticized decision on another mine disaster in Southern Turkey (Afşin-Elbistan) in which he merely imposed a fine on the defendants who were responsible for the death of 11 miners.

Furthermore, there were considerable interventions in the legal process by the coal companies as well. Following the disaster, the Soma Eynez Mine (SEM) was shut down, and the contracts of 2831 miners were terminated. As a result, the problem of unemployment started for the first time in the basin. As frequently mentioned during the interviews, once the workers who witnessed the disaster gave evidence against the company, they would lose their jobs and could not find a job in any of the pits in the Basin. As a result, many workers did not give evidence during the trials. For example, as stated by one of the miners after a trial in 2016 who survived the disaster with an injury: 'I have been unemployed for two years. I have two kids. Even to come to Akhisar from Soma for this trial, I had to borrow money. I am sorry, but I have to drop the charge.'

Additionally, there were strong signs of collaboration between the Soma Coal Company and some of the witnesses who gave evidence during the trials. It was frequently mentioned that the firm provided benefits such as employment opportunities or cash transfers in return for the witnesses not to file a complaint. Three of the unemployed interviewees mentioned that the company had offered them money. For example, one of them stated:

> The company offered me money. But I didn't accept it. They offered me 80,000 Liras not to give evidence against the company. That money would have changed my life, but I did not accept it. Look, I am unemployed now. And looks like I won't be able to find a job under these circumstances.

Similarly, there were several inconsistencies between the statements of the same miners, which were made in the prosecution office immediately after the disaster and the statements during the trials. Also, there were inconsistencies between the statements of the miners who filed a complaint and those who did not. For example, the former mentioned the production pressure implemented by the informal subcontractors, whereas the latter rejected the existence of the informal subcontracting system in the company.

Almost all employees (including miners and engineers) who gave evidence during the trials stated that they had been aware of the existence of self-burning coal over a couple of months before the disaster. They frequently mentioned that the temperature in the galleries had increased drastically, and warning systems showed rising levels of carbon monoxide and carbon dioxide. As revealed in the report prepared by the Boğaziçi University Soma Research Group, the temperature almost doubled between May 1, 2014 and May 13, 2014 – it rose from 22.7 degrees on May 1 and 45 degrees on May 13. According to the report, the maximum expected temperature of the pit was 20–21 degrees; therefore, coal extraction should have stopped once the temperature exceeded 21 degrees (Ersoy, 2015: 36). Similarly, the interviewees frequently mentioned the temperature increase. For example, as stated by a miner: 'It was impossible to touch the coal. It was that hot! It was burning ... The pit was also burning.' Additionally, as stated by a 48-year-old miner who worked at another shift:

> I worked as a miner for several years. I was a sergeant. I know the underground pits inside out. I was aware that the coal was burning. I warned them, but they told me, 'do your own business!' If you do not consider warnings ... So to say, it was natural or it was the will of God! Come on! Think about it as if you are driving a car. You don't fasten your seatbelt, you are drunk, and you go overspeed. If you have an accident under such conditions, could you call it the will of God?.

The relatives of the deceased miners also mentioned the signs of a disaster over a couple of months before the disaster in their statements. On the one hand, there are several deceased miners whose fathers had worked in the same pit. They mentioned their conversations with their sons on the difference between their working conditions and the production pressure experienced by their sons. Secondly, statements of women (miners' wives or mothers) who were responsible for the social reproduction of the miners mentioned the changing physical and psychological conditions of the miners over the last couple of months before the disaster. Almost all women mentioned the physical suffering of their husbands or sons, including headaches, extreme fatigue, vomiting, dehydration, and intoxication. For instance, as stated by a miner's wife during the trials of December 2015:

> My husband was working at the S panel. Over the two months before the disaster, he was taking extra underwear, and they were all wet because of sweating. Four days before the incident, he got poisoned. He vomited for hours ... He was suffering from a headache anyway. He used to

take painkillers all the time. He was always sleeping at home during his last days.

Similarly, as revealed by the lawyers of the families, there were large numbers of applications to the public hospital at the centre of Soma due to carbon monoxide poisoning.

Finally, a variety of instances of neglect regarding health and safety was underlined during the trials. The first one was the absence of reliable worker training. Legally, there should be at least two weeks of compulsory worker training in the underground mines. However, two of the interviewees whose husbands died in the disaster stated that their husbands started working in the Soma Coal Company three days before the disaster and died at the most dangerous gallery. Secondly, neglect of the maintenance and repair of the oxygen masks was frequently underlined. Witnesses mentioned that even when the masks gave error, they were expected to keep working. Finally, insufficient inspections by the Turkish Coal Enterprises and the Ministry of Labour and Social Security were frequently mentioned. Almost all witnesses of the trial and the interviewees argued that the dates were known prior to the inspections, and they were making necessary arrangements. Furthermore, many workers mentioned that the inspectors did not even visit the underground production units but they were merely visiting the main galleries. For instance, an interviewee who formerly worked in the Eynez Mine and lost his two brothers in the disaster state:

> They keep talking about the inspectors during the trials. I worked there for nine years and never saw an inspector. We used to hear that they were visiting, but we did not used to see them. As far as I heard, they were merely visiting the main galleries.

All in all, the Soma Mine Disaster unveiled how the coal rush policies of the government and the profit-maximization objectives of the companies risk the lives of miners. Particularly, the implementation of royalty tender and the guarantee of purchase provided by the state for the companies regardless of the amount of the coal have encouraged the companies to accelerate coal production and exceed the natural limits of the pit through labour-intensive techniques. The clearest summary of the process that led to the Soma Mine Disaster can be found in the following witness statement in the trial:

> There was a pressure for overproduction. Sometimes, the supervisors, even the engineers, were oppressing the miners by insulting them.

> I remember the times when I could not even have the time to take my gas mask or boots with me because of their rush. Miners were hired by illegal subcontractors. The chief executive of the company employs the workers like slaves. They always oppress workers to work more … When the inspectors visited, they let us know before. Some deficiencies in the mine were fixed, and some were hidden. Workers were forced not to tell about the deficiencies to the inspectors.

Additionally, the lack or insufficiency of inspections allowed the companies to neglect health and safety measures, which would increase the cost of production. As long as the final rule of the prosecution of the disaster would have an impact on the whole sector, not merely on the Soma Coal Company, and the consecutive AKP governments have been reluctant to abandon the coal rush plan, the disaster could not have been prosecuted independently from the government interventions.

3 Local Labour Control and Discipline Strategies

As underlined by Jonas (1996), local labour control is developed through interrelationships among workplace, family and community institutions, local trade union organizations, employment associations, and local political parties by using mechanisms such as paternalism and corporate welfarism. In the Soma Coal Basin, this is exemplified in the interrelationship among the AKP government, coal companies, hometown associations, and the Maden İş trade union. Local labour control strategies implemented through these institutions and communities have taken different forms since the Soma Mine Disaster.

The informal subcontracting system operates as a control mechanism beyond the workplace, within local relations in general. As mentioned in the third chapter, labour processes in the underground pits are designed through subcontracting teams, which are usually formed through kinship and hometown networks. Therefore, workers from other mining towns in Turkey migrate to Soma as subcontracting teams. Migrant workers frequently mentioned that they could find a job in the mines because their relatives gave their names to the labour intermediaries. Moreover, they established hometown associations in Soma, which I define as the aboveground reflections of the informal subcontracting system. Miners frequently mentioned during the interviews that informal subcontractors themselves established those associations.

First, as underlined in Chapter 4, migrant families' conditions of social reproduction are more precarious compared to the local ones due to factors such as having relatively more cash-dependent and higher-cost means of subsistence and lack of access to the non-market means of social reproduction such as family housing, land, clean water, firewood etc. Hometown associations tend to function as 'invisible economies of care' (Shah and Lerche, 2020) to cope with insecure conditions of social reproduction. In the Soma Coal Basin, hometown associations are significant community institutions for the migrant households' survival. They are very effective both as labour control and discipline mechanisms as they constitute alternatives for the oppositional unionization of miners and as a means of survival for the migrant workers. On the one hand, through these associations, migrant households build care networks with folks from their hometowns and act with solidarity in times of need. As stated by a woman:

> We feel lonely in Soma; it has never felt like home, to be honest. But at least there are other families from Kütahya. If we need something, morally or materially, we immediately call our association. Whatever we need, they do their best to support us. We also have collective circumcises or sometimes we collect money to support when a family from Kütahya is indigent.

These associations have coffeehouses or clubs, and people from the same town mostly live in the same neighbourhood. They mostly call their neighbourhoods a neighbourhood of people from Kütahya, Ordu, Zonguldak, etc. Therefore, the sphere of social reproduction is mostly divided through kinship and hometown networks. For example, as explained by a woman from Ordu who is an agricultural worker:

> I mean, could people from Zonguldak, Kütahya, and Ordu be the same? We work on the same farms; we are separated there too. People from Kütahya have lunch together, those from Zonguldak have it together, we eat together ... We also have an association. I go there and say I need something; they would help me. We don't have our own house in Soma, but if we buy one day, I would prefer to buy a house in the neighbourhood of people from Ordu.

On the other hand, hometown associations are instrumental in preventing the formation of a united struggle of workers by dividing the local labour market on religious, cultural, and spatial bases. For example, religious networks are functional, especially because almost all migrant workers are Sunni Muslims, whereas the majority of local workers are Alevis. Instead of a class-based organization, such as an alternative trade union to the existing one, these associations constitute a straightforward and trustworthy social network for migrant families. As explained by a miner:

> Now, I made Ali be recruited, and then Ali made Samet be recruited. I mean, we are about one-fourth of Soma as people from Kütahya people. If its population is 100 thousand, there are at least 15–20 thousand people from Kütahya. We have our own neighborhoods here. I mean, this is tempting. For example, friends from our hometown call us and ask whether they should come here if they can find a job here … There was something called an informal subcontractor in the past before these incidents. We should not deny this. We used to tell them we had a friend willing to get a job, namely telling these big brothers. They were making benefits, helps. (…) We also have an association where we can visit and spend time by just saying that we are from Kütahya … We can also look after and collaborate when one of our men falls into trouble. For example, when someone has an accident or something like that … Under the name of an association, if someone needs it, we can immediately collect money for solidarity.

The insights shared by local activists, who were the primary sources in the initial phase of the fieldwork, are of significant importance. They revealed that the number and influence of hometown associations have been on the rise since the early 2000s. This underscores the strong correlation between the establishment of these associations and the transformation of local class relations in the basin, a transformation driven by the neoliberal shift in agriculture and coal mining. The spread of these associations, as noted by a local activist who lived in Soma for more than 60 years, is a direct response to the gap left by the loss of the secure conditions of miners, previously guaranteed by the state:

> I figured out how these associations have become so widespread in this way. In the past, a relationship with agriculture was established over the state before the neoliberal policies were implemented. The relationship between workers and the mine was through the state. The relationship established by the government with people was over the establishments like Tekel, ELI. What is completely dissolved now is these relationships. The state is out of the frame. The necessity for another relationship has risen when it becomes excluded. In my opinion, these hometown associations directly fills this gap. Because there is actually a mafia-type organization: the existing ELI, district governorate, shipping agents,

cooperatives, local associations ... These local associations are even effective in ensuring everyone votes in election periods. Which are marketing the votes of all these countrymen, their own members, acting in concert with the district governor in policies to be implemented ... I think an instrument applied by the state is included in this organization. The time when local associations became widespread and became significant powers was in late 2002. They were provided with buildings. The existing district governorate did this. If you visit, you will see that they have considerable possibilities, and the state itself has encouraged and developed them. Therefore, a triangle of union-capital-state is mentioned, but actually, it is multi-dimensional.

As stated above, therefore, hometown associations and informal networks constructed through them fill the gap resulting from the dissolution of the previous relations of the local population to the state, such as tobacco production under the purchase guarantee of Tekel or employment in state-operated mines and living like a community in the personnel houses and the social facilities provided by the Turkish Coal Enterprise. They trust these associations, especially to meet their social reproduction needs in order to cope with the gap created as a result of the "hollowing out of the social reproductive roles of the public institutions" (Yalman et al., 2023).

Secondly, therefore, as associations are established by and operated through the informal subcontractors, the informal subcontracting system is directly reproduced in the trade union. Miners Union of Turkey (Maden İş) was established in 1958 and became a member of the Confederation of Turkish Trade Unions (Türk-İş) in the 1960s. Türk-İş Confederation was founded in 1952. Its member unions have experienced a significant transformation during the AKP period as a result of the restructuring of the general trade union profile in the country. During the AKP governments, the Hak İş Confederation was explicitly supported by the government, and a new form of unionization based on control and discipline of workers instead of the defense of their social rights was developed. Under the AKP rule, the Confederation of Progressive Trade Unions (DISK) maintained its pro-labour position, whereas Türk-İş failed to take a firm stand on the side of workers (Çelik, 2012; Erdinç, 2014). Similarly, Maden İş trade union has turned into a control and discipline mechanism of the mining companies and the AKP government upon the workers. In fact, relatively older miners mentioned during the interviews that coal companies were against unionization between 2005 and 2008. Accordingly, the chair of the executive board of the Soma Coal Company used to say, 'as long as I am here, there will be no trade union in this company.' Yet, since 2008, coal companies, except for

Demir Export, have been forcing their workers to become members of Maden Iş. As claimed by older or retired miners, it is because collaboration between the coal companies and the union started in 2008, which has taken several forms, including the nomination of candidates for union representatives by the employers, distribution of already signed ballots or cheating in the union elections. As stated by an interviewee:

> Previously, Maden Iş was a well-operated union. We didn't use to know its close relations to the employers. They were in contact with the workers when necessary. Or they used to ask for the workers' opinions in the decision-making processes. For example, they were telling that 'the company offered a 5 percent increase in wages, but we requested 10 percent, and we tried to reach an agreement.' Now they do not even let us in the union office … This has become apparent since 2008–9. They started not to deal with the workers at all or just meet the employers when they visited the company.

The majority of the workers explained their relation to unionization by referring to the decisions of the companies. For example, miners who work for Soma Coal Company or Imbat Coal Company used statements such as 'They said we had to be a member of Maden Iş, so I did,' whereas miners who work in Demir Export answered either 'Our company does not accept trade union' or 'There is no trade Union in Demir Export.' Furthermore, miners who work in Demir Export explained why they were not unionized by claiming that workers of a strong company such as Demir Export and Koç Holding would not need trade unions because these strong business groups could protect the rights of their workers.

Answers to my questions regarding the miners' opinion about the Maden Iş union can be grouped into three: neutral, positive, and negative. Neutral responses mostly belong to the depoliticized workers who do not have sufficient knowledge about, therefore, expectations from unionization. They often used statements such as 'trade union membership has not changed anything' or 'the only thing I know is that they cut a per diem amount from my monthly salary.' Miners who were glad to be a member of Maden Iş tended to refer to the material benefits specified in the collective bargaining, such as soap or coal aid, instead of their social rights. Finally, workers who criticized the union constituted three-quarters of the interviewees. They can be divided into two groups: those who are still members of Maden Iş and those who resigned from Maden Iş and joined oppositional unions. The former group is composed of miners who are not satisfied with the union but do not resign due to the fear of unemployment or to keep receiving the benefits, especially coal aid. The details about the second group will be discussed in the next section on the moments of resistance.

Thirdly, the AKP government is successful not only in implementing effective labour control and discipline strategies in the Basin but also in receiving electoral support from Soma. Although the expert report revealed that the Soma Mine Disaster was a direct result of the coal policies of the AKP governments, there has been no mass resistance against these policies in Soma. In fact, AKP has been the leading party in Soma in all the general and local elections between 2002 and 2023. As argued by Adaman and Akbulut (2021), extractive investments constitute a significant consent-making mechanism for the AKP governments. It was observable in the Soma Coal Basin despite the death of 301 miners because of wrong coal policies. During the fieldwork, the most significant concern for the miner families was the continuity of employment opportunities in the mines, even more than health and safety in the coal pits or the impact of CFPPs on their health. After the disaster, three pits operated by the Soma Coal Basin were shut down. For six months, workers were on paid leave. In November 2014, two of the pits re-started production, but the contracts of 2831 miners were terminated because the SEM was not active. Therefore, the disaster also marks a turning point in terms of the problem of unemployment. Almost all the interviewees identified unemployment as the main issue after the disaster, and they were hoping that SEM would be reopened soon so that they could be rehired.

Meanwhile, through the local community and institutional networks, it is imposed upon miner families that they have jobs with a regular income thanks to the coal investments encouraged by the AKP government. Therefore, a possible change of the government is presented as a risk of diminishing coal investments, closure of the active pits, and, therefore, a rise in unemployment. During our interview, the secretary-general of the Soma Chamber of Industry and Trade stated:

> First of all, coal has become more important in every sense following the change of the government. Needy families receive coal aid every year at the moment. A production increase has occurred because of this. Moreover, there were reserves not operated by ELI; they have given these to private firms. We call this royalty here. They are paid some amount per ton they produce through ELI and TKI. Currently, 80–85 percent of production is made via the private sector, with royalty. The number of firms has increased; they have put new sites out to tender. ELI has an awkward situation; this government solved this. This would probably

sound odd, but coal is a blessing from God to Soma. None of the former governments were willing to value coal to such an extent until now. Now the production has increased. Surely some troubles are experienced, we cannot deny … Soma was not a place visible from Ankara, for example, till the accident. You know what they say? There is no such thing as bad advertising; our accident was such that. The name of Soma was heard by the whole world. It is always attractive for investment. This attraction was not known until this government. They have a very good logic on this subject. In terms of privatization, in terms of giving to the private sector … They also provide employment. They found a very good method.

This was reflected in the narratives of some workers as well. During my visit two weeks before the 2017 Constitutional Referendum on the Presidential System, interviewees stated that they would vote yes to the presidential system proposed by the AKP because Turkey needed political stability to become an 'independent and strong country' and because political stability would influence the future of the coal industry, and therefore, their employment. As an unemployed miner stated: 'If stability comes, our pit will be reopened, unemployment will end.' Therefore, the local population views coal investment as an employment opportunity and the AKP as the only guarantor of these investments. That is one of the reasons why the AKP received strong support from the basin until very recently.

Fourth, the close relationship between the coal firms and the AKP government is a significant factor determining labour control and discipline in the basin. The miners frequently mentioned that companies forced them to attend the public meetings of the AKP in nearby towns. Accordingly, those who attended the meetings received additional per diem wages, whereas those who refused saw that their salaries were cut down and were blacklisted. Additionally, it is quite common for the workers to become members of the AKP to find a job in the pits. For example:

> Probably others don't admit it, but I confess: I became a member of the AKP to get this job. People suggested me this way. Then I became a member. In the district branch, they said there was an engineer in the company. Go and see him, say hello to him for me … Then, I was immediately hired. All of the miners in our village are members of the AKP. But we all support CHP.

Fifth, in line with the rest of the country, Islamic networks successfully operate as labour control and discipline mechanisms in the Basin. I could not concretely observe the religious networks because they are entirely closed and isolated communities. Yet, there were strong claims about their effectiveness in local community relations. For example, a worker stressed the significance of *tarikat* networks in Soma as follows:

> *Tarikats* are very active here in Soma. I was also a member of one. They have meeting places, slaughtering spaces ... Now they are building a dormitory. They are widespread and effective.

Additionally, local activists underlined the existence of *tarikat* networks within the hometown associations. These communities function both as social networks to find a job or ask for assistance in times of need and as pedagogic institutions imposing Islamic notions such as *fıtrat, şükür*, and *benevolence* to prevent potential resistance movements. As stated by a local activist:

> Religion is very effective. Especially migrant families prefer to socialize in Islamic communities. *Tarikats* also get involved. Now, if you ask, most families consider the disaster as fate. It is imposed on the workers in those religious communities.

All in all, in parallel to the strategic significance of the coal industry, various political, institutional, and community dynamics within the Soma basin have been in the spheres of reproduction in order to guarantee the sustainability of the investments. As argued by Jonas (1996: 327), the methods of local labour control regimes are developed through the interrelationships among work place, family and community institutions, local trade union organizations, employer associations, and local political parties through the use of various methods of control convenient to localities such as paternalism or corporate welfarism. In Soma, this is clearly exemplified in the interrelationship among the AKP government, coal companies, hometown associations and informal subcontractors, and the Maden İş trade union. The most convenient method preferred by these actors has been the use of conflicting characteristics and interests of local and migrant workers stemming from different patterns of reproduction of labour power or denominational differences. To a certain extent, this has been maintained following the Soma Mine Disaster, but under the crisis conditions following the death of 301 miners, they developed additional discipline and control mechanisms.

4 Local Labour Control and Discipline after the Soma Mine Disaster: Clientelism – Wage Increases – Unemployment

Following the Soma Mine Disaster, the then Minister of Energy and Natural Resources Taner Yıldız and the then Prime Minister Recep Tayyip Erdoğan made successive statements in the media. The statements of the minister of energy and natural resources were mostly about the situation of the miners in the pit and the rescue operations, whereas Tayyip Erdoğan adopted a tone marked by a 'combination of defiance and fatalism' (Adaman et al., 2019: 514). As underlined earlier, he referred to the conditions of miners in 19th-century England, and by referring to an Islamic term, *fitrat*, he underlined that such tragedies are natural and inevitable for coal miners. Moreover, he visited the Soma district the day after the disaster and faced fierce protests from the local population. He had to hide in a grocery store to escape from the protestors, whereas one of his advisors kicked a miner protesting them.

As mentioned in the previous section, three pits operated by the Soma Coal Company were closed for six months. During that six-month period, miners were on paid leave. Six months after the disaster, there were three important developments which have determined the local class relations since then. First, in November 2014, the contracts of 2831 miners employed in different pits operated by the Soma Coal Company were terminated due to the financial bottleneck of the company since the disaster. Secondly, in the context of the Omnibus Bill No. 6552 enacted in September 2014, the minimum wage for the underground coal miners was set as double the minimum wage in the country and weekly working hours were diminished to 36 hours (i.e. two days off). Finally, the families of the miners who died in the disaster received compensation for wrongful death. Additionally, they received significant amounts of financial aid from different regions of the country, especially from celebrities such as artists, football players, etc. Furthermore, the Housing Development Administration of Turkey (TOKI) initiated a housing project of 602 flats, two for each family. As a result of these, rising income inequality among miner families and the problem of unemployment have become significant factors triggering intra-class conflict within the local labour market. During the fieldwork, hostility between the families of the deceased miners, miners who still work in the underground pits, unemployed miners, and between landowner and landless miners was observable. For instance, in February 2016, during the monthly commemoration of the families of the deceased miners, someone yelled at the families, 'you received 500 thousand liras; why do you still make a fuss?' Later, I learned that the man who yelled at them was an unemployed migrant miner.

Unemployed miners have experienced a deepening of poverty, and during the interviews, all of them complained about the invisibility of their situation. Statements such as 'Did we have to die to be seen?' 'I wish I died; at least my children would not be starving.' 'Nobody sees us because we did not die' were frequently used. Yet, among the 2831 unemployed miners, only 53 of them filed a reemployment lawsuit. This is mainly explained by referring to the fear of being blacklisted by the companies and not being employed in the pits any longer.

Additionally, there is a significant difference in the ways in which local and migrant workers experience unemployment. All local unemployed miners stated that they started working as unregistered daily agricultural wage workers together with their wives. For example, as stated by an unemployed miner from Kınık in the summer of 2016:

> Now, I am working at the farm with my wife ... We receive 50 liras daily wage, no insurance ... My wife has been working there for years. Yet, before, she used to benefit from my insurance. Now, we are both unregistered. We have no social security. Working conditions ... Of course, there is no work safety. Look, recently, there was an accident ... 15 women farmworkers died in Gölmarmara. Nothing ... If we have an accident or something like that or if we get sick ... What would we do?.

As for the migrant workers, the financial burden stemming from unemployment was more severe due to their relatively higher cost of social reproduction stemming from lack of access to the means of subsistence such as land or family housing. Moreover, as they migrated to Soma due to the precarious conditions of work in their hometowns, many of them did not consider moving back to their hometowns. For example, as explained by a miner from Zonguldak:

> I cannot return back to Zonguldak. They don't give money there too! Besides, the pits are illegal. Everything is under your responsibility in an illegal pit. Even if you died, nobody would be informed about this anyway.

Meanwhile, since the disaster, some of the coal companies have enlarged their pits and two new pits were opened in 2015 and 2020. Even though more than 5 thousand jobs were created as a result of these, the number of unemployed miners did not drop under 3 thousand since 2014. On the one hand, the employment of the miners who were blacklisted workers for taking part in alternative unionization attempts or attending demonstrations to criticize the coal policies were suspended. On the other hand, according to the narratives of most interviewees, as a labour discipline strategy, mining companies have tended to prefer migrant workers since the disaster. Accordingly, factors such as having the opportunity to maintain agricultural production (as a petty commodity producer or as a subsistence producer) and lower costs of social reproduction for the local families strengthen the local families' bargaining power. As a result, they are more likely to be an active part of alternative unionization attempts or other forms of social movements against coal companies and coal policies. Particularly, as reactions and resistance movements of the Alevi workers from Kınık after the disaster were stronger compared to the other groups of miners, it became more difficult for them to be employed in the underground mines. For example, a 48-year-old miner who was fired in November 2014 states:

> They no longer accept the people of Kınık. Because we were on TV after the accidents. If you apply to a company, once they see on your identity card that your birthplace is Kınık. They would never hire you. We had farming in the past. They deprived us of farming; we were forced to work in the mines. Now, they are taking this option too. What will the people of Kınık do? We have always been impoverished. We have always been impoverished more and more!

Similarly, migrant workers explained the stronger opposition of the local populations, especially from Kınık, because of Kınık's ongoing relation to the land and agriculture and the availability of fertile land. For instance, as stated by a migrant miner: 'Kınık people are braver because they can survive even when they cannot work in the mines. Everywhere is fertile; they can cultivate the land.' As a result, local workers blame migrant workers for being extremely obedient to the employees and weakening their bargaining power. For example, as stated by a miner from Kınık:

> We cannot be organized because of the cowardice of migrant families. Most of them are tenants, or they are indebted. If their sergeant asks them to enter where they could die, they will accept entering there.

In short, the intra-class conflict between the local and migrant workers constitutes a significant impediment to a possible organized class movement.

Both for the local and migrant families, the unemployment of miners directly affects women's work in production and social reproduction. Historically, employment patterns, social security systems and power relations they generate are shaped by the male breadwinner, female caregiver type of proletarian households. This inevitably deems women as dependents of their husbands or fathers. Yet, women's participation in wage employment, especially as informal workers, tends to increase in times of crisis, given that women are considered as reserve army of labour to be utilized in the last resort. When men are discouraged in the job market or the income they generate is not sufficient for the reproduction of the households, women may participate in wage work (cf. Akgöz and Balta, 2015; Elson, 2010; Yaman, 2009). In the Soma Coal Basin, unemployment of miners tends to result in the over-exploitation of women's work in agriculture or in other unregistered wage employments on the one hand, their unpaid reproductive and emotional work on the other hand. As exemplified in the narratives of women, even though they used to work in agriculture when their husbands were working in the mines, due to their unemployment they started to work for seven days a week and in the harvest of all products in the region. As stated by the wife of an unemployed miner:

> Things are much more difficult now. For example, before I could say 'I am tired, I could not go to the farm today.' I am 46 years old. You were here; it was almost 50 degrees yesterday. I would not have worked in such weather in the past. Now, I have to go for seven days. Or for example, I would not have gone to olive farming in Akhisar in the past. Now, I have no chance to choose. I go to work at any time. We have two children and my husband is unemployed.

Similarly, the exploitation of the emotional work of women has also intensified because of the unemployment of their husbands. Especially women whose husbands survived the disaster have frequently mentioned that their husbands had been mentally depressed since the disaster, and this resulted in increasing pressure on women. Or, as traditionally it is women's responsibility to take care of the household under financial bottleneck, income loss leads to an emotional burden on women. Many of them mentioned the difficulty they had in feeding the family. For instance, I witnessed a striking conversation between two women (the former lost his son in the disaster, whereas the latter is married to an unemployed miner):

- Are you still making lace?
- Yes. What else can I do? We have three children; we live in a rented flat. Would a family eat plain pasta for three meals, even for breakfast? We are doing it .
- Never mind, God bless your husband.
- Amen.

Meanwhile, the threat of unemployment affects the condition of all the miners in the basin, and it is used as a means of labour discipline and further production pressure. For example, as stated by a miner:

> The unemployment concern is big. And the company uses this against us. Mostly, subcontractors use this. They keep saying that there are many people looking for a job outside, if you don't work, you are replaceable!

Wage increases made employment in Soma even more attractive for the miners across the country. Wage increases, along with the rise of unemployment, triggered competition among workers. Due to the lack of sectoral diversity in the region and massive dispossession of land and agriculture, competition for employment in mining, which offers relatively stable and well-paid employment, has increased. As frequently stated by the interviewees, 'People have to choose between dying of starvation and dying in the mine,' or they are forced to choose 'the lesser of two evils.' For instance, one of the interviewees mentioned his apprehension due to the gas leak in his production unit as follows: 'There is a methane leak in our unit. It would be too bad if our section is closed. They could let us unpaid leave or even dismiss' As can be seen, he feared losing his job even more than methane poisoning.

All in all, wage increases along with the threat of unemployment, created a local labour market, largely obedient to the coal companies. Most of the workers explained why they did not take part in alternative attempts for unionization or in the local social movements by referring to the risk of unemployment. For example, a miner who was formerly among the leaders of a famous strike in Zonguldak in 2014 argued that it was not possible to organize that kind of strike in Soma:

> Let me explain the fundamental difference between Zonguldak and Soma ... If you tell these people to protest the company, they would not. Workers' only concern is their wages. In Soma or in Zonguldak, it doesn't matter. If the workers' wages are not paid for two months, if they do not get a raise, then they would protest their company. There is no financial trouble for the miners of Soma. Wage levels are good. Protests, as in the case of Zonguldak, would not rise here. Besides, our education level is apparent. We cannot easily find this wage level with our education level.

Finally, since the disaster, local institutional and community networks successfully operate to explain the reason behind the disaster either as workers' fault or as faith instead of paying attention to the responsibilities of the company or shortcomings of the coal policies of the government. When I asked workers questions regarding the health and safety in the coal pits, the majority of them underlined the responsibilities of the workers. For example, the workers of the Imbat Mining Company appreciated the company for being *'the number one in safety.'* Yet, when I questioned the measures taken by the company, almost all the miners underlined how the company disciplined them to overcome a possible disaster. In other words, as mine disasters are regarded as the outcomes of workers' failure, health and safety measures are designed to 'educate' and 'discipline' the workers instead of investing in health and safety technologies. I frequently heard narratives such as, 'If we bang a nail on the wrong place, our supervisors immediately report, and the company cuts off our daily wage.' Additionally, workers who have chronic illnesses or mental issues are under extremely precarious conditions. For example, many workers who took anti-depressant pills after surviving the disaster were fired for being 'mentally unstable' and at risk of causing an accident due to their mental conditions. For example, as underlined by a worker in the interview he gave to BBC Turkish:

> I don't work now. I also applied to other mines. Honestly, I don't want to work in the mine, but I am paying the mortgage. I wasn't hired because of the drugs. I took those because they were prescribed by a psychiatrist. One year of drug breakdown is included in the requested hiring documents.

Similarly, during the interviews, workers who have chronic illnesses such as epilepsy, diabetes, and hernia told that their contracts were terminated. For instance:

> We have always engaged in agriculture, I started working in the mine to get the pension rights. I worked as a miner for 11 years. I fell sick in May. I fainted. When I opened my eyes, I was in the hospital. They took me to the hospital. ... Then, it appeared that I had epilepsy. They terminated my contract. I did not want to quit. I was at least expecting to complete this year. They didn't let me. They told me that this disease could lead to an accident underground. Actually, they could shift my task to the ground, but they didn't do this. Then I applied for a disability retirement. Yeti the Social Security Institution rejected it.

Therefore, by imposing on the workers that mine disasters stem from the defects of the workers, coal firms not only get rid of the responsibility of the disasters but also discipline the workers to work more efficiently.

According to the findings of the fieldwork, this strategy was successful to a significant extent, and it was frequently argued by the miners that the reason behind the Soma Mine Disaster could be the lack of attention or even sabotage of the workers. For example, the response of a worker from Soma working in Soma Coal Company to the question, "what is the reason behind the accident, what do you think?" was as follows:

> Workers' fault. Even ... The man would have burned the band because he got angry at his subcontractor. But he could not estimate the things would reach to such an extent. He is an uneducated man in the end.

One final point to be underlined regarding the period after the massacre is the reflection of the statements of the representatives of the government on the local population and the means through which they have been imposed. Naturalizing the "accident" by referring to Islamic notions imposed through the mechanisms mentioned earlier. A lot of people mentioned the visits of people wearing religious dress immediately after the Soma Mine Disaster. Accordingly, they were visiting the families of the deceased miners. Also, as mentioned before, hometown associations have strong religious networks. During the interviews, there were more than ten workers who explained the Soma Mine Disaster by referring to religious/Islamic notions. For example, as stated by a miner retired from Soma Coal Company:

> This accident was an act of God. Nobody could understand the reason of it. These people are in prison, far away from their family. Who wants this? Who does this intentionally?

Or as stated by a woman from Zonguldak whose husband works in İmbat Coal Company:

> They told us we should return back to Zonguldak after the accident. But nobody knows what will happen in the future. There is no guarantee that I would not have a car accident and die after going out. Death finds a person everywhere if the fatal date comes.

Consequently, local labour control mechanisms established to prevent workers' integration in the production and social reproduction spheres, and the networks operated through the informal subcontracting system, hometown associations, and religious relations constitute significant impediments to the formation of an organized class movement in the basin. For example, one of the workers whose job contract was terminated for being an active member of the trade union of the Confederation of Progressive Trade Unions (DISK) stated that one of his relatives, who is an informal subcontractor and in the executive committee of Maden İş trade union warned him as follows:

> Break off your organization (DISK Dev Maden Sen), break with people there, agree to become a member of our Maden İş, I will make you get a job just tomorrow. But I can't find you a job even if you stand by them.

On the other hand, unemployed miners are under the threat of not being able to be employed in the mines, whereas others are threatened by losing their jobs, and in this way, they are set against each other by the use of money and material conditions. As a result, participation in the oppositional demonstrations fell, and workers did not prefer to take a stand in the criminal court. They were afraid of being blacklisted. As a matter of fact, workers who were blacklisted due to their critiques to the company could not find jobs in other firms as well.

Also, shopkeepers on the main street of the Soma district were mobilized against the workers who attended the meetings or other demonstrations in return for incentives such as interest-free loans. It is frequently argued that they videotaped the demonstrations and showed them to the coal companies and to the trade union. Therefore, workers confined within these networks of revelation, targeting, competition, and coercion could not develop a strong alternative power against these local labour control strategies. Still, there have been certain attempts at organization and moments of resistance since 2014. In the next section, these attempts will be discussed.

5   Moments of Resistance: Attempts for Alternative Unionizations and Local Social Movements in the Basin

Under these conditions of labour control and discipline organized by the extractive capital, state, and local political and community institutions in the Basin, and the consent of the majority of the miner families mentioned so far, there have been moments of resistance since the Soma Mine Disaster as well. In this section, attempts to establish alternative unionizations and two significant local social movements are examined.

Immediately after the disaster, the Progressive Union of Miners (Dev Maden Sen), affiliated with the Confederation of Progressive Trade Unions (DISK), opened a branch in Soma. DISK was established in 1967 when the organized working-class movement was relatively strong in Turkey. Then, it was closed down in 1980, following the September 12 military coup, for 12 years. Dev Maden Sen was established in 1959 as a union of the workers of the Mineral Research and Exploration Institute (MTA). It had been affiliated with the Confederation of Turkish Trade Unions (Türk-İş) until it became a member of DISK in 1975. Between 1975 and 1980, the Dev Maden Sen had almost 25 thousand members. In 1999, it was merged with another trade union of DISK, namely, Underground Miners' Union (Yeraltı Maden İş) under the name of Dev Maden Sen.

According to the narratives of the representatives of the Dev Maden Sen, the union attracted significant attention at the beginning. Almost all the representatives and members mentioned that in its first days, 'people lined up to become a member of DISK' and the number of members reached around one thousand workers within three days. Then, the number of members continuously fell due to the labour control mechanisms, including the threat of unemployment and the collective redundancies of the DISK members. In the summer of 2015, the number of members was around 400, which is less today.

In addition to the pressure over DISK by the state, capital, and their collaborators, internal disputes within the union constituted a significant impediment to organizing more workers. A Regular General Assembly of the Union was held in April 2016, in which two groups competed. The first group supported the existing administration, whereas the second group underlined the need for a change in the union. The latter group was critical of the union bureaucracy employed by the then chair who was not a miner and 'unwilling to leave his seat to a miner.' They were insistent on the need for a chair who is a miner, and their slogan was, 'We are the ones who produce; we shall be the ones who govern.' As a result, the first group won the elections, whereas the second group filed a lawsuit against the union by claiming that the first group cheated in the elections. Eventually, against the union bureaucracy of DISK, the second group resigned from the Dev Maden Sen and established a new union under the name of Independent Miners Union in June 2018.

In the opening press release of the trade union, besides the coal companies and Maden İş trade Union, Dev Maden Sen and DISK were criticized as follows[1]:

> In a business line where nearly two hundred thousand people are working, only 35 thousand workers are trade union members. Despite the unions existing in this business line being seized by the state and

---

1 http://bagimsizmaden.org/2018/06/12/bagimsiz-maden-iscileri-sendikasi-kuruldu/.

employers, they continue to function, albeit as instruments of attack against the working class. Trade unionists, despite receiving high wages and engaging in questionable financial practices, are still fighting for the rights of the workers. The trade union affiliated to DISK, though labeled as a signboard union, is a testament to the resilience of the workers. They reject our membership application on the excuse that we may be opponents to them, but we continue to fight for our rights. We have obtained certain concrete achievements in certain basins in the direction of the Miners' Councils attempt we have carried out in our business line after the Soma massacre. We made decision for establishment of an independent mine workers union head office of which will be located in Soma where 16 thousand miners work collectively as a result of meetings organized in Soma, Divriği, Çetinkaya, İliç, Kangal, Hekimhan, Zonguldak, Bartın, Murgul, Yatağan, Afşin-Elbistan and Akçakale.

Therefore, currently, there are two opposition trade unions in Soma, both with limited number of members, but united in their goal to organize workers under the conditions of intense pressure. During the interviews with the representatives of both trade unions, interviewees insistently underlined the difficulties of organizing workers in the Soma basin. For example, as stated by a local representative of Dev Maden Sen during an interview in July 2015 (before the split):

> At the beginning, we saw about 1000 members. At that time, a significant number of workers was coming. But they prevent this by putting something into practice. We can also criticize us. We probably had the wrong discussions. Of course, we had some fault; I don't justify us. But in a general sense, the state applied serious pressure. This necessarily inflicted the union. Besides, when you talk about a union, the thing coming to mind is very different here ... For example, we do a training practice in every village we visit. About how a trade union should be, so-and-so. We start telling the process, so basically ... How can a worker be unaware of collective bargaining articles? We even have to tell what collective bargaining means.

Therefore, there are currently two oppositional trade unions in the Basin, with a limited number of members. During the interviews, representatives of both unions underlined how difficult organizing workers in Soma was. For example, the former General Secretary of the Independent Miners Union, Kamil Kartal, used the following metaphor: 'Labour organization in Soma is like acting as a minefield donkey' (Bütün, 2015: 255). What he means is that it was quite difficult to organize workers in a Basin where the word trade union almost connotates mining capital because of the collaboration between the Maden İş union and coal companies.

Furthermore, the Social Rights Association (SHD) opened a branch in Soma in November 2014. SHD is an association whose centre is in Istanbul and has three local branches in Iskenderun (Hatay), Adana, and Soma. Under the slogan of 'social rights for everyone,' SHD is engaged in following up and struggling against the violation of social rights in issues including workers' rights, women's rights, right to the city, and ecology. In the Soma Coal Basin, over the last nine years, SHD has been pursuing a struggle by (i) following the legal prosecution of the Soma Mine Disaster by advocating for the families of the deceased miners, (ii) working conditions and rights of miners, (iii) the conditions of small-scale agricultural producers and agricultural workers, and (iv) the ecological impacts of the mine and CFPP investments in the region. In this context, they organized a variety of activities in the Basin, including miners' councils, summer schools for the children of miners and agricultural workers, and struggle against new extractive investments. Yet, similar to the oppositional trade unions, the power of SHD has been limited to a small number of members due to the pressures over the miner families mentioned so far.

Since 2014, there have been a couple of moments of resistance in the Basin. Yet, I will mention two of them, which were successful to a certain degree. The first one was against the construction of a CFPP and the grab of olive groves in the village of Yırca in November 2014. The second was against the collective redundancy of DİSK members by the Imbat Coal Company.

5.1   Anti-coal Resistance in Yırca

Yırca is a small village of Soma with around 130 households. Just like the rest of the villages, in Yırca the local population was engaged in tobacco farming before the neoliberal transformation of agriculture. Yet, residents of Yırca have not experienced a proletarianization pattern as in the case of other villages. Instead, they have kept cultivating their land for other crops. Today, the primary means of living in Yırca is olive farming, and the number of miners is quite limited (there were four miners in the summer of 2016) compared to the other villages in the Basin. However, Yırca has been affected by the coal rush of the AKP governments in a rather different way.

In April 2014, the then Council of Ministers decided on an urgent expropriation of olive groves for a CFPP construction. As soon as they received the notification, olive farmers in Yırca appealed against the decision. Yet, when the file was on appeal, Kolin Incorporated Company entered Yırca and cut 511 olive trees. The company faced strong resistance from the residents of Yırca, who started guarding the olive grove to protect the rest of the trees. On November 7, 2014, the company cut down 6 thousands of olive trees at 6 a.m. in the morning with the help of private security forces. On the very same day, the Council of State adopted a motion stay for execution. As indicated in the decision of the Council of State, construction of a CFPP on an oil grove was illegal. As a result, despite the grab of oil groves, the struggle in Yırca was successful in preventing the construction of CFPP.

The resistance movement against the extractive capital in Yırca is a typical example of a social reproduction struggle. Firstly, the leaders of the movement in Yırca were women, and they defined their main motivation as preventing the condemnation of their lives to coal like other villages of the Basin. They basically defended their means of social reproduction, such as land, ecology, air, clean water, and healthy food. For example, protestors have used phrases such as 'We will not give up our land,' 'We will not give up our olives,' 'Don't they have children? What do they eat? Olives or coal?' 'the Kolin Incorporated cut off our lifeblood,' 'Olive oils yield fruit in ten years. Until the age of ten, you need to take care of an olive tree as if you are taking care of the child. Then it takes care of you. It feeds you.' In fact, they defined protecting olive trees as a form of protecting life and defined their main motivation as preventing condemnation of their lives to the coal industry like other villages of the Basin. For example, as stated by a woman during the protests: '[miners] died in the mine for once, we would die slowly' (Tuncer, 2016) because of the ecological impacts of the CFPP.

Since then, the residents of Yırca have kept rejecting the condemnation of their lives by the coal industry by stating that 'we can plant new olive trees. It will take time, but still, we managed to protect our lands.' Moreover, women in Yırca established a women's cooperative through which they formed a collective means of living. They produce hand-made products such as olive oil soaps, candles, spices, lace, tomato or pepper paste, tarhana, etc. and sell them either online or through other means. Women in Yırca keep underlining the empowering impact of their struggle for the olive groves and how they learned collective means of living and producing. For example: 'We have learned unionizing in the olive resistance. We have interlocked each other. Look, our olives were cut, but we kept our lands. Now, we are united together in a soup house.'

5.2 *Resistance against Redundancy of Miners*

Another striking resistance movement since the Soma Mine Disaster was organized by the DISK member miners whose contracts were terminated by the Imbat Coal Company in December 2015. On December 17, 2015, 29 workers figured out that they were fired when their personnel card was not scanned at the gate. As stated by a miner who was among the first ones to realize that they were fired:

> I went to the day shift on the 17th. This morning, I saw that the driver did not accept my card at the entrance. I asked ... They told me to go see the personnel management office. A man had 3–4 pages in his hand. He checked the list ... He said, "your contract has been terminated." I asked why. He said, nonconformity ... The employers are not happy with your productivity. You may cause an accident. I yelled at him, "tell me the real reason!" No answer ... I yelled and asked if it was because of my union membership. He asked what my union was. I said Dev Maden Sen. He said he did not know such a union. Then came the other union member friends.

The next morning, workers went to the company with their lawyers to learn "the real reason" why they got fired. They waited until the evening, then, the lawyer of the company declared that the contracts of 29 workers were terminated. On the exact spot where they learned this, 12 of them started a protest under a banner on which 'We want their jobs back' was written. That night, all of them were detained by the military police.

Once they were released the next day, miners had a meeting to plan the rest of the protest. As a result, four workers decided to maintain the protest. Those four workers pitched a tent in front of the entrance of the mine. Even though they were members of the DISK, there was a continuous dispute about the role of Dev Maden Sen in their resistance. In time, one of the miners, who was also a delegate of Dev Maden Sen, stated that he started to feel uncomfortable without the union as well as because of the criminalization of their struggle. He left the tent on the 24th day of the resistance. The rest three workers maintained the struggle for more than 60 days, and they were detained more than 10 times.

Meanwhile, several meetings were arranged to negotiate with the general director of the Imbat Coal Company. Yet, he refused to rehire them. For instance, as narrated by the brother of one of the protestors, the general director of the company told the following during one of their meetings:

> If they took legal action, they would have the chance to take their jobs back. Yet, if I rehire them, all the workers we dismiss would attempt to put up a tent in front of the mine. Our workers see their tents every day

while entering the mine. It is impossible for the company to rehire them under such circumstances.

On the last day of the protests, one of the miners decided to make this resistance 'even more radical,' and he climbed the high-voltage tower located in front of the mine. Once the military police arrived, he stated: 'We want our jobs back. If you do not comply with our request, I will jump off this tower and kill myself.' He waited seven hours at the tower, and then the company declared that they had accepted their requests. Eventually, the three protestors were hired by two other coal companies in the Basin (one by Soma Coal Company and two by Demir Export).

Albeit limited, the resistance movement was significant and successful as the demands of the workers were complied with. Yet, it had two serious shortcomings. First of all, it was limited to the issue of unemployment and lacked dynamics regarding the social rights of the miners, such as health and safety in the coal mines. It remained restricted to the employment of three workers. Secondly, workers were not hired by the company, which terminated their contracts in the first place. Therefore, the Imbat resistance showed a strong collaboration among the companies more than that of workers. As mentioned by the general director of the company, it would be a loss of power and control for the company over the workers if they hired them back, whereas there was a need to put an end to the resistance. Coal companies solved the issue by collaborating without leading to a major crisis for the coal sector. As a matter of fact, during the interviews with the miners from the Imbat Company, they frequently mentioned that this resistance was used as a threat against them by their supervisors. For example, as stated by a miner:

> The company told us that they were dismissed because they did not work, they were absent. Our sergeant was showing us their tent and say, 'if you do not work hard, you will be under that tent.' Following their resistance, extraction increased further and absence completely ended in the company. The company did not hire them back. The manager told that he would never hire back a man who did something wrong to him.

6   Conclusion

Overall, there have been two significant resistance movements in the Basin against the extractive capital, one for the sphere of production and the other for the sphere of social reproduction. The most important shortcoming in this respect has been the lack of connection between the ecology movement organized by the villagers of Yırca and the labour movement organized by the miners. In other words, while the extractive capital and the state expropriate the spheres of both production and social reproduction, movements against them have failed to embrace both. For example, even though it was a significant success to prevent the construction of a CFPP in Yırca, it remained place-based and failed both to turn into a broad-ranged anti-extractive movement and to include a class dynamic. As a matter of fact, Kolin Incorporated relocated the CFPP construction to a nearby village in the Basin. As mentioned by the chair of the Farmers' Union in our virtual interview in 2021: 'Once the urgent expropriation in Yırca was cancelled, the company bought the farmlands of five villages. The dwellers of those villages accepted selling their lands because they could not make money from tobacco farming.' The difference in the case of Yırca is directly related to the proletarianization and impoverishment of tobacco farmers. As the main agricultural activity in Yırca is olive farming, farmers can still earn their living from agriculture; they could resist the expropriation of their land by extractive capital. Yet, as long as tobacco farmers could not survive by cultivating their lands, they had to choose between 'dying from hunger or dying in the mines' or dying due to the ecological impacts of coal. Similarly, even though three miners of the Imbat Resistance were successful in keeping their mining jobs, both the problem of unemployment (especially for the members of oppositional trade unions and political parties) and the shortcomings of health and safety in mining and agricultural work still continue.

The limitations of the resistance movements are related to the success of labour control and discipline strategies developed by the extractive capital and the state, in other words, success of the authoritarian neoliberalism in Turkey. In fact, two decades of AKP rule in Turkey is characterized by an accumulation model built upon the exploitation of a cheap, disposable, unorganized, and depoliticized labour force. As aptly put by Bozkurt Güngen (2021), there were two fundamental conditions for the power bloc to achieve this. The first one was to keep the working classes collectively weak, reduce their organizational capacities, and thereby keep the conditions of accumulation and distribution immune from the impacts of democratic demands and constraints. The political and institutional structure inherited from the 1980 military coup, which was against organized labour, provided a favorable ground for the AKP in this respect. The second condition was to keep alive the promise of increasing the consumption capacity and improving the living conditions of the working classes. The AKP was, to a significant degree, successful in fulfilling this promise until the second half of the 2010s. Local labour control and discipline strategies in the Soma Coal Basin constitute a typical example of the AKP governments' "commitment to a workforce that has been organizationally weakened, individually disciplined, and forced to work for long hours for low wages and under precarious conditions." (Bozkurt-Güngen, 2021).

CHAPTER 6

Conclusion

This book has suggested a relational approach to the analysis of class relations in rural extractive regions. In examining the labouring populations in rural extractive regions, I adopt a class-relational approach (Pattenden, 2016), which sees class as a process, relationship, and a plural category. Therefore, on the one hand, I view the processes of dispossession and proletarianization of small-scale agricultural producers as an integral part of the class formation processes in the rural extractive regions. On the other hand, I take into-account plurality of proletarian conditions across exploitation and domination, as well as across urban/rural, agricultural/non-agricultural, land-owning/landless, and paid/unpaid. Following Bernstein's (2007; 2010) analytical framework, I define the partly dispossessed populations in rural extractive regions as classes of extractive labour.

The book has argued that natural resource extraction in the agrarian South is a multi-dimensional development strategy whose holistic analysis necessitates attention to (i) the significance of the natural resource in question for macro development plans and global value chains, (ii) the formation of the classes of extractive labour across production and social reproduction, (iii) gender division of labour within rural extractive households and rural labour markets, and (iv) labour process and control strategies in the spheres of production and social reproduction. This way, the book represents the significance of overcoming the formal externalities between (i) different scales (global, national, local), (ii) production and social reproduction, and (iii) class and gender in development studies.

Coal extraction in rural Turkey has been related to the aim of utilizing domestic resources to meet the increasing demand for electricity since the mid-2000s. This is related to the structural fragilities of the Turkish economy, especially the widened current account deficits, one of the significant reasons behind which is dependency on imported energy. The book has sought to address how the labour processes in the coal pits of the Soma Coal Basin and local labour control and discipline strategies are shaped by the strategic significance of the coal industry for the Turkish economy. The simultaneous experience of commodification of agriculture and the privatization of coal extraction and the rising significance of the coal industry in general and the coal of Soma in particular for the Turkish economy have determined the labour processes, labour control strategies, and moments of resistance in the

CONCLUSION 153

Basin since the mid-2000s. One important implication of these processes has been proletarianization of the local agricultural producers and migration to Soma from other mining regions of Turkey.

In 2014, the labour regime in the mines of Soma which is characterized by production pressure has resulted in a fatal disaster which killed 301 miners. Even though it was shown in the expert reports that one of the most significant reasons behind the disaster was the coal policies of the AKP governments and the extraction of the amount of coal beyond the mechanical capacity of the Basin, neither the coal companies not the government abandoned coal rush policies. As the state-capital-labour-nature relations determine the labour control strategies in the extractive regions and investments cannot simply be relocated due to the spatial fixity of the resources, the government and coal investors developed labour control mechanisms to sustain the rhytms of investments despite the geological limitations of the Basin.

Even though the patterns of proletarianization in the mining region are mostly elaborated on by referring merely to the transformation of agricultural producer men into miners, such a framework fails to represent the holistic picture. The experiences of women in the Soma Coal Basin exemplify the ways in which neoliberal transformation of agriculture and large-scale investments in natural resource industries in rural Turkey have restructured the imperatives of social reproduction for the classes of extractive labour. Firstly, despite the dramatic fall of the share of agriculture in the GDP and massive urbanization since the 1980s, this book shows that the neoliberal transformation in rural Turkey is a lot more complex than a simple deagrarianization process. The main transformation under neoliberalism has been a shift from a smallholder based to an agribusiness-based agrarian structure and dispossession of the small-scale farmers as a result of the decline of state support, rising production costs and falling farm incomes. Secondly, proletarianization in rural Turkey has not been straightforward, and more than 20 percent of the population is still rural. Neoliberal policies have created under-reproduced classes of rural labour who have lost non-market access to the means of production and social reproduction. Under this reproduction squeeze, rural households have relied on the combination of a multiplicity of and highly fragmented forms of rural and urban, waged and unwaged work to cope with the precarious conditions of social reproduction. In this context, the employment creation potential of the large capitalist farms that produce crops prioritized by agribusiness and the rising extractive investments in the countryside have been pivotal. Thirdly, this rural social differentiation is inherently gendered and determined by the mutual and internal relationship between production and social reproduction. On the one hand, as the classes of rural labour became unable to meet the conditions of social reproduction solely with family farming, these households searched for income diversification strategies. Although the literature on natural resource extraction largely focuses on the proletarianization of male members of these households, the case of Turkey and the Soma Coal Basin shows that reproduction squeeze of the households resulted in super-exploitation of rural women both on their own land as unpaid family workers and as extremely low-waged agricultural workers. On the other hand, new forms of working conditions of the classes of extractive labour have restructured social reproduction and intensified reproductive work of women. In this study, I referred to the category of 'miners' wives' as the producers and reproducers of the classes of extractive labour. Transformation from small-scale farmer households to miner households has restructured and intensified women's work in the reproduction of workers who work under extremely severe conditions. Therefore, women's reproductive work does not only guarantee the survival of the household but also provides the extractive capital with the opportunity of expropriating and exploiting unpaid work of women without assuming responsibility for it.

This central yet invisible role of women's labour within the classes of extractive labour is located at the intersection of capitalism and patriarchy. Capitalism owes the opportunity of expropriating and exploiting the invisible labour of women to patriarchy (Acar-Savran & Yaman, 2020) and housewife ideology (Mies, 1986). Patriarchy and housewife ideology both guarantee the conditions of continuous exploitation of women's unpaid work and determine the conditions of wage work. By naturalizing housewife ideology, capitalist patriarchy defined women's paid work as a temporary income-generating activity to support the male breadwinner of the household. This has, in turn, brought extremely precarious, informal and low-wage work of women. Eventually, capitalist patriarchy has defined women's unpaid work as activity (not as work) and paid work as supplementary work to support the male breadwinner of the family. It is this mystification what makes super-exploitation of women's unpaid work invisible and justifies low wages in their paid work (Mies, 1986).

All in all, the processes of exploitation and expropriation in Soma have had several dimensions, including expropriation of the control over agricultural production, expropriation of commons and private farmland, super-exploitation of the labour power of miners, agricultural workers, petty-commodity producers, and housewives in paid and unpaid forms, and expropriation of access to fresh air, clean water, and healthy food. As the processes of expropriation and exploitation in Soma include all these dimensions, the struggle against these should be multi-dimensional. The reason behind the failure of the resistance movements and alternative organizations attempted so far has been the limitation of their endeavour to the rights of the miners and/or conditions of employment in the mines. Yet, since the impact of neoliberalism in Soma has not been limited to the working conditions in the coal mines but has entailed the expropriation of land, dispossession and impoverishment of the small producers, over-exploitation of women and ecocide, the struggle should encompass all these processes and actors in the sphere of production and social reproduction. Therefore, the struggle for the rights of the miners should not be independent of the struggle of the farmers, land struggles, the struggle of women, and the struggle against ecocide.

Postscript: The Condition of Coal Mining and Agricultural Production Amid the Overlapping Crises in Turkey during the 2020s

In May 2024, on the tenth anniversary of the Soma Mine Disaster, I embarked on a new journey of research in the Soma Coal Basin. In our joint research with Dr. Sinem Ayhan, we aim to uncover the potential implications of just transition on coal miners, offering a new perspective. We[1] conducted interviews with the representatives of the Turkish Coal Enterprises, three managers from two coal companies, and eight coal miners working in different firms. Additionally, I did interviews with four small-scale farmers. Our joint project with Dr. Ayhan questions the dilemma between the country's dependence on fossil fuels and the policy actions in response to the European Green Deal and how this dilemma will be reflected in the coal miners in Turkey (Ayhan and Çelik, 2024). In this postscript, I will discuss the changing conditions of small-scale farmers, changing state-capital relations in the coal industry, and the condition of coal miners under the overlapping crises in the country, namely, the crises of social reproduction in the 2020s.

The prominent Marxist economist in Turkey, Korkut Boratav, in a recent interview, argued that Turkey experienced the most severe redistribution shock of its history between 2015 and 2022. Accordingly, workers lost 10.1 points of their share in the GDP over the seven years. Conversely, all forms of non-labour income have grown by the same amount. This indicates a period when capital has thrived while labour has suffered. Moreover, the workers haven't received any compensatory benefits during the AKP's neoliberal period; consumption has not been offset because real incomes have also fallen (Boratav and Aktan, 2024). Presenting a more detailed framework, Orhangazi and Yeldan (2023: 1219) explain the unequalizing characteristics of the growth impetus of the 2020s as follows:

> [L]eaving aside the issues of quality and sustainability of this achievements aside, it is clear that the patterns of growth were unequalizing and immeserizing. Wage labour has not benefited from positive rates of growth achieved thus far; and as the TurkStat data reveal, income share

---

[1] I would like to thank Dr. Sinem Ayhan for letting me include some updates from the field in this postscript.

of wage labour has fallen from 31.3 per cent in 2020 to 24.7 per cent in the fourth quarter of 2022. In contrast, capital incomes (corporate surplus) increased their share from 59.6 per cent to 67.3 per cent over the same period.

Therefore, as can be exemplified by the analyses of critical economists, the ongoing economic crisis in Turkey is characterized by deepening social and economic inequalities as a result of the depreciation of the Turkish Lira, high inflation rates, impoverishment of labouring classes in contrast to the rising share of capital in the national economy. This impoverishing growth, along with the disasters such as the pandemic and the 2023 earthquake in Southeast Turkey, has been manifested in the form of overlapping crisis in the "daily and intergenerational processes involved in producing, maintaining and reproducing labouring populations, such as the provision of food, clothing, housing, healthcare, education, and basic safety" (Bezanson and Luxton, 2006:3), i.e. in the processes of social reproduction.

In this study, I define the crisis of social reproduction by referring to the analysis of Nancy Fraser (2017, 2022), according to which different regimes of social reproduction regimes having different forms of relationship among the states, markets, and households bring different crisis tendencies under different phases of capitalism. As put by Fraser (2017: 22), social reproductive contradictions and crises are endemic to capitalism as such since, on the one hand, social reproduction is a necessary precondition for sustained accumulation; on the other hand, capitalism's need for unlimited accumulation destabilizes the patterns of social reproduction upon which it relies. The periodization of different regimes of social reproduction and their corresponding crisis tendencies indicate changing forms of the capitalist state. For example, the neoliberal regime of social reproduction is characterized by state and corporate disinvestment from social welfare and externalization of care work onto households and unpaid work of women. Yet, the neoliberal regime of social reproduction also brought a shift from the male breadwinner and female caregiver model of the household of the state-managed capitalism of the 20th century to the two-earner family through the feminization of paid workforce (Fraser, 2017, as cited in Çelik, 2023b). Therefore, there is a need to link social reproduction to the changing balances or power and contexts of production (Bakker and Silvey, 2008). As we argue elsewhere (Yalman et al., 2023), authoritarian neoliberal regime of social reproduction brought a new paradox. Accordingly, neoliberal authoritarian governments are equally committed to the neoliberal orthodoxy, while at the same time consolidating their power. In this context, the authoritarian neoliberal regime of social reproduction is characterized by the hollowed-out social reproduction roles and apparatuses of the state along with its fully employed coercive power.

The overlapping crises of the 21st century, including the pandemic, climate crisis, food crisis, wars, and the disasters such as the wildfires or catastrophic earthquake in Turkey, may differ in terms of their content and reasons, but these crises are the expressions of the structural contradictions of global capitalism and lead to even deeper crises (Çelik, 2024; Saad-Filho, 2021; Yalman,, 2021). For example, the pandemic-initiated crisis has been defined as a crisis of social reproduction (Mezzadri, 2020; Stevano et al., 2021) as it unveiled the social reproductive contradictions inherent in capitalism as such, as well as that of neoliberalism. Indeed, the current global economic and social crises have exposed a structural contradiction inherent in capitalism more clearly than ever: Capitalism is based on the production of life, it is a system that produces massive death. These crises made crystal clear that: "in the trade-off between *economic* health and *workers'* health, capitalism sides with the former, which is another way of saying that capitalism sides with death over life" (Ferguson, 2021). Similarly, overlapping crises in Turkey, including food crisis, housing crisis, care crisis, deepening income inequality, ecocide, and the February 2023 earthquakes, have revealed that, when necessary for the "economic health" of capitalism, "the working classes can die at work, from a virus, starvation, war, police brutality, air pollution caused by thermal power plants, ecological destruction, lack of water, or the collapse of their house that has been robbed of its iron in an earthquake while sleeping to prepare for the next working day" (Çelik, 2024).

In the Soma Coal Basin, along with the overall crises experienced worldwide and across the country, classes of labour are affected severely by the food crisis and deepening income inequality. In this Postscript, building upon the revisit to the Basin between May 11 and May 19, 2024, changing relations between the state, capital, and labour in the coal industry and the impact of the ongoing food crisis on the producers of food will be elaborated on.

1 Food Crises and Agricultural Production of Small-scale Farmers

Globally, the number of people facing acute food insecurity and the threat of hunger has significantly increased over the past four years. According to the data from the Food and Agricultural Organization of the United Nations (FAO, 2022a), approximately 193 million people in 53 countries were experiencing acute food insecurity in 2021. In 2020, around 3.1 billion people worldwide could not afford a sufficient and healthy diet (FAO, 2022b). The 2023 report prepared by the Global Network Against Food Crises (GNAFC) shows that the numbers continue to rise and by the end of 2022, 258 million people in 58 countries were experiencing food insecurity and the threat of hunger on a global scale (GNAFC, 2024) and this situation continued throughout 2023 (FAO, 2024).

Reports and policy programs prepared by international organizations such as the World Food Programme (WFP, 2023), World Bank (2022a), IMF, and the World Trade Organization (WTO) have so far identified the pandemic, international conflicts, and the climate crisis as the key factors triggering the global food crisis. To fight against the risk of hunger, the World Food Programme called private sector actors, high net-worth individuals, celebrities, etc., for technical assistance, knowledge transfers, financial contributions, and raising their voices. The World Bank announced a 30-billion-dollar aid package over 15 months aimed at boosting food and fertilizer production, improving food systems, facilitating greater trade and supporting vulnerable households in several Latin American and African countries. Additionally, in their Joint Statement (World Bank, 2022b), the WFP, WB, IMF, and WTO call for urgent measures to tackle food insecurity and support vulnerable groups and countries through emergency food supplies, financial aid, and increased agricultural production. The Statement also urges the international community to meet urgent financing needs and calls on governments to keep trade open and avoid restrictive measures like export bans on food or fertilizer, which worsen the plight of the most vulnerable. These international organizations view food insecurity as a supply-side issue and believe that food security can be achieved through the trickle-down effects of agricultural growth driven by the private sector (Vercillo, 2020: 237). As I argued elsewhere (2023b: 193–194):

> Even though the pandemic and the political conflicts have severely impacted the food security of the working classes worldwide, it would be wrong to consider the global food crisis as a conjunctural issue stemming from fluctuations in demand and supply. (…) Global food crises under neoliberalism, including today's food crisis, reflect the contradictions of global value relations formed under the corporate food regime since the 1980s, and they cannot simply be resolved through demand-supply management. Today's food crisis and food insecurity of the classes of (rural and urban) labour are the expressions of the structural shifts, including the development of capitalism in agriculture; the commodification of the production, circulation, distribution and consumption of food; and dispossession, impoverishment and proletarianization of small-scale farmers of the South. Therefore, its analysis necessitates attention to the

internal relationship between the social reproduction of those who cannot consume and those who cannot produce enough and healthy food.

Turkey has the highest food inflation among the OECD (Organization for Economic Co-operation and Development) countries and the fourth-highest in the world (World Bank, 2023). Accordingly, whereas the food inflation averaged 18.99 percent between 2004 and 2024, it reached 102.55 percent in November 2022. Even though it fell to 72.01 percent in December 2023 and 70.14 in May 2024, it still dramatically exceeds the thirty year average (Trading Economics, 2024). Even though the rising food prices in Turkey correspond to global crises such as the post-pandemic, the war in Ukraine, and the climate crisis, the most significant factor triggering food inflation is the rising costs of production. In fact, dependency on imported agricultural inputs, along with the fast depreciation of money in the 2020s, accelerated the rise of food prices (Demirkılıç et al., 2022).

Consequently, rising costs of production (see Figure 4) led not only to precarious conditions of food consumption but also precarious conditions of production. Therefore, today's food crisis is rooted in the agrarian change in the context of neoliberalism discussed in Chapter 3, and the rising food crisis impoverishes not only the consumers but also the producers of food. For instance, as stated by a small-scale tomato producer during our interview:

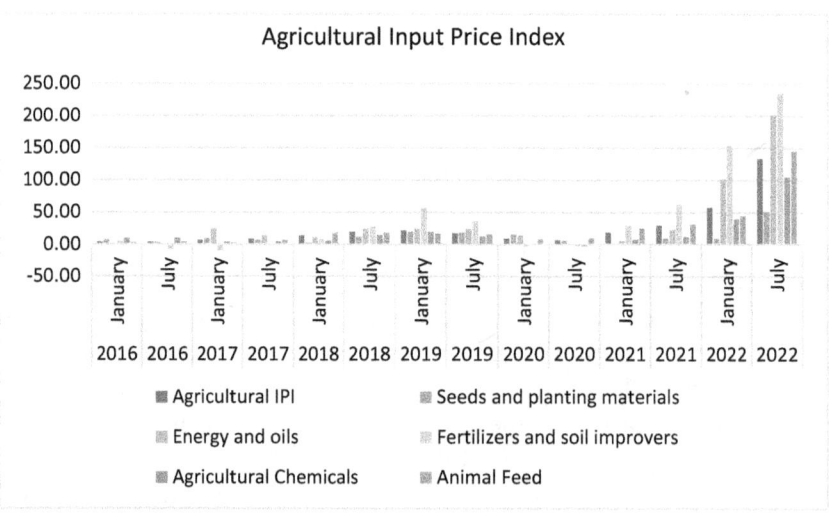

FIGURE 4 Agricultural input price index, 2016–2022
SOURCE: TURKSTAT

POSTSCRIPT 161

> No one cared about agriculture until our crisis was reflected in the cities. We have been suffering from the rising input prices since the mid-2000s. Of course, it got worse recently. But it was obvious.

It is essential to underline that farmer families mentioned their experiences of food insecurity merely by referring to the production process. The fact that they have the opportunity to produce for their own consumption puts them immune from the food inflation in their consumption processes. For example, as mentioned by an agricultural wage worker who lives in his family's village house in Kınık:

> We have no problems regarding consumption. When we plant a little bit in our garden at home, it is enough for our family for the whole summer. We have eggplants, peppers, tomatoes, etc. That is enough for us, there is no problem. We do not buy vegetables from the markets anyway. But how about those who live in the center of Soma?

In terms of the precarious conditions of food production, they mention two milestones. The first one is the neoliberal transformation of agriculture, as detailed in Chapter 4. The second one is the rising input prices in the 2020s. Even though I received limited information, during the interviews, farmers and agricultural workers underlined three major interrelated changes: rising production costs relative to farm incomes, rising indebtedness, and property transfers.

First of all, as it is frequently discussed in the food sovereignty literature (Shiva, 2016), small-scale farmers do not benefit from the rising food prices. As long as food production has increasingly become dependent upon the inputs produced and circulated by agribusiness, economic and financial crises have directly led to the rise of food prices in the 21st century. Yet, rising food prices do not benefit farmers as the cost of production also increases. For example, as explained by a tomato producer in Kınık:

> Those prices are market prices ... They do not benefit the producer at all. The costs increase even faster. The price of tomatoes in the groceries is at least 30 Turkish Liras, even 40–45 depending on the market ... If I can sell it for 10 Liras from the farm, that would be enough for me. But I can sell it for around 3 or 4 Liras. Maximum, 5 Liras ... In this way, it is a loss! And the production costs are huge! Seeds, fertilizers, diesel, chemicals, daily wages of the workers.

Secondly, as underlined in Chapter 4, several miner families used to finance the cost of agriculture with the wage income they received from mining. During the interviews, I asked if that was still possible under the rising production costs. All the interviewees argued that, for family farmers, maintaining production has not been possible without indebtedness over the last four or five years. For example, as explained by a retired miner:

> Well, my monthly retirement pension is 14 thousand Liras. Yesterday, the farmer paid 16 thousand Liras only for the workers' daily payments. I cannot do farming any longer. Well, I am retired, but it is impossible even for a miner who receives double-minimum wage. Before, I used to finance seeds, fertilizers, and diesel using my mining salary. Now, it is not possible. Everything is extremely expensive ... Only rich farmers and firms can maintain farming. Families try to maintain through bank credits, which is not sustainable, I think.

Furthermore, according to the farmers' narratives, being eligible for bank credits also became very difficult. Due to the rising production costs and falling farm incomes, banks no longer accept the land as collateral.

Thirdly, therefore, property transfer has become a dramatic issue in the Basin over the last four years. Especially, farmers whose lands have been distrained because of their mortgage are dispossessed of their lands. As frequently underlined during the interviews, small and medium-scale firms, as well as rich farmers, follow those whose lands are pledged in order to buy their lands. For example, as mentioned by a farmer:

> My uncle mortgaged his land and took out a loan. But he could not pay it back. The bank sold it through the foreclosure system. A company bought it for 90 thousand Liras. Soon, there a dam will be built near his land. It will be worth at least 10 million Liras.

Similarly:

> The number of families selling their lands increased significantly. The rich are buying up the land. And they are waiting for it ... A man who could not pay his loan, it went to foreclosure ... The bank puts his land up for sale. Well, he has nothing to do, he is indebted. A rich person or a company buys it for very low prices and makes big money through contract farming or selling it to the state for an off-farm investment such as highways.

Consequently, the current food crisis and food inflation in Turkey lead to further dispossession and impoverishment of farmer families. Until the 2020s, they could develop survival strategies by diversifying their livelihood. As an outcome of overlapping crises, including food inflation and redistribution shortcomings in the country, it is likely for them to be forced to develop new survival strategies.

2   Changing State-Capital-Labour Relations in the Coal Industry

Turkey, a significant player in global coal production, has long been heavily reliant on fossil fuels, with over three-fourths of its energy demand being met by them. This stark reality has led to a lag in the country's decarbonization efforts. However, the government has recently taken significant policy actions in response to the European Green Deal and the Carbon Border Adjustment Mechanism. By 2021, Turkey started to align itself with the European Green Deal, ratified the Paris Agreement, and committed to achieving net-zero emissions by 2053 at COP26. In late 2023, Turkey also introduced a draft of the Climate Change Law, which emphasizes the implementation of an Emissions Trading System and subsequent Carbon Market Regulation. Despite the absence of a detailed plan for phasing out fossil fuels and ensuring a just transition, Turkey's international commitments and private sector pressures to comply with the Carbon Border Adjustment Mechanism may push policymakers to accelerate decarbonization efforts and consider phasing out coal and abandoning a decade of coal rush policies (Ayhan and Çelik, 2024). In our joint research with Dr. Sinem Ayhan, we argue that for transition policies to be politically and socially acceptable, it is essential to understand the potential risks and costs to workers and communities resulting from phasing out coal. Comprehensive planning, including the necessary social protection measures, is necessary to achieve a just transition. In line with this argument, we focus on coal miners in the hard coal and lignite extraction sectors in order to reveal their potential welfare losses from leaving the coal sector. In order to do that, we combine descriptive evidence from the administrative data of the Entrepreneur Information System and qualitative fieldwork. A detailed analysis of just transition exceeds the limits of this book. Instead, in this part of the postscript, I will discuss the implications of a possible phasing out of coal in the Soma Coal Basin and the impact of the ongoing economic crisis on coal companies and coal miners by referring to the interviews.

The most striking change in terms of the state-capital relations in the coal industry has been the removal of royalty tender and, therefore, the guarantee of purchase provided by Turkish Coal Enterprises for the coal companies. As explained in Chapter 3, the state, as the sole customer of coal, was buying all the extracted coal irrespective of its amount. The state no longer signs royalty tender with the coal companies; instead, the license of the mines is transferred to the coal companies, and they are expected to sell only certain amounts of the extracted coal to the state. This amount is determined in accordance with the size of the pit and the terms and conditions included in the contract. A representative from Turkish Coal Enterprises (TKI) explained why they no longer prefer royalty tender by referring to the Soma Mine Disaster and mentioned the legal burdens stemming from the royalty tender. In fact, in 2024, a new prosecution process for the disaster started, in which some of the public personnel of the TKI were also among the defendants. As explained by a representative of the TKI:

> In the past, there was a royalty tender system. We have now moved to the license transfer system. The mining law says that the license holder is also responsible as an operator. We have started to be held jointly responsible for all accidents, all deaths, disabilities, and injuries. This has become a great burden for both the state and our institution.

During our interviews with deputy general managers from two coal companies, they did not mention a malcontent stemming from the lack of guarantee of purchase, yet they mentioned the insecure conditions of coal firms because of the economic crisis in the country, specifically high inflation rates and depreciation of money. In fact, one of the deputy general managers mentioned that, in 2020 and 2021, they made significant gains because of the rising energy and coal prices in the world and how it was more profitable to sell their coal in the market instead of selling the whole product to the state. Yet, especially due to the high inflation rates in the company and the condition of global energy markets, the removal of royalty tender has turned into a significant barrier for the coal companies to make profits. For example, as explained by a deputy general manager of one of the coal companies:

> The removal of royalty tender is of course a disadvantage for us. Even if some freedom is granted, even if the free market is an advantage under normal conditions; the current state of the coal market is evident. When we first started, only TKI (Turkish Coal Enterprises) was buying the coal. We said that we wanted to open up to international markets. At that time, cement factories and power plants were also buying the coal we produced from TKI. To be honest, we experienced a golden age when

energy and coal prices rose during the pandemic. But now, energy prices are falling worldwide. Inflation in Turkey is obvious … Since imported coal is cheaper, power plants have started to prefer coal from Ukraine, for example. What happened to energy supply security? The state should impose restrictions on imports. Power plants are buying cheaply from abroad. Who am I going to sell the coal extracted?

Another very important transformation in terms of the state, capital, and labour relations in the coal industry is related to the government's austerity plans to cope with the ongoing crisis. A couple of days before my visit to the Basin, the Minister of Finance announced the Savings and Efficiency Plan in the Public sector, which includes a variety of plans to cut costs and improve fiscal discipline for the next three years. Even though there is no explicit statement regarding the coal industry, the representatives of the coal companies mentioned the fact that they could not receive their annual state subsidy in 2024, and that could be related to the government's plan to cut its spending. As mentioned in Chapter 3, after the Soma Mine Disaster, the minimum wage level in the underground coal pits has become double the minimum wage. According to the statements of the deputy general managers of the coal companies, the government was supporting them by paying around half of the labour costs, and for the first time, in 2024, they did not receive any payments. For example:

> After the Soma accident, the government made some regulations. They told us to pay at least twice the minimum wage to the miners. Well, these are good things. We are not against decent payment. However, the then government said, I increased your costs, so I will support you. And this support continued untik December 2023. It is now May, 2024, it is still unclear whether the support will be provided or not. It looks like, as coal producers, we are caught up in the government's austerity measures. Now, both zero-duty imported coal is entering the Turkish market; they said the current account deficit should be reduced, but they do not cover the costs they themselves increased. So, looks like the government is going to bankrupt us. This is the most important problem for the coal industry now. Our highest cost is labour cost. And there are concerns whether the government will keep supporting us or not. Our employees are also stressed out. They have always known that we receive support from the government. They also know that we are facing financial difficulties because of the removal of supports. We have survived thanks to

the state support, our employees know this. Our uncertainty gives them future anxiety as well.

As a matter of fact, during the interviews with the miners, they mentioned the existence of redundancies and their fear about that. Just like it was mentioned during the main phases of my fieldwork, mining still constitutes the most tempting job opportunity for the local population. Similarly, their biggest concern is still the sustainability of coal subsidies for the investors in order for them to secure their employment. Almost all the miners mentioned the possible unrest that would occur in the basin if coal mining would be phased out.

3 Conclusion

Both the agriculture and coal industries are severely impacted by the crisis conditions in the country. In fact, for the first time since 2002, the Justice and Development Party lost elections in the Soma Coal Basin in the local elections of March 2024. The main opposition party, Republican People's Party won the municipal elections. Furthermore, on May 29, 2024, the Maden Iş union, which has had close relations with the companies and the government since the mid-2000s, organized a protest with the workers, representatives of coal companies, and the mayor of Soma. Under the slogan of "the state should protect its miners!" they protested the use of imported coal by underlining that it would lead to unemployment. They called on the government to put restrictions on coal imports and bring the former support for domestic coal back.

All in all, despite the experience of a fatal disaster, injuries of many workers, shortcomings regarding the health and safety measures in the coalmines, expropriation of farmlands, and ecological destruction of coal such as air pollution, water pollution, and land degradation, miners in Soma still tend to defend their employment in the mines. On the one hand, this is a clear outcome of lack alternative means of living in the region in agriculture or in other sectors. On the other hand, this shows that authoritarian neoliberalism in Turkey is not limited to the AKP government and the leadership of Erdoğan. In contrast, as part of the power bloc, the main opposition does not offer an alternative to the authoritarian neoliberal accumulation and political regime.

References

Acar, S., Kitson, L., and Bridle, R. (2015) Türkiye'de Kömür ve Yenilenebilir Enerji Teşvikleri. *Global Studies Initiative Report*. Retrieved from: https://www.iisd.org/gsi/sites/default/files/ffsandrens_turkey_coal_tk.pdf (Accessed 20.12.2023).

Acar, S., Challe, S., Christopoulos, S., and Christo, G. (2018) Fossil fuel subsidies as a lose-lose: Fiscal and environmental burdens in Turkey. *New Perspectives on Turkey* 58: 93–124.

Acar, S. and Kızılkaya, S. (2021) Türkiye'de Kömüre Dayalı Istihdamın ve Ekonominin Analizi. *Climate Action Network (CAN) Europe*. Retrieved from: https://caneurope.org/content/uploads/2021/11/Komure-Dayali-Istihdam-ve-Ekonomi_CAN-Europe.pdf (Accessed 27.05.2024).

Acar, S. and Yeldan, E. (2016) Environmental impacts of coal subsidies in Turkey: A general equilibrium analysis. *Energy Policy* 90: 1–15.

Acar-Savran, G. and Yaman, M. (2020) Kapitalizm ile Ataerkinin Kesişiminde Kadın Emeği. *Praksis* 52: 9–34.

Adaman, F. and Akbulut, B. (2021) Erdoğan's three-pillared neoliberalism: authoritarianism, populism, and developmentalism. *Geoforum* 124: 279–289.

Adaman, F., Arsel, M., and Akbulut, B. (2019) Neoliberal developmentalism, authoritarian populism, and extractivism in the countryside: The Soma mining disaster in Turkey. *The Journal of Peasant Studies* 46(3): 514–536.

Akbulut, B. (2019) The 'state' of degrowth: Economic growth and the making of state hegemony in Turkey. *Nature and Space* 2(3): 513–527.

Akgöz, G. and Balta, E. (2015) Kapitalizmin Krizine Toplumsal Cinsiyet Perspektifinden Bakmak: Analitik Bir Çerçeve Önerisi. *Hacettepe Üniversitesi Sosyolojik Araştırmalar E-Dergisi* 1–17.

Akram-Lodhi, H. and Kay, C. (2009) The agrarian question: peasants and rural change. In Akram-Lodhi, H. and Kay, H. (eds.) *Peasants and Globalization: Political economy, rural transformation and the agrarian question* (pp. 3–34). New York: Routledge.

Alavi, H. and Shanin, T. (1988) Introduction to the English Edition: Peasantry and Capitalism. In Kautsky, K. *Agrarian Question*. London: Zwen.

Albo, G. (2013) Capital, crisis and state economic policy: a neoliberal exit. In Karaagac, B. (ed) *Accumulations, Crises, Struggles: Capital and Labour in Contemporary Capitalism* (pp 13–38). Berlin: LIT.

Ali, M. Y., Shahrier, M., Kafy, A. A. Ara, I., Javed, A. Fattah, M. A. Rahaman, Z. A. Tripura, K. (2023)., ... (2023) Environmental Impact Assessment of Tobacco Farming in Northern Bangladesh. *Heliyon* 9(3).

Angın, M. and Bedirhanoğlu, P. (2012) Privatization processes as ideological moments: the block sales of largescale state enterprises in Turkey in the 2000s. *New Perspectives on Turkey* 47: 139–167.

Araghi, F. (1995) Global Depeasantization, 1945–1990. *Sociological Quarterly* 36(2): 337–368.

Araghi, F. (2000) The Great Global Enclosure of Our Times: Peasants and the Agrarian Question at the Beginning of the Twenty-First Century. In Magdoff, F., Foster, J. B., and Buttel, F. H. (eds.) *Hungry for Profit: The Agribusiness Threat to Farmers, Food, and the Environment* (pp. 145–160). Monthly Review Press.

Araghi, F. (2009a) The invisible hand and the visible foot: peasants, dispossession and globalization. In Akram-Lodhi, H. and Kay, H. (eds.) *Peasants and Globalization: Political economy, rural transformation and the agrarian question* (pp. 111–147). New York: Routledge.

Araghi, F. (2009b) Accumulation by Displacement: Global Enclosures, Food Crisis, and the Ecological Contradictions of Capitalism. *Review* 32(1): 113–146.

Arsel, M., Akbulut, B., and Adaman, F. (2015) Environmentalism of the malcontent: anatomy of an anti-coal power plant struggle in Turkey. *The Journal of Peasant Studies* 42(2): 371–395.

Arsel, M., Adaman, F., and Saad-Filho, A. (2021) Authoritarian developmentalism: The latest stage of neoliberalism? *Geoforum* 124: 261–266.

Atkinson, P. and Hammersley, M. (1994) Ethnography and Participant Observation. In Denzin, N. K. and Lincoln, Y. S. (eds.) *Handbook of Qualitative Research* (pp. 248–261). Thousand Oaks: Sage Publications.

Aydın, Z. (1986) Kapitalizm, Tarım Sorunu ve Azgelişmiş Ülkeler 1. *Onbirinci Tez* 3: 126–156.

Aydın, Z. (2002) The new right, structural adjustment and Turkish agriculture: Rural responses and survival strategies. *The European Journal of Development Research* 14(2): 183–208.

Aydın, Z. (2010) Neo-liberal transformation of Turkish agriculture. *Journal of Agrarian Change* 10(2): 149–187.

Aydın, Z. (2022) Türkiye Tarımında Kriz ve Finansallaşma: El Koyma Yoluyla Birikim ve Toprak Gaspı. In Topal, A., Birler, Ö., Çelik, C., and Göksel, A. (eds.) *21. Yüzyılda Devletin Dönüşümü: Otoriterleşme, Kriz ve Hegemonya (Galip Yalman'a Armağan)* (pp. 225–255). Ankara: Imge Publishing.

Ayelazuno, J. A. (2014) The 'new extractivism' in Ghana: A critical review of its development prospects. *The Extractive Industries and Society* 1(2): 292–302.

Ayers, A. J. and Saad-Filho, A. (2015) Democracy Against Neoliberalism: Paradoxes, Limitations, Transcendence. *Critical Sociology* 44(4–5): 597–618.

Ayhan, S. and Çelik, C. (2024) *Unveiling the Just Transition: Policy Implications and Descriptive Data Insights for Coal Miners in Türkiye.* Sabancı University, Istanbul Policy

Centre (IPC), IPC-Mercator Analysis. Retrieved from: https://ipc.sabanciuniv.edu/Content/Images/CKeditorImages/20240516-11054259.pdf (Accessed: 27.05.2024).

Aysu, A. and Kayalıoğlu, M. S. (2014) Sunuş. In Aysu, A. and Kayalıoğlı M. S. (eds.) *Köylülükten Sonra Tarım: Osmanlı'dan Günümüze Çiftçinin Ilgası ve Şirketleşme* (pp. 11–16). Ankara: Epos Yayınları.

Baglioni, E. (2018) Labour control and the labour question in global production networks: exploitation and disciplining in Senegalese export horticulture. *Journal of Economic Geography* 18(1): 111–137.

Baglioni, E. (2022) The making of cheap labour across production and reproduction: Control and resistance in the Senegalese horticultural value chain. *Work, Employment and Society* 36(3): 445–464.

Baglioni, E. (2023) Some reflections on the capitalist labour process, nature, and social reproduction. *Sociologia Del Lavoro* 167: 9–32.

Baglioni, E. and Campling, L. (2017) Natural resource industries as global value chains: frontiers, fetishism, and the state. *Environment and Planning A: Economy and Space* 49(11): 2437–2456.

Baglioni, E. and Mezzadri, A. (2020) Labour Control Regimes and Social Reproduction: Some Reflections on the Strengths and Weaknesses of an Evolving Framework. In Hammer, A. and Fishwick, A. (eds.) *The Political Economy of Work in the Global South* (pp. 115–129). London: Macmillan.

Baglioni, E., Campling, L., Mezzadri, A., Miyamura, S., Pattenden, J. and Selwyn, B. (2022) Exploitation and labour regimes: production, circulation, social reproduction, ecology. In Baglioni, E., Campling, L., Coe, N. M. and Smith, A. (eds.) *Labour Regimes and Global Production* (pp. 81–99). Newcastle upon Tyne: Agenda Publishing.

Bağımsız Sosyal Bilimciler (BSB) (2015) *AKP'li Yıllarda Emeğin Durumu*. Istanbul: Yordam Kitap.

Bakker, I. And Silvey, R. (2008) Introduction: social reproduction and global transformations – from the everyday to the global. In Bakker, I. And Silvey, R. (eds.) *Beyond States and Markets: The challenges of social reproduction* (pp. 1–15). New York: Routledge.

Banaji, J. (1977) Capitalist domination and the small peasantry. Deccan Districts in the late 19th century. *Economic and Political Weekly* 12(33–34): 1375–1404.

Banaji, J. (2002) The metamorphoses of agrarian capitalism. *Journal of Agrarian Change* 2(1): 96–119.

Banaji, J. (2003) The fictions of free labour: contract, coercion and the so-called unfree labour. *Historical Materialism* 11(3): 69–95.

Banaji, J. (2012) Mode of production. In Fine, B., Saad-Filho, A. and Boffo, M. (eds.) *The Elgar Companion to Marxist Economics* (pp. 227–232). Cheltenham: Edward Elgar Publishing.

Barrios de Chungara, D. and Viezzer, M. (1978) *Let me speak: Testimony of Domitila, a woman of the Bolivian mines* (Translated by Ortiz, V.). New York: Monthly Review Press.

Benlisoy, F. (2021) *Kapitalist Kıyamet: Sermaye mi Dünya mı?* İstanbul: Habitus Kitap.

Bennholdt-Thomsen, V. (1982) Subsistence production and extended reproduction. A contribution to the discussion about modes of production. *The Journal of Peasant Studies* 9(4): 241–254.

Bernstein, H. (1977) Notes on capital and peasantry. *Review of African Political Economy* 10: 60–73.

Bernstein, H. (2001) 'The peasantry' in global capitalism: Who, where, why. *Socialist Register* 37: 25–51.

Bernstein, H. (2007) *Capital and labour from centre to margins.* Keynote speech at the conference "Living on the Margins" Stellenbosch University (26–28 March).

Bernstein, H. (2009) V. I. Lenin and A. V. Chayanov: looking back, looking forward. *The Journal of Peasant Studies* 36(1): 55–81.

Bernstein, H. (2010) *Class Dynamics of Agrarian Change.* London: Fernwood Publishing.

Bezanson, K. and Luxton, M. (2006) Introduction: Social reproduction and feminist political economy. In Bezanson, K. and Luxton, M. (eds.) *Social Reproduction: Feminist Political Economy Challenges Neoliberalism* (pp. 3–11). Montreal and Kingston: McGill-Queens University Press.

Bhaduri, A. (1973) A study on agricultural backwardness under semi-feudalism. *The Economic Journal* 329(83): 120–137.

Bhanumathi, K. (2002) The status of women affected by mining in India. In Macdonals, I. and Rowland, C. (eds.) *Tunnel vision: Women, mining, and communities.* Oxfam Community Aid Abroad. Retrieved from: https://www.oxfam.org.au/wp-content/uploads/2011/11/OAus-TunnelVisionWomenMining-1102.pdf (Accessed: 21.12.2023).

Bloomberg New Energy and Finance (BNEF) and World Wide Fund for Nature (WWF) Turkey (2014) Türkiye'nin Değişen Elektrik Piyasaları Raporu. Retrieved from: https://tenva.org/wp-content/uploads/2014/12/Bloomberg-Turkiye-Elektrik-Piyasasi-Raporu.pdf (Accessed: 20.12.2023).

Boffo, M., Saad-Filho, A., and Fine, B. (2019) Neoliberal Capitalism: The Authoritarian Turn. *Socialist Register* 55: 247–270.

Bonefeld, W. (2011) Primitive Accumulation and Capitalist Accumulation: Notes on Social Constitution and Expropriation. *Science and Society* 75(3): 379–399.

Bonefeld, W. (2014) Kapitalist Birikim ve Özgür Emek: Toplumsal Kuruluş Üzerine. In Göztepe, Ö. (ed.) *İlkel Birikim: Sermayenin Kaldıracı* (pp. 65–87). Ankara: Notabene.

Bor, Ö. (2014) Yeni Tarım Düzeni. In Aysu, A. And Kayalıoğlu, M. S. (eds.) *Köylülükten Sonra Tarım: Osmanlı'dan Günümüze Çiftçinin Ilgası ve Şirketleşme* (pp. 82–121). Ankara: Epos Yayınları.

Boratav, K. (2004) *Tarımsal Yapılar ve Kapitalizm*. Ankara: İmge.

Boratav, K. (2010) *Türkiye İktisat Tarihi: 1908–2010*. Ankara: İmge Kitabevi.

Boratav, K. and Aktan, İ. (2024) Muhalif kitle örgüt bulamayınca lider arıyor. Interview with Korkut Boratav. *Artı Gerçek* Retrieved from: https://artigercek.com/makale/korkut-boratav-muhalif-kitle-orgut-bulamayinca-lider-ariyor-306696 (Accesssed: 12.06.2024.).

Bozkurt-Güngen, S. (2017) Labour markets, labour relations and the state: a comparative – historical analysis of Argentina and Turkey, 2001–2015. Unpublished Ph.D. dissertation. Ankara: Middle East Technical University, Institute for Social Sciences.

Bozkurt-Güngen, S. (2018) Labour and authoritarian neoliberalism: Changes and continuities under the AKP governments in Turkey. *South European Society and Politics* 23(2): 219–238.

Bozkurt-Güngen, S. (2021) AKP'nin emek rejimi, otoriterleşme ve Türkiye'nin zombie neoliberalizmi. Retrieved from: https://textumdergi.net/akpnin-emek-rejimi-otoriterlesme-ve-turkiyenin-zombi-neoliberalizmi/ (Accessed: 13.04.2024).

Brass, T. (1999) *Towards a political economy of unfree labour: case studies and debates*. London: Routledge.

Brass, T. (2010) Unfree labour as primitive accumulation? *Capital and Class* 35(1): 23–38.

Braverman, H. (1974) *Labour and monopoly capital: The degradation of work in the twentieth century*. New York: Monthly Review Press.

Bridge, G. (2008) Global production networks and the extractive sector: governing resource-based development. *Journal of Economic Geography* 8(3): 839–419.

Bruff, I. (2014) The rise of authoritarian neoliberalism. *Rethinking Marxism* 26(1): 113–129.

Bruff, I. and Tansel, C B. (2019) Authoritarian neoliberalism: trajectories of knowledge production and praxis. *Globalizations* 16(3): 233–244.

Burawoy, M. (1976) The functions and reproduction of Migrant Labor: comparative material from Southern Africa and the United States. *American Journal of Sociology* 81(5): 1050–1087.

Burawoy, M. (1979) *Manufacturing Consent: Changes in the Labour Process under Monopoly Capitalism*. Chicago: University of Chicago Press.

Burawoy, M. (1985) *Politics of production: Factory regimes under capitalism and socialism*. London: Verso.

Burkett, P. (1999) *Marx and Nature: A Red and Green Perspective*. Chicago: Haymarket Books.

Bütün, O. (2015) *Yedi Kat Yerin Altından Uğultular Geliyor: Yeni Çeltek'ten Soma'ya Maden İşçileri*. Ankara: Dinpot Yayınevi.

Byres, T. (1991) Agrarian question and differing forms of capitalist agrarian transition: An essay with reference to Asia. In Breman, J. and Mundle, S. (eds.) *Rural Transformation in Asia* (pp. 3–76). Delhi: Oxford University Press.

Byres, T. (2012) The Agrarian Question and Peasantry. In Fine, B., Saad-Filho, A. and Boffo, M. (eds.) *The Elgar Companion to Marxist Economics* (pp. 19–15). Cheltenham: Edward Elgar Publishing.

Cardoso, A. and Turhan, E. (2018) Examining new geographies of coal: dissenting energyscapes in Colombia and Turkey. *Applied Energy* 224: 398–408.

Çelik, A. (2012) Sendikal Ayrımcılık ve Yasaklar Manzumesi. Retrieved from: http://www.kesk.org.tr/2012/10/30/sendikal-ayrimcilik-ve-yasaklar-manzumesi/ (accessed 21.12.2021).

Çelik, A. (2015) Turkey's new labour regime under the Justice and Development Party in the first decade of the twenty-first century: Authoritarian flexibilization. *Middle Eastern Studies* 51(4): 618–635.

Çelik, C. (2017) Kırsal Dönüşüm ve Metalaşan Yaşamlar: Soma Havzasında İşçileşme Süreçleri ve Sınıf İlişkileri. *Praksis* 43(1): 785–810.

Çelik, C. (2019) Extractive industries and changing means of rural livelihood: patterns of proletarianization and labour processes in Soma coal basin. Unpublished Ph.D. Dissertation, Middle East Technica University, Ankara, Turkey.

Çelik, C. (2021) The making of the rural proletariat in neoliberal Turkey. In Şahin, E. C. and Erol, M. E. (eds.) *The Condition of the working class in Turkey: Labour under neoliberal authoritarianism* (pp. 116–134). London: Pluto Press.

Çelik, C. (2023a) Extractivism and Labour Control: Reflections of 'Turkey's Coal Rush' in Local Labour Regimes. *Critical Sociology* 49(1): 59–76.

Çelik, C. (2023b) Global food insecurity as a crisis of social reproduction for the classes of labour. *Human Geography* 16(2): 193–199.

Çelik, C. (2023c) The social reproduction of natural resource extraction and gendered labour regimes in rural Turkey. *Journal of Agrarian Change* DOI: https://doi.org/10.1111/joac.12535.

Çelik, C. (2024) Disaster capitalism, women's labour and class struggle. *Çatlak Zemin* https://en.catlakzemin.com/disaster-capitalism-womens-labor-and-class-struggle/ (Accessed: 10.06.2024).

Çelik, C. and Erkuş-Öztürk, H. (2016) Role of precariousness and space on class formation process: The case of Antalya's tourism workers. *Capital and Class* 40(3): 419–445.

Çınar, S. (2014) *Öteki Proletarya: De-Proletarizasyon ve Mevsimlik Tarım İşçileri.* Ankara: Notabene.

Dalla Costa, M. (1995) Capitalism and reproduction. In Bonefeld, W., Holloway, J., and Psychopedis, J. (eds.) *Open Marxism Volume III (Emancipating Marx)* (pp. 7–16). London: Pluto Press.

Dalla Costa, M. and James, S. (1972) The Power of Women and Subversion of the Community. Retrieved from: https://libcom.org/article/power-women-and-subversion-community-mariarosa-dalla-costa-and-selma-james (23.12.2023).

De Angelis, M. (2001) Marx and Primitive Accumulation: The Continuous Character of Capital's "Enclosures." *The Commoner* No: 2.

REFERENCES

Deere, C. D. (2005) *The Feminization of Agriculture? Economic Restructuring in Rural Latin America*. Occasional Paper No.1 Geneva: United Nations Research Institute for Social Development. Retrieved from: https://www.unrisd.org/en/library/publications/the-feminization-of-agriculture-economic-restructuring-in-rural-latin-america (Accessed: 21.12.2023).

Değirmenci, S. (2021) *Türkiye'de Tarım Kapitalistleşirken: Talepler ve Yasalar*. Istanbul: Sosyal Araştırmalar Vakfı.

Demirkılıç, S., Özertan, G., and Tekgüç, H. (2022) The evolution of unprocessed food inflation in Turkey: an exploratory study on select products. *New Perspectives on Turkey* 67: 57–82.

Denzin, N. and Lincoln, Y. (2003) *Collecting and Interpreting Qualitative Materials*. London: Sage.

Düzgün, H. S. and Yaylacı, E. D. (2016) An evaluation of Soma underground coal mine disaster with respect to risk acceptance and risk perception. In *3rd International Symposium on Mine Safety Science and Engineering* (pp. 368–374). Montreal, Canada, 13–19 August 2016. Montreal: McGill University.

Düzgün, H. S. and Leveson, N. (2018) Analysis of Soma mine disaster using causal analysis based on systems theory. *Safety Science* 110: 37–57.

Ellem, B. (2006) Scaling Labour: Australian Unions and Global Mining. *Work, Employment and Society* 20(2): 369–387.

Ellem, B. (2016) Geographies of the Labour Process: Automation and Spatiality of Mining. *Work, Employment and Society* 30(6): 932–948.

Ellis, F. (1998) Household Strategies and Rural Livelihood Diversification. *The Journal of Development Studies* 35(1): 1–38.

Elson, D. (1998) The economic, the political, and the domestic: Businesses, states, and households in the organisation of production. *New Political Economy* 3(2): 189–208..

Elson, D. (2010) Gender and the global economic crisis in developing countries: a framework for analysis. *Gender and Development* 18(2): 201–212.

Engels, F. (1950) *Peasant Question in France and Germany*. Moscow: Progress Publishers.

Ercan, F. and Oğuz, Ş. (2015) From Gezi resistance to Soma Massacre: capital accumulation and class struggle in Turkey. *Socialist Register* 51: 114–135.

Ercan, H. (2007) *Youth Unemployment in Turkey*. International Labour Office: Ankara, Turkey.

Ercan, M. R. and Öniş, Z. (2001) Turkish Privatization: Institutions and Dilemmas. *Turkish Studies* 2(1): 109–134.

Erdinç, I. (2014) AKP Döneminde Sendikal Alanın Yeniden Yapılanması ve Kutuplaşma: Hak-İş ve Ötekiler. *Çalışma ve Toplum* 41: 155–174.

Eren, Z. C. (2019) Gendered Rural Transformation and Peasant Workers: The Case of the Women of the Greenhouse, Western Anatolia, Turkey. Unpublished Ph.D. Dissertation. Middle East Technical University, Ankara: Turkey.

Eren, Z. C. (2022) Rising Authoritarian Neoliberalism in Rural Turkey: Change and Negotiation of Women ina Gendered Agribusiness in Western Anatolia. In Borsuk, I., Dinç, P., Kavak, S. ve Sayan, P. (eds.) *Authoritarian Neoliberalism and Resistance in Turkey: Construction, Consolidation, and Contestation* (pp. 61–80). New York: Palgrave Macmillan.

Erensü, S. (2017) Turkey's hydropower renaissance: Nature, neoliberalism, and development in the cracks of infrastructure. In Adaman, F., Akbulut, B., and Arsel, M. (eds.) *Neoliberal Turkey and its Discontents: Economic Policy and the Environment under Erdoğan* (pp. 120–146). London and New York: I.B. Tauris.

Erensü, S. (2018a) Powering neoliberalization: Energy and politics in the making of a new Turkey. *Energy Research and Social Science* 41: 148–157.

Erensü, S. (2018b) The contradictions of Turkey's rush to energy. Retrieved from: https://merip.org/2018/12/the-contradictions-of-turkeys-rush-to-energy/ (Accessed: 20.12.2023).

Erensü, S., Evren, E., and Aksu, C. (2016) Giriş: Yeğin Sular Daim Engine Akar. In Aksu, C., Erensü, S. and Evren, E. (eds.) *Sudan Sebepler: Türkiye'de Su-Enerji Politikaları ve Direnişler* (pp. 9–33). Istanbul: İletişim Yayınları.

Eres, B. (2007) Economic Policy Regimes and the Profitability: The Turkish Economy, 1968–2000. In Köse, A. H., Şenses, F., and Yeldan E. (eds.) *Neoliberal Globalization as New Imperialism: Case Studies on Reconstruction of the Periphery* (pp. 115–127). New York: Nova Science Publishers.

Ergün, İ. (1997) *Soma Belediyesi Tanıtım Kitabı*. İzmir: NEŞA Ofset.

Ersoy, N. (2015) Giriş: İşleneceğini Herkesin Bildiği Bir Cinayetin Öyküsü. In *Boğaziçi Üniversitesi Soma Araştırma Grubu Raporu*. Retrieved from: https://busomarastirmagrubu.bogazici.edu.tr/sites/default/files/calismaraporu (Accessed: 20.12.2023).

Ertürk-Keskin, N. and Yaman, M. (2013) *Türkiye'de Tütün: Reji'den Tekel'e Tekel'den Bugüne*. Ankara: Notabene.

Erwiza, E. (2002) *Hidden Stories: Gender, Family, and Community in the Ombilin Coalmines (1892–1965)*. Clara Working Paper No: 13, Amsterdam.

FAO (2022a) Global Report on Food Crises: Joint Analysis for Better Decisions. Retrieved from: https://www.fao.org/3/cb9997en/cb9997en.pdf. (Accessed: 08.06.2024).

FAO (2022b) The State of Food Security and Nutrition in the World. Retrieved from: https://www.fao.org/3/cb9997en/cb9997en.pdf. (Accessed 08.06.2024).

FAO (2024) The State of Food Security and Nutrition in the World. Retrieved from: https://openknowledge.fao.org/items/09ed8fec-480e-4432-832c-5b56c672edg2 (Accessed 08.10.2024)

Federici, S. (2004) *Caliban and the Witch: Women, The Body and Primitive Accumulation*. New York: Autonomedia.

Federici, S. (2012) *Revolution at point zero: Housework, reproduction and feminist struggle*. New York: PM Press.

Federici, S. (2014) Notes on Elder-Care Work and the Limits of Marxism. *Beyond Marx: Theorising the Global Labour Relations of the Twenty-First Century* (pp. 239–250). Leiden and Boston: Brill.

Federici, S. (2021) *Patriarchy of the Wage: Notes on Marx, Gender, and Feminism*. New York: PM Press.

Ferguson, S. (2021) Life-Making or Death-Making?. *Midnight Sun Magazine* Retrieved from: https://www.midnightsunmag.ca/life-making-or-death-making/ (Accessed 02.06.2024).

Ferguson, S. and McNally, D. (2015) Precarious migrants: gender, race and the social reproduction of a Global Working Class. *Socialist Register* 51: 1–23.

Fine, B. (1994) Coal, diamonds and oil: toward a comparative theory of mining? *Review of Political Economy* 6(3): 279–302.

Fine, B. and Saad-Filho, A. (2016) Thirteen Things You Need to Know about Neoliberalism. *Critical Sociology* 43(4–5): 1–22.

Fortunati, L. (1995) *Arcane of Reproduction: Housework, Prostitution, Labor and Capital*. New York: Autonomedia.

Fraser, N. (2017) Crisis of care? On the social-reproductive contradictions of contemporary capitalism. In Bhattacharya, T. (ed.) *Social reproduction theory: Remapping class, recentring oppression* (pp. 21–36). London: Pluto Press.

Fraser, N. (2022) *Cannibal Capitalism: How our System is Devouring Democracy, Care, and the Planet and What We Can Do About It?* London: Verso.

Freidberg, S. (2001) On the trail of the global green bean. *Global Networks* 1(4): 353–368.

Friedmann, H. (1992) Distance and durability: Shaky foundations of the world food economy. *Third World Quarterly* 13(2): 371–383.

Friedmann, H. (1993) The Political Economy of Food: A Global Crisis. *New Left Review* 197: 29–57.

Friedmann, H. (2006) Focusing on Agriculture: A Comment on Henry Bernstein's 'Is There an Agrarian Question in the 21st Century?.' *Canadian Journal of Development Studies* 27(4): 461–465.

Gacal, F. and Stauffer, A. (2018) *Toolkit: Coal power generation and health in three regions of Turkey; Çanakkale, İzmir, and Tekirdağ*. Istanbul: Printworld Matbaa. Retrieved from:https://www.env-health.org/IMG/pdf/20180223_heal_toolkit_turkey_coal_power_plants_health_izmir_canakkale_tekirdag.pdf (Accessed: 21.12.2023).

Glassman, J. (2006) Primitive Accumulation, Accumulation by Dispossession, Accumulation by "Extra-Economic" Means. *Progress in Human Geography* 30(5): 608–625.

Global Network Against Food Crisis (GNAFC) (2024) Financing Flows and Food Crises Report. Retrieved From: https://www.fightfoodcrises.net/fileadmin/user_upload/fightfoodcrises/doc/resources/Financing_Flows_and_Food_Crises_Report_2023.pdf (Accessed: 04.06.2024).

Gough, J. (2003) *Work locality and the rhythms of capital.* London: Continuum.

Günaydın, G. (2009) Türkiye Tarım Politikalarında 'Yapısal Uyum': 2000'li Yıllar. *Mülkiye Dergisi* 3(162): 175–221.

Gürel, B. (2011) Agrarian change and labour supply in Turkey, 1950–1980. *Journal of Agrarian Change* 11(2): 195–219.

Gürel, B. (2014) Türkiye'de Kırda Sınıf Mücadelelerinin Tarihsel Gelişimi. In Savran, S., Tanyılmaz, K., and Tonak, E. A. (eds.) *Marksizm ve Sınıflar: Dünyada ve Türkiye'de Sınıflar ve Mücadeleleri* (pp. 303–385). Istanbul: Yordam Kitap.

Gürel, B. Küçük, B., and Taş, S. (2019) The rural roots of the Justice and Development Party in Turkey. *The Journal of Peasant Studies* 46(3): 457–479.

Harriss-White, B. (2005) Commercialisation, commodification, and gender relations in post-harvest systems for rice in South Asia. *Economic and Political Weekly* 40: 2530–2542.

Hartmann, H. (1976) Capitalism, Patriarchy, and Job Segregation by Sex. *Signs* 1(3): 137–169.

Harvey, D. (2003) *The New Imperialism.* Oxford: Oxford University Press.

Herod, A., Rainnie, A., and McGrath-Champ, S. (2007) Working space: why incorporating the geographical is central to theorizing work and employment practices. *Work, Employment and Society* 21(2): 247–264.

Hobsbawm, E. (1984) *Worlds of Labour: Further Studies in the History of Labour.* London: Weidenfeld and Nicolson.

Islamoğlu, H. (2017) The Politics of Agricultural Production in Turkey. In Adaman, F., Akbulut, B., and Arsel, M. (eds.) *Neoliberal Turkey and its Discontents: Economic Policy and Environment under Erdoğan* (pp. 75–102). London and New York: I. B. Tauris.

Islar, M. (2012) Privatised hydropower development in Turkey: a case of water grabbing? *Water Alternatives* 5(2): 376–391.

Jessop, B. (2019) Authoritarian Neoliberalism: Periodization and Critique. *South Atlantic Quarterly* 118(2): 343–361.

Johnson, H. (2004) Subsistence and control: The persistence of the peasantry in the developing world. *Undercurrent* 1(1): 54–65.

Jonas, A. E. G. (1996) Local labour control regimes: Uneven development and the social regulation of production. *Regional Studies* 30(4): 323–338.

Katz, E. (2003) The changing role of women in the rural economies of Latin America. In Davis, D. (ed.) *Food agriculture and rural development: Current and emerging issues for economic analysis and policy research volume 1 (Latin America and Caribbean).* Food and Agricultural Organization of the United Nations (FAO).

Kaup, B. Z. (2014) Divergent paths of counter-neoliberalization: materiality and the labor process in Bolivia's natural resource sectors. *Environment and Planning A: Economy and Space* 46: 1836–1851.

Kautsky, K. (1988) *The Agrarian Question*. London: Zwen.

Kaygusuz, K., Toklu, E., and Avcı, A. C. (2015) Energy security in a developing world: a case of Turkey. *Journal of Engineering Research and Applied Science* 4(1): 265–277.

Keyder, Ç. And Yenal, Z. (2011) Agrarian change under globalization. Markets and insecurity in Turkish agriculture. *Journal of Agrarian Change* 11(1): 60–86.

Kleiber, P. B. (2004) Focus Groups: More than a Method of Inquiry. In deMarrais, K. and Lapan, S. D. (eds.) *Foundation for Social Research: Methods of Inquiry in Education and Social Sciences* (pp. 87–102). London: Lawrence Erlbaum Associates Publishers.

Klein, N. (2007) *The Shock Doctrine: The Rise of Disaster Capitalism*. London: Penguin Books.

Kocabicak, E. (2022) Gendered property and labour relations in agriculture: Implications for social change in Turkey. *Oxford Development Studies* 50(2): 91–113.

Köse, A. H. and Yeldan, E. (1998) Turkish Economy in the 1990s: An Assessment of Fiscal Policies, Labor Markets and Foreign Trade. *New Perspectives on Turkey* 18: 51–78.

Kumar, M. (2022) Fossil neoliberalism and its limits: Governing coal in South India. *Environment and Planning E: Nature and Space* 5(4): 1853–1871.

Kumbamu, A. (2020) Saffron Fascism: The Conflux of Hindutva Ultra-Nationalism, Neoliberal Extractivism, and the Rise of Authoritarian Populism in Modi's India. In Berberoglu, B. (ed.) *The Global Rise of Authoritarianism in the 21st Century: Crisis of Neoliberal Globalization and the Nationalist Response* (pp. 161–177). New York: Routledge.

Lahiri-Dutt, K. (2015) The feminisation of mining. *Geography Compass* 9(9): 523–541.

Lozeva, S. and Marinova, D. (2010) Negotiating gender: Experience from Western Australian mining industry. *Journal of Economic and Social Policy* 13(2): 1–24.

Lutz-Ley, A. N. and Buechler, S. J. (2020) Mining and women in northwest Mexico. A feminist political ecology approach to impacts on rural livelihoods. *Human Geography* 13(1): 74–84.

Lenin, V. I. (1974) *The Development of Capitalism in Russia*. Moscow: Progress Publishers.

Luxemburg, R. (2003) *Accumulation of Capital*. London: Routledge.

Makhhijani, S. (2014) *Fossil fuel exploration subsidies*: Turkey. Oil Change International Country Study. Retrieved from: https://odi.org/sites/odi.org.uk/files/odi-assets/publications-opinion-files/9257.pdf (accessed: 20.12.2023).

Mason, J. (2002) *Qualitative Researching* (Second Edition). London: Sage.

May, T. (2004) *Social Research* (Third Edition). Norfolk: Open University Press.

Marx, K. (1973) *Grundrisse: Foundations of the Critique of Political Economy*. Harmondsworth: Penguin Books.

Marx, K. (1995) *Capital: A Critique of Political Economy Volume 1*. Moscow: Progress Publishers.

Marx, K. (1999) *Capital: A Critique of Political Economy Volume 3*. NY: International Publishers.

McMichael, P. (1997) Rethinking globalization: The agrarian question revisited. *Review of International Political Economy* 4(4): 630–662.

McMichael, P. (2009) A food regime genealogy. *The Journal of Peasant Studies* 36(1): 139–169.

McMichael, P. (2012) The land grab and corporate food regime restructuring. *The Journal of Peasant Studies* 39(3–4): 681–701.

McMichael, P. (2021) Food Regimes. In Ahram-Lodhi, H. A., Dietz, K., Engels, B., and McKay B. M. (eds.) *Handbook of Critical Agrarian Studies* (pp. 218–231). Cheltenham: Edward Elgar Publishing.

McMichael, P. and Mhyre, D. (1991) Global regulation vs. the nation state: Agro-food systems and new politics of capital. *Capital and Class* 15(1): 83–105.

Mercier, L. and Gier, I. (2007) Reconsidering women and gender in mining. *History Compass* 5(3): 995–1001.

Mezzadri, A. (2010) Neoliberalism, industrial restructuring and labour: Lessons from Delhi garment industry. In Saad Filho, A. and Yalman G. L. (eds.) *Economic Transitions to Neoliberalism in Middle-Income Countries* (pp. 128–140). London and New York: Routledge.

Mezzadri, A. (2016) Class, gender, and the sweatshop: On the nexus between labour commodification and exploitation. *Third World Quarterly* 37(10): 1877–1900.

Mezzadri, A. (2019) On the value of social reproduction. *Radical Philosophy 2.04*, Spring 2019: 33–41.

Mezzadri, A. (2020) A Crisis like no other: social reproduction and the regeneration of capitalist life during the COVID-19 pandemic. *Developing Economics* Retrieved from: https://developingeconomics.org/2020/04/20/a-crisis-like-no-other-social-reproduction-and-the-regeneration-of-capitalist-life-during-the-covid-19-pandemic/ (Accessed: 09.06.2024). .

Mezzadri, A. (2021) A value theory of inclusion: Informal labour, the homeworker, and the social reproduction of value. *Antipode* 53(4): 1186–1205.

Mezzadri, A., Newman, S., and Stevano, S. (2022) Feminist global political economies of work and social reproduction. *Review of International Political Economy.* 29(6): 1783–1803.

Mies, M. (1982) *The Lace Makers of Narsapaur: Indian Housewives Producing for the World Market.* London: Zed.

Mies, M. (1986) *Patriarchy and Accumulation on a World Scale: Women in the International Division of Labour.* London: Zed.

Mies, M. (1988) "Introduction". In Mies, M., Bennholdt-Thomsen, V. and Von Werlhof, C. (eds.), *Women: The Last Colony* (pp. 1–10). London: Zed.

Mies, M. (1998) Globalization of the Economy and Women's Work in a Sustainable Society. *Gender, Technology and Development* 2 (1): 3–37.

Mies, M. (2014) Housewifisation – Globalisation – Subsistence Perspective. In Budgen, S., Edwards, S., van der Linden, M. (eds.) *Beyond Marx: Theorising the Global Labour Relations of the Twenty-First Century* (pp. 209–237). Leiden and Boston: Brill.

Ministry of Development, Tenth Development Plan 2014–2018. Retrieved from: https://www.sbb.gov.tr/wpcontent/uploads/2018/11/The_Tenth_Development_Plan_2014–2018.pdf (Accessed 20.12.2023).

Ministry of Development, Eleventh Development Plan 2014–2018. Retrieved from: https://www.sbb.gov.tr/wpcontent/uploads/2020/06/Eleventh_Development_Plan-2019–2023.pdf (20.12.2023).

Naudi, S. C. and Rao, S. (2018) *Reproductive Work and Female Labour Force Participation in Rural India*. Political Economy Research Institute, University of Massachusetts, Amherst, Working Paper 458. Retrieved from: https://peri.umass.edu/publication/item/1070-reproductive-workand-female-labor-force-participation-in-rural-india (Accessed 23.12.2023).

Nizam, D. and Yenal, Z. (2020) Seed politics in Turkey: The awakening of a landrace wheat and its prospects. *The Journal of Peasant Studies* 47(4): 741–766.

Oil Change International (2014) Turkey's Coal Subsidies and Public Finance. Retrieved from: https://priceofoil.org/content/uploads/2014/07/Turkey-Coal-Subsidies-Full-07.28.14.pdf (accessed 20 December 2023).

O'Laughlin, B. (1996) Through a divided glass: Dualism, class and the agrarian question in Mozambique. *The Journal of Peasant Studies* 23(4): 1–39.

O'Laughlin, B. (2009) Gender justice, land and the agrarian question in Southern Africa. In Akram-Lodhi, H. and Kay, H. (eds.) *Peasants and Globalization: Political economy, rural transformation and the agrarian question* (pp. 190–203). New York: Routledge.

Ollman, B. (2003) *Dance of the Dialectic: Steps in Marx's Method*. Chicago: University of Illinois Press.

Oral, N., Sarıbal, O., and Şengül, H. (2015) Cumhuriyet Döneminde Uygulanan Tarım Politikaları. In Oral, N. (ed.) *Türkiye'de Tarımın Ekonomi Politiği, 1923–2013* (pp. 71–89). Ankara: Notabene.

Orhangazi, Ö. (2020) *Türkiye Ekonomisinin Yapısı: Sorunlar, Kırılganlıklar ve Kriz Dinamikleri*. Ankara: Imge Kitabevi.

Orhangazi, Ö. and Yeldan, E. (2021) The Re-making of the Turkish Crisis. *Development and Change* 52(3): 460–503.

Orhangazi, Ö. And Yeldan, E. (2023) Turkey in Turbulence: Heteredoxy or a New Chapter in Neoliberal Peripheral Development? *Development and Change* 54(5): 1197–1225.

Önder, Z. (2022) The Economics of Tobacco in Turkey: New Evidence and Demand Estimates. Economics of Tobacco Control Paper No. 2. Retrieved from: https://openknowledge.worldbank.org/bitstream/handle/10986/13733/multiopage.pdf?sequence=1&isAllowed=y (Accessed 21.12.2023).

Öniş, Z. (2011) Power, interests, and coalitions: the political economy of mass privatization in Turkey. *Third World Quarterly* 32(4): 707–724.

Oyan, O. (2015) Tarımda IMF-DB Gözetiminde 2000'li Yıllar. In Oral, N. (ed.) *Türkiye'de Tarımın Ekonomi Politiği, 1923–2013* (pp. 111–130). Ankara: Notabene.

Özen, E. N. and Aşık, G. (2021) Kömüre Dayalı İstihdamdan Çıkış: Sorun Alanları ve Çözüm Önerileri. *Climate Action Network (CAN) Europe*. Retrieved from: https://sefia.org/wp-content/uploads/2023/08/komure-dayali-istihdamdan-cikis-web.pdf (Accessed 27.05.2024).

Özuğurlu, M. (2011) *Küçük Köylülüğe Sermaye Kapanı*. Ankara: Notabene Yayınları.

Pamir, N. (2015) *Enerjinin İktidarı: Enerji Kaynaklarını Elinde Tutan Dünyayı Elinde Tutar*. Istanbul: Hayy Kitap.

Pamuk, Ş. (2008) Agriculture and Economic Development in Turkey, 1870–2000. In Lanis, P. and Pinilla, V. (eds.) *Agriculture and Economic Development in Europe since 1870* (pp. 375–396). Oxon: Routledge.

Panitch, L. and Leys, C. (2001) Preface. *Socialist Register* 37: vii–xi.

Parpart, J. L. (1983) *Class and Gender on the Copperbelt: Women in Northern Rhodesian Copper Mining Areas 1926–1964*. Working Papers No: 77 African Studies Center, Boston University.

Pattenden, J. (2016) *Labour, state, and society in rural India: A class-relational approach*. Manchester: Manchester University Press.

Pattenden, J. (2018) The politics of classes of labour: Fragmentation, reproduction zones and collective action in Karnataka, India. *The Journal of Peasant Studies* 45(5–6): 1039–1059.

Pattnaik, I., Lahiri-Dutt, K., Lockie, S., and Pritchard, B. (2018) The feminization of agriculture or the feminization of agrarian distress? Tracking the trajectory of women in agriculture in India. *Journal of the Asia Pacific Economy* 23(1): 138–155.

Pattnaik, I. and Lahiri-Dutt, K. (2020) What determines women's agricultural production? A comparative study of landholding households in rural India. *Journal of Rural Studies* 76: 25–39.

Perelman, M. (2000) *The Invention of Capitalism: Classical Political Economy and Secret History of Capital Accumulation*. Durham: Duke University Press.

Poulantzas, N. (2014) *State Power Socialism*. London and New York: Verso.

Radel, C., Schmook, B., Mcevoy, J., Mendez, C., and Pedrzelka, P. (2012) Labour migration and gendered agricultural relations: The feminisation of agriculture in the Ejidal sector of Calakmul, Mexico. *Journal of Agrarian Change* 12(1): 98–119.

Rainnie, A., McGrath-Champ, S., and Herod, A. (2010) Making space for geography in labour process theory. In Thomson, P. and Smith, C. (eds.) *Working Life: Renewing Labour Process Analysis* (pp. 297–315). Basingstoke: Palgrave.

Rao, S. (2018) Gender and class relations in rural India. *The Journal of Peasant Studies* 45(5): 950–968.

Rao, M. (2018) Reframing the Environment in Neoliberal India: Introduction to the Theme. *Sociological Bulletin*. 67(3): 259–274.

Razavi, S. (2003) Introduction: Agrarian change, gender and land rights. *Journal of Agrarian Change* 3(1): 2–32.

Razavi, S. (2009) Engendering the political economy of agrarian change. *The Journal of Peasant Studies* 36(1): 197–226.

Roberts, M. J. (2014) Critical Realism, Dialectics, and Qualitative Research Methods. *Journal for the Theory of Social Behaviour* 44 (1): 1–23.

Saad Filho, A. (2011) Crisis in neoliberalism or crisis of neoliberalism? *Socialist Register* 47: 242–259.

Saad-Filho, A. (2021) Neoliberalism and the pandemic. *Notebooks: The Journal for Studies on Power* 1(1): 179–186.

Saad-Filho, A. and Johnston, D. (2005) Introduction. In Saad-Filho and Johnston D. (eds.) *Neoliberalism: A Critical Reader* (pp. 1–16). London: Pluto Press.

Scheyvens, R. and Lagisa, L. (1998) Women disempowerment and resistance: An analysis of logging and mining activities in the Pacific. *Journal of Tropical Geography* 19(1): 51–70.

Shah, A. and Lerche, J. (2020) Migration and the invisible economies of care: Production, social reproduction and seasonal migrant labour in India. *TIBG* 45(4): 719–734.

Shiva, V. (2014) GATT; agriculture and third world women. In Mies, M. and Shiva, V. (eds.) *Ecofeminism* (pp. 231–245). London: Zed Books.

Shiva, V. (2016) *Staying alive: Women, ecology and development.* Berkeley: North Atlantic Books.

Sinha, S. (2021) Strong leaders, authoritarian populism, and Indian developmentalism: The Modi Moment in historical context. *Geoforum* 124: 320–333.

Soliland, T. (2016) A Feminist Approach to Primitive Accumulation. In Dellheim, J. and Wolf, F. O. (eds.) *Rosa Luxemburg: A Permanent Challenge for Political Economy.* London: Palgrave.

Soma Municipality Strategic Plan (2019) Retrieved from: http://www.sp.gov.tr/tr/stratejik-plan/s/815/Soma+Belediyesi+_Manisa_+2015-2019 (accessed: 22.12.2023).

Somel, K. (2021) Agricultural Support Policies in Turkey, 1950–1980: An Overview. In Richard, A. (ed.) *Food, States, and Peasants: Analyses of the Agrarian Question in the Middle East* (pp. 97–130). New York and London: Routledge.

Stevano, S. (2022) Classes of working women in Mozambique. An integrated framework to understand working lives. *Review of International Political Economy* 29(6): 1847–1869.

Stevano S. Mezzadri, A., Lombardozzi, L. Bargawi, H. (2021) Hidden Abodes in Plain Sight: The Social Reproduction of Households and Labor in the COVID-19 Pandemic. *Feminist Economics* 27(1–2): 271–287.

Şengül, H. T. and Aytekin, A. (2012) Zonguldak Coalfield and the past and future of Turkish coal-mining communities. In Kirk, J., Contrepois, S., and Jeffreys, S. (eds.) *Changing Work and Community Identities in European Regions: Perspectives on the Past and Present* (pp. 154–183). London: Palgrave Macmillan.

Şenses, F. and Koyuncu, M. (2007) Socioeconomic effects of economic crises: a comparative analysis of the experiences of Indonesia, Argentina and Turkey. In Köse, A. H., Şenses, F., and Yeldan E. (eds.) *Neoliberal Globalization as New Imperialism: Case Studies on Reconstruction of the Periphery* (pp. 1–20). New York: Nova Science Publishers.

State Planning Organization (SPO) (2008) Electricity Market and Supply Security Strategy Document. Retrieved from: https://ww4.ticaret.edu.tr/enerji/wp-content/uploads/sites/79/2015/11/Elektrik-Enerjisi-Piyasas%C4%B1-Ve-Arz-G%C3%BCvenli%C4%9Fi-Strateji-Belgesi.pdf (accessed 22 December 2023).

Tamzok, N. (2014) Soma: Bir Facianın Tarihçesi Yazı Dizisi. Retrieved from: https://www.enerjigunlugu.net/yazi-dizisi-soma-bir-facianin-tarihcesi-9187h.htm (accessed 20.12.2023).

Tamzok, N. (2016) Yerli Kömürler Türkiye için Kurtarıcı Olur mu? Retrieved From: (accessed: 12.03.2024).

Tansel, C. B. (2017) Authoritarian Neoliberalism: Towards A New Research Agenda. In Tansel, C. B: (ed.) *States of Discipline: Authoritarian Neoliberalism and the Contested Reproduction of Capitalist Order* (pp. 1–28). London: Rowman & Littlefield International.

Tansel, C. B. (2018) Authoritarian Neoliberalism and Democratic Backsliding in Turkey: Beyond the Narratives of Progress. *South European Society and Politics* 23(2): 197–217.

Taylor, M. and Rioux, S. (2017) *Global Labour Studies*. Cambridge: Polity Press.

Telli, Ç., Voyvoda, E., and Yeldan, E. (2006) Modelling general equilibrium for socially responsible macroeconomics: seeking for the alternatives to fight jobless growth in Turkey. *METU Studies in Development* 33(2): 255–293.

Thompson, E. P. (1963) *The Making of the English Working Class*. London: Penguin Press.

Thompson, E. P. (1978) Eighteenth-century English society: Class struggle without class. *Social History* 3: 133–165.

Tilly, C. (1979) Proletarianization: Theory and Research. CRSO Working Paper No: 202.

TBB (2014) *Soma Maden Faciası Raporu*. Ankara: Şen Matbaa.

The Union of Agricultural Chambers (2021) October 21. World Women Farmers Day. Retrieved from: https://www.tzob.org.tr/basin-odasi/haberler/15-ekim-dunya-kadin-ciftciler-gunu20211015085915 (accessed: 23.12.2023).

Trading Economics (2024) Turkey: Food Inflation. Retrieved from: https://tradingeconomics.com/turkey/food-inflation#:~:text=Cost%20of%20food%20in%20Turkey,percent%20in%20April%20of%202016 (Accessed: 10.06.2024).

Türk Sosyal Bilimler Derneği (TSBD) (2016) *İki Yılın Ardından Soma Maden Faciası Raporu*. Ankara, Turkey.

Tuncer, Ö. (2016) Ölmez ağaç; Yırca direnişi ve direnişin öznesi kadınlar. *Başlangıç*. Retrieved from: https://baslangicdergi.org/olmez-agac-yirca-direnisi-ve-direnisin-oznesi-kadinlar/ (Accessed: 17.02.2023).

TURKSTAT (2017) Women in Statistics. Retrieved from: https://data.tuik.gov.tr/Bulten/Index?p=Istatistiklerle-Kadin-2017-27594 (accessed 21.12.2023).

TURKSTAT (2020) Annual GDP, 2019. Retrieved from: https://data.tuik.gov.tr/Bulten/Index?p=Yillik-Gayrisafi-Yurt-Ici-Hasila-2019-33671 (accessed 23.12.2023).

Veltmeyer, H. (2013) The political economy of natural resource extraction: A new model or extractive imperialism? *Canadian Journal of Development Studies* 34(1): 79–95.

Veltmeyer, H. and Petras, J. (2014) *The new extractivism: A post-neoliberal development model or imperialism of the twenty-first century*. London: Zed Books.

Vercillo, S. (2020) The complicated gendering of farming and household foos responsibilities in Northern Ghana. *Journal of Rural Studies* 79: 235–245.

Von Werlhof, C. (1988) Women's work: The blind spot in the critique of political economy. In Mies, M., Bennholdt-Thomsen, V. and Von Werlhof, C. (eds.), *Women: The Last Colony* (pp. 13–26). London: Zed.

Von Werlhof, C. (2007) No Critique of Capitalism Without a Critique of Patriarchy! Why The Left Is No Alternative. *Capitalism Nature Socialism*. 18(1): 13–27.

Wood, E. M. (1995) *Democracy against capitalism: Renewing historical materialism*. Cambridge: Cambridge University Press.

Wood, E. M. (2009) Peasants and the market imperative: the origins of capitalism. In Akram-Lodhi, H. and Kay, H. (eds.) *Peasants and Globalization: Political economy, rural transformation and the agrarian question* (pp. 37–56). New York: Routledge.

World Bank (2020) Rural population (% of total population) – Turkey. Retrieved from:https://data.worldbank.org/indicator/SP.RUR.TOTL.ZS?locations=TR(accessed: 20.12.2023).

World Bank (2022a) Food Security Update. Retrieved From: https://www.worldbank.org/en/topic/agriculture/brief/food-security-update (Accessed: 08.06.2024).

World Bank (2022b) Joint Statement: The Heads of the World Bank Group, IMF, WFP, and WTO Calling for Urgent Coordinated Action on Food Security. Retrieved from: https://www.worldbank.org/en/news/statement/2023/02/08/joint-statement-on-the-global-food-and-nutrition-security-crisis#:~:text=The%20World%20Bank%20is%20providing,and%20nutrition%20security%20in%20hotspots. (Accessed: 04.06.2024).

World Bank (2023) Food Security Update. Retrieved from: https://thedocs.worldbank.org/en/doc/40ebbf38f5a6b68bfc11e5273e1405d4-0090012022/related/Food-Security-Update-XCIX-February-01-24.pdf (Accessed: 08.10.2024).

World Food Programme (2023) A global food crisis. 2023: Another Year of Extreme Jeopardy for Those Struggling to Feed Their Families. Retrieved from: https://www.wfp.org/global-hunger-crisis (Accessed: 09.06.2024).

Wright, M. (2006) *Disposable women and other myths of global capitalism*. New York: Routledge.

Yaman Öztürk, M. (2009) *Geç Kapitalistleşen Ülkelerde Krizin Kadınların Hayatında Yarattığı Güçlükler*. Paper Presented at *EconAnadolu 2009*, 7–19 June 2008. Eskişehir, Turkey.

Yalman, G. L. (2009) *Transition to Neoliberalism: The Case of Turkey in the 1980s*. Istanbul: Bilgi University Press.

Yalman, G. L. (2016) Crises as Driving Forces of Neoliberal "Trasformismo": The Contours of the Turkish Political Economy since the 2000s. In Cafruny, A., Talani, L. S., and Martin, G. P. *The Palgrave Handbook of Critical International Political Economy* (pp. 239–266). London: Palgrave Macmillan.

Yalman, G. L. (2019) The Neoliberal Transformation of State and Market in Turkey: An Overview of Financial Developments from 1980 to 2000. In Yalman, G. L., Marois, T., and Güngen, A. R. (eds.) *The Political Economy of Financial Transformation in Turkey* (pp. 51–87). London and New York: Routledge.

Yalman, G. L. (2021) Crisis of what? Crisis in or of neoliberalism? A brief encounter with the debate on the authoritarian turn. In Babacan, E., Kutun, M., Pınar, E., and Yılmaz, Z. (eds.) *Regime Change in Turkey: Neoliberal Authoritarianism, Islamism, and Hegemony* (pp. 15–31). London and New York: Routledge.

Yalman, G. L. and Topal, A. (2017) Labour containment strategies and working class struggle in the neoliberal era: The case of TEKEL workers in Turkey. *Critical Sociology* 45(1): 447–461.

Yalman, G. L., Çelik, C., Topal, A. (2023) *From Containment of Labour to Containment of Solidarity of People for Survival: Authuritarian State's Responses to Covid19 Pandemic and 2023 Earthquake in Turkey*. Paper Presented in the Critical Political Economy Research Network of the European Sociological Association Workshop, 8–10 June 2023, Naples, Italy: University ıf Naples L'orientale.

Yeldan, E. and Ünüvar, B. (2016) An assessment of the Turkish economy in the AKP Era. *Research and Policy on Turkey* 1(1): 11–28.

Yıldırmaz, S. (2009) *From 'Imaginary' to 'Real': A Social History of the Peasantry in Turkey (1945–1960)*. Unpublished Ph.D. dissertation. Istanbul: Boğaziçi University, Atatürk Institute for Modern Turkish History.

Yılmaz, Z. and Turner, B. D. (2019) Turkey's deepening authoritarianism and the fall of electoral democracy. *British Journal of Middle Eastern Studies* 46(5): 691–698.

Yorulmaz, Ş. (1998) Türkiye'de Kömürün Keşfi ve Kömür İşletme İmtiyazları (1829–1938). In *Türkiye Kömür Kongresi Bildiri Kitabı* (pp. 283–298). Bartın.

Zaifer, A. (2018) The acceleration of privatization: understanding state, power bloc, and capital accumulation in Turkey. *Review of Radical Political Economics* 50(4): 810–829.

Zaifer, A. (2020) Variegated privatisation: class, capital accumulation and state in Turkey's privatisation process in the 1980s and 1990s. *Critical Sociology* 46(1): 141–156.

Zaifer, A. (2022) *Privatization in Turkey: Power Bloc, Capital Accumulation and State*. Leiden and Boston: Brill.

Index

2001 financial crisis   IX, X, 2, 50, 51, 53, 92, 98

accumulation
   by dispossession   9, 32, 122
   by displacement   1, 122
   capitalist   26, 27, 31, 33, 39
   of capital   27, 36, 38, 47, 88, 121, 122, 123
   See also primitive accumulation
agrarian
   change   IX, XIII, 20, 45, 85, 95, 103, 160
   structure   2, 10, 24, 86, 90, 93, 96, 153
agribusiness
   capital   2, 57, 92, 93, 118
   firms   1, 43, 94
agricultural
   employment   91, 95
   producer   1, 7, 8, 13, 24, 30, 57, 94, 146, 152, 153
   state economic enterprises   1, 2, 40, 43, 57, 90, 92
   support   91, 91
Alevi   129, 138
austerity   165
authoritarian
   authoritarian neoliberalism   15, 22, 119, 120, 121, 123, 150, 166
   authoritarianism   120

capitalist patriarchy   84, 88, 154
care
   economies of   129
   work   20, 115, 116, 157
cash dependency   30, 67, 78, 89 112, 129
class
   classes of extractive labour   7, 8, 20, 21, 22, 24, 43, 44, 45, 84, 85, 86, 88, 94, 95, 118, 152, 153, 154
   classes of labour   XI, 6, 43, 44, 86, 103, 121, 158
   differentiation   26, 27, 86
   formation   7, 21, 24, 41, 42, 44, 56, 86, 152
   relations   6, 15, 16, 19, 31, 42, 44, 45, 46, 48, 49, 86, 90, 120, 121, 130, 136, 152
   relational approach   4, 5, 21, 24, 42, 152
coal
   exploration   55

extraction   X, 9, 19, 50, 52, 56, 58, 60, 61, 62, 64, 70, 76, 79, 95, 96, 124, 126, 152
imports   54, 57, 165, 166
industry   X, 21–23, 45, 49, 54–58, 61, 71, 83, 96, 104, 119, 123, 124, 134, 135, 147, 152, 156, 158, 163, 165
miners   9, 23, 58, 96, 136, 156, 163
mining   IX, X, 3, 9, 12, 19, 49, 57, 58, 67, 69, 105, 112, 122, 130, 156, 166
policies   10, 122, 123, 124, 133, 137, 141, 153
rush   9, 10, 21, 45, 52, 54, 57, 58, 61, 69, 79, 80, 82, 85, 95, 127, 128, 146, 153, 163
commodification   28, 31, 33, 39–41, 49, 78, 84–86, 91, 112, 152, 159
consent   15, 16, 22, 37, 47, 57, 88, 119, 121, 123, 133, 143
construction (sector)   2, 40, 43, 51 55, 57, 69, 78, 94, 121
contract farming   XI, 86, 94, 101, 106, 162
contradictory role of the capitalist state   47, 120, 121
control over production   2, 21, 28, 44, 87, 93, 94, 154
current account deficit   2, 51, 54, 57, 124, 152, 165

deagrarianization   2, 93, 153
decarbonization   163
depeasantization   40, 42, 43
deproletarian   41, 42
dispossession
   forms of   32, 33, 39
   of peasantry   5, 25, 28, 43
   of small-scale agricultural producers   1, 30, 56–57, 155
   of small-scale farmers   1, 2, 25, 38, 93, 117, 153, 159, 163
   of rural population   1, 3, 8
   of tobacco farmers   63
   partly dispossessed   1, 5, 6, 29, 43, 118, 152
   patterns of   1, 3, 10–12, 20–22, 24, 83, 84, 91, 95, 101, 118
   process of   40, 82, 94, 152
   See also accumulation by & land dispossession

diversification
    livelihood   1, 6, 22, 24, 84–87, 94, 95, 102, 105, 106
    income   94, 154
domestic
    coal   9, 55, 57, 59, 83, 124, 166
    energy   61
    resources   2, 3, 52, 54, 59, 152
    violence   37, 88, 116

ecological   8, 40, 89, 104, 121, 146, 147, 150, 158, 166
emotional work   34, 89, 115, 139
employment
    creation   56, 58, 153
    generation   8, 51, 57, 58, 84, 87
    in the mines   58, 67, 131, 140, 155
    opportunity   1, 9, 64, 66, 67, 78, 95, 125, 133, 134
    See also agricultural employment, precarious employment, and unregistered employment
enclosure   2, 9, 32, 35, 39, 46
energy supply security   52, 54, 57–59, 165
export
    led agricultural growth   89
    oriented agriculture   90
    oriented development   46, 50
extractive
    capital   1, 3, 7, 8, 22, 24, 43, 48, 49, 68, 84, 89, 118, 119, 122, 123, 143, 147, 149, 150, 154
    developmentalism   3, 7, 8, 21, 45, 122
    household   8, 84, 152
    investment   X, 4, 20, 22, 24, 25, 43, 46, 57, 87–89, 95, 133, 146, 153
    regions   3, 4, 7, 20, 21, 22, 24, 43, 44, 47, 49, 84, 87, 89, 94, 119, 152, 153
    sectors/industries   3, 21, 44–46, 49, 56, 82, 87, 122

factory regime   46
feminization
    of agriculture   8, 87, 95, 106
    of workforce   157
focus group interviews   10, 12, 13, 16, 19, 20, 98
food
    crisis   23, 158–160, 163

    inflation   160, 161, 163
    insecurity   158, 159, 161
fossil fuels   54, 156, 163
fractions of capital   52, 53, 55, 56, 58, 71

gender
    division of work   45, 86, 87, 94, 102, 110, 117, 118, 152
    gendered   XI, 3, 19, 22, 31, 44, 83–85, 87, 91, 153
Global South   IX, 1, 3, 5, 6, 34, 37, 40, 43, 45, 52, 87, 102, 103, 106, 112, 122
global value chains   3, 8, 47, 152

health and safety in the mines   60, 71, 75, 80, 123, 124, 127, 128, 133, 141, 149, 150, 166
housewife
    housewifization   34, 37, 113
    ideology   84, 88, 117, 154
housework   XI, 34, 37, 88, 115–117

iceberg economy   34, 117
illegal mine   65, 66, 72, 78, 96, 137
import
    dependency   2, 3, 9, 51, 54, 59, 83, 95, 124, 152, 160
    substitution   50, 91
    See also coal imports
income security   9, 100
indebtedness   2, 68, 110, 112, 138, 161, 162
informal subcontracting   72–77, 81, 82, 125, 128, 131, 135, 142
international
    division of labour   40, 90, 91, 117
    tobacco corporations   63, 100
Islam   51, 123, 134–136, 142

jobless growth   51, 56
just transition   23, 156, 163

labour control
    local   3, 13, 15, 22, 46, 47, 58, 119, 128, 135, 136, 142, 143, 151, 152
    mechanisms   15, 16, 58, 69, 77, 119, 142, 144, 153
    regimes   8, 46–48, 135
    strategies   X, 3, 5, 22, 46, 47, 49, 119, 128, 143, 152, 153

INDEX   187

labour regime   x, 3, 4, 8, 10, 11, 14, 15, 20, 21,
    22, 43, 46, 48, 49, 51, 86, 109, 119, 153
labour discipline   3, 4, 8, 13, 22, 25, 41, 48, 51,
    80, 81, 119, 121, 128, 129, 131, 133–136, 138,
    140, 141, 143, 150–152
labour intermediaries   72, 109, 128
labour process theory   8, 21, 45, 46, 48, 49, 82
labour regime   x, 3, 4, 8, 10, 11, 14, 15, 20–22,
    43, 45, 46, 48, 49, 51, 86, 109, 119, 153
    See also labour control regime
labour supply   3, 8, 9, 21, 24, 63, 64, 82,
    96, 100
land
    degradation   22, 104, 107, 166
    dispossession   5, 11, 16, 155
    expropriation   1, 21, 26, 28, 43, 44, 89, 93,
        103, 104, 146, 150, 154, 155, 166
    grabs   112
landless   6, 30–32, 43, 44, 86, 98, 136, 152
lignite   9, 17, 54, 56–61, 66, 69, 78, 163
local
    class relations   15, 16, 19, 130, 136
    labour market   3, 8, 46, 69, 86, 119, 129,
        136, 140
    See also labour control

market
    dependency   40, 43, 92
    imperative   5, 39, 120
    See also local labour market & rural
        labour market
Marxist   4, 5, 6, 21, 24, 25, 28, 33–35, 39, 42,
    46, 88, 156
Marxist feminism   21, 24, 25, 31, 44
means of
    production   1, 4, 5, 8, 24–28, 30–33, 38–
        46, 85, 86, 94, 122, 153
    social reproduction   1, 5, 8, 24, 38, 40, 44,
        86, 106, 122, 129, 147, 153
    subsistence   6, 25, 28, 30, 32, 41, 43, 78, 89,
        103, 112, 129, 137
migrant
    family/household   16, 18, 67, 68, 106, 113,
        128, 129, 130, 135, 138
    labour   67, 113
    women   20, 105, 106, 109, 110, 112, 113
    worker   19, 29, 64, 66–68, 78, 82, 86, 95,
        128, 129, 137, 138
mine

coal   x, 9, 10, 12, 14–16, 18, 20, 21, 45,
    59, 63, 64, 69, 82, 96, 102, 133, 141, 152,
    165, 166
    investments   8, 56, 78, 84, 112, 146
    operated by the state   19, 53, 59–61, 64,
        65, 67, 77, 131
    surface   9, 59, 60, 61, 63, 69, 104
    underground   9, 14, 15, 18, 20, 21, 45, 57,
        59, 61, 63, 64, 69, 72–79, 82, 96, 100–104,
        111, 123–128, 138, 144
miner
    miner families   8, 10, 14, 16, 18, 19, 22, 68,
        84, 96, 104–106, 111, 113, 114, 119, 133, 136,
        143, 146, 154, 162
    miner's wife   7, 115, 126
Ministry of Energy and Natural
    Resources   17, 124

National Energy and Mining Policy   54
neoliberal
    agricultural policies   1–3, 10, 43, 93, 117
    rural development   1, 117
    transformation of agriculture   1, 2, 5, 19,
        57, 58, 63, 78, 89, 92, 101, 102, 112, 146,
        153, 161
    transformation of coal   x, 9, 19, 22,
        61, 105
    See also authoritarian neoliberalism
non-capitalist   5, 6, 26, 27, 33, 34, 36,
    37, 39, 88

ownership
    land   6 38, 86, 90, 101, 136
    of means of production   27, 31, 41, 43

pandemic   11, 16, 111, 157–160, 165
participant observation   10, 13, 14, 16–18, 20
patriarchal
    household   20, 38, 84, 154
    oppression   37, 88
    peasant   30
    relations   35, 117
patriarchy. See also capitalist patriarchy
peasant
    differentiation of peasantry   26, 27, 30,
        86, 153
    household   30, 85, 89
    production   27
    traditional peasantry   5, 29, 85

petty commodity production   8, 20, 21, 29, 31, 40, 44, 49, 84, 86, 87, 92, 94, 95, 102, 105, 106, 112, 117, 138, 154
philosophy of internal relations   4, 24
politics of production   46
power bloc   47, 53, 55, 56, 58, 71, 121, 150, 166
precarious
  labour   1, 14, 37, 51, 57, 65, 78, 85, 87, 88, 106, 122, 137, 141, 151, 154
  conditions of food production   160, 161
  conditions of social reproduction   67, 68, 106, 128, 153
primitive accumulation   5, 6, 21, 24, 25–35, 38, 39, 44
  See also accumulation
private sector
  energy investments   3, 53–55
  mine investments   9, 19, 56, 61, 96, 133, 134, 163
privatization
  of energy   53, 3
  of coal extraction   56, 61, 63, 152
  of public services   32, 33
  of state economic enterprises   x, 1, 2, 40, 43, 51, 52, 57, 92, 98, 100
production pressure   15, 21, 69, 71, 72, 74, 79–82, 123, 125, 126, 140, 153
proletarianization
  of peasantry/rural populations   1, 2, 4–6, 9–11, 13, 20–22, 24–31, 38, 40, 42, 56, 63, 87, 93, 96, 102, 117, 150, 152–154, 159
  patterns of   XI, 1, 10, 11, 13, 19–22, 43, 83, 84, 91, 101, 146
protectionism   2, 40, 90, 91

qualitative research   11, 95

renewable energy   54
reproduction of labour power   7, 8, 20, 47, 48, 88, 89, 111, 126, 135, 154
resistance
  anti-coal   104, 146, 147
  moments of   15, 16, 22, 119, 133, 143, 146, 154
  movements   3, 84, 135, 138, 147, 150
  against collective redundancy   147–149, 152
royalty tender   9, 10, 55, 56, 61–64, 67, 69–71, 80, 81, 95, 96, 124, 127, 163, 164

rural
  class structure   28, 43
  commons   43, 44, 103
  development   1, 22, 117
  household   1, 8, 19, 49, 84, 86, 87, 94, 117, 153
  labour markets   1, 45, 86, 117, 152
  population   1, 3, 5, 6, 24, 26, 30, 40, 43, 85, 90, 94
  proletariat   27, 29–31
  social differentiation   105, 153

savings and efficiency plan   165
semi-feudal   37, 41, 42
semi-structured interviews   10–12, 14, 16, 20
simple reproduction squeeze   43, 93, 102, 106, 112
small scale farmer/farming   1, 2, 5, 8, 9, 2–25, 38–40, 43, 57, 59, 61, 84–86, 91–97, 109, 117, 146, 153, 154, 156, 158–161
snowball sampling   18
social reproduction
  crisis of   157, 158
  early social reproduction analysis   6, 7, 21, 33–37, 88
  imperatives of   4, 12, 20–22, 44, 83–85, 105, 119, 153
  of extractive/mining communities   89, 111–117, 126
  of migrant workers   106
  regimes of   157
Soma Mine Disaster   10, 12–19, 22, 62, 63, 65, 66, 69, 70, 72, 79–81, 113, 114, 119, 122–128, 133, 135–143, 146, 147, 153, 156, 164–166
state
  subsidies   1, 40, 43, 91, 94
  support for agricultural producers   9, 63, 90, 91, 93, 94, 97, 98, 100, 153
  support for the coal industry   55, 166
state-capital-labour-nature relations   11, 21, 45, 82, 153
subsistence
  crisis   43, 87
  farming   XI, 20, 27, 34, 37, 49, 68, 87–90, 103, 105, 111, 112, 117
  producer   6, 8, 21, 33, 34, 36, 37, 84, 87–89, 95, 102, 112, 113, 116, 138
  See also means of subsistence

super-exploitation   2, 21, 44, 45, 79, 84, 88, 89, 115, 118, 154
surplus
    labour   1, 6, 29, 43, 46
    value   4, 27, 42, 47
survival strategy   6, 43, 57, 84, 87, 94, 163

Tekel   X, 2, 9, 63, 97–100, 130, 131
TKI   X, 9, 14, 17, 56, 59–61, 63, 80, 82, 133, 164
tobacco
    factories   63, 100
    farmer   X, XI, 9, 63–65, 82, 96–102, 104, 106, 107, 109, 111, 112, 150
    farming   9, 20, 97–99, 101–103, 106–108, 112, 131, 146, 150
trade union
    Dev Maden Sen   14, 143, 144, 148
    DISK   14, 131, 143–147
    Maden Iş   17, 124, 128, 131, 135, 143, 144, 146, 166
    Türk Iş   131, 144
    Independent Miners Union   144, 145
TTK   56, 65

unemployment   51, 69, 110, 122, 125, 133–140, 144, 149, 150, 166
unemployed miners   76, 79, 81, 82, 100, 110, 125, 134, 136, 137, 139, 143
unpaid
    unpaid family worker   8, 84, 95, 106, 108, 109, 116, 154
    unpaid reproductive work   37, 84, 88, 105, 111, 115–117, 139
unregistered   58, 65, 72, 95, 109, 110, 117, 137, 139

wage
    income   9, 63, 68, 78, 87, 103, 106, 113, 162
    relation   30, 35
    daily wage worker   13, 98, 102, 104, 105, 108, 161
Western Anatolia   3, 9, 10, 86
Workforce   1, 3, 6, 8, 41, 43, 44, 46, 57, 74, 87, 89, 95, 151, 157
Workplace   8, 10, 18, 22, 45–48, 74, 77, 111, 114, 119, 123, 128, 135

www.ingramcontent.com/pod-product-compliance
Lightning Source LLC
Chambersburg PA
CBHW070623030426
42337CB00020B/3898